Christian Jihad does many things, and all of them well. It gives us an insıdc view of the religious right while humanizing its participants. It proposes a way forward in the culture wars while transcending warfare rhetoric. It gives a first-hand account of an important and ongoing movement in American political and religious history while suggesting both the appeal and weaknesses of that movement. Concerned observers of the Religious Right and the New Apostolic Reformation will benefit from Colonel Doner's eyewitness testimony, and participants may gain even more.

BRIAN McLAREN, AUTHOR, SPEAKER, BLOGGER (BRIANMCLAREN.NET)

Fascinating . . . A superbly detailed insider's account of the war waged by much of the Christian Right against the rest of us - and against American values, and against the heart of the Bible.

MARCUS BORG, BIBLICAL AND JESUS SCHOLAR, BEST-SELLING AUTHOR OF *SPEAKING CHRISTIAN*

The mindset behind the Christian Right, as well as the Christian (or secular) Left, is far more alike than we realize. Colonel Doner, once an insider and founding leader of the Christian Right, pulls back the curtain in this well-written memoir so we can see what really brought about the constant culture wars that threaten to destroy public life and civility in America. This well-conceived book gave me hope that Christians can do better and stop spreading movements rooted in fear and loathing. Doner is hopeful and so am I. He shows how humble Christians, who give up false certitude for the love of Jesus, can actually help to create a culture rooted in God's love, one that results in healthy pluralism and human respect.

DR. JOHN H. ARMSTRONG, AUTHOR OF *YOUR CHURCH IS TOO SMALL*, PRESIDENT ACT 3

Christian Jihad is almost too hot to pick up, almost impossible to put down. The most mesmerizing part of the book, though, is Colonel Doner's portrayal of a way forward without these civil wars of religion that are anything but civil and everything but religious.

LEONARD SWEET, BEST-SELLING AUTHOR AND PROFESSOR (DREW UNIVERSITY, GEORGE FOX UNIVERSITY) AND CHIEF CONTRIBUTOR TO SERMONS.COM

Christian Jihad

Christian Jihad

Neo-Fundamentalists and the
Polarization of America

Colonel V. Doner

Denver   Los Angeles

SAMIZDAT CREATIVE
A Division of Samizdat Publishing Group, LLC.

Christian Jihad. Copyright © 2012 by Colonel V Doner. All rights reserved. Printed in the United States of America. No part of this book may be used or reproduced in any manner whatsoever without written permission except in the case of brief quotations embodied in critical articles and reviews. For information, email comrade@samizdatcreative.com.

The author can be reached at christian-jihad.com.

ISBN: 978-0-9846852-5-7

Library of Congress Cataloging-in-Publication Data is available upon request.

Samizdat Creative books may be purchased with bulk discounts for educational, business, or sales promotional use. For information please email: comrade@samizdatcreative.com

Samizdat Creative online: samizdatcreative.com

Cover Design: White Bread Design

Scripture quotations in this publication are taken from the Holy Bible, New International Version® (NIV®). Copyright © 1973, 1978, 1984 by International Bible Society. Used by permission of Zondervan. All rights reserved; the New American Standard Bible® (NASB), Copyright © 1960, 1962, 1963, 1968, 1971, 1972, 1973, 1975, 1977, 1995 by The Lockman Foundation. Used by permission; the Amplified Bible (AMP), © The Lockman Foundation 1954, 1958, 1962, 1964, 1965, 1987; The Living Bible (TLB), copyright © 1971, used by permission of Tyndale House Publishers, Inc., Wheaton, IL 60189, all rights reserved; and the King James Version (KJV).

For Brant and Bella—
Leaders of the next generation.

Contents

Acknowledgments

To acknowledge everyone who contributed to a work like this is all but impossible. How to remember the countless conversations over the decades that contributed to rethinking my faith, worldview, life, and purpose? Should I thank those who dislodged me from my comfortable sense of objective certainty? Or should I blame them for deconstructing my blind ignorance? While ignorance may be blissful, it is not how I choose to live my life. I would rather embrace truth or reality to the best of my limited ability. Nevertheless, let me start this important tribute by thanking the Christian thinkers, like Andrew Sandlin, Bob Mumford, Brian McLaren, Leonard Sweet, and Ron Martoia, who first opened new vistas to me through their written works and later were kind enough to invest their time and energy in helping me transition from my exclusive, "objective" rigid fundamentalist paradigm for one that is open, inclusive, and fluid.

I am deeply indebted to the many scholars and authors whose groundbreaking work helped me to break my own new ground. It is an all too limited list due to my less than photographic memory, but just a few of these authors include:

Karen Armstrong
Frank Schaeffer
Rob Bell
Hamilton Smith
Marcus Borg
Leonard Sweet
Stanley Grenz
Richard Tarnas
Nathan Hatch
Ken Wilber
Mark Noll
N. T. Wright
George Marsden

I am also thankful for the rare blessing of friends who also are well-read, thoughtful, and wise—true friends who helped me think through, reshape, and hone my questions, observations and conclusions. These invaluable and patient friends include:

John Armstrong
Wayne McNamara
Mario Aviles
Barret Orteg
Kurt Bruder
Daniel Tocchini
Mike Bresnan
Monte Wilson
Theo Geyser

JR Young
Warren Hayes
Davide Zaccariello
Betel Lopez
Caleb Seeling
Lynda Terry
Daniela Innocenti Beem
Joseph Spiccia
Gabriele Schmitz

Without Terry Grave, Derek Hammond, Kathleen McCall, and Wendy Swezy keeping our worldwide humanitarian relief efforts humming smoothly, I would not have been able to take the time needed to think, write, reflect, write, rewrite, and endlessly edit.

Last but not least, painstakingly navigating shifting paradigms with my twenty-one-year-old son, Brant (CJ) Eric Vaughn Doner, has been an inspiration, joy, and blessing. As he reexamined his own fundamentalist paradigm, he freed me to fully experience my own questions and finally uncover what I really believed.

Part I

On the Front Lines of the Culture War

1

Torn Apart by Hate

IN NOVEMBER 1963, as the public address system at a high school in Orange County, California, solemnly announced the assassination of President John F. Kennedy, a fifteen-year-old boy shot from his seat, stunning his classmates with his spontaneous outburst that JFK was not assassinated. "He was executed for treason," he claimed, referring to his "soft on communism" policies. This youngster, already well trained in a Christian worldview that allowed for no gray areas or nuances in diplomacy, knew one thing: JFK was a liberal, and liberals were clearly betraying God, America, and all of Western civilization. So he also offered that JFK's assassin, whoever it turned out to be, should be awarded the Congressional Medal of Honor.

Rather than being reprimanded, his stridency elevated him within three years to the ranks of national leadership in the Christian anticommunist movement, the '60s forerunner of the Christian Right.

Within another twelve short years he became one of the most prominent leaders of the Christian Right, threatening to defeat "any and every congressman who failed to support 'traditional values'" (code words for the hard-right agenda). In another decade, he became first the strategist, then the spokesperson, and finally the chief polemicist for Christian Reconstructionism. This is the Christian neo-fundamentalist flip side of Islamic fundamentalism, preparing a stealth strategy to ensure all Americans submit to God's law (just as the term Islam means "submission").

That young boy was me.

From 1966 to 1996, over a span of three decades, I was a neo-fundamentalist strategist, spokesman, apologist, and author—an insider in the deepest sense. In the obscurant and xenophobic world of the Christian anticommunist movement in the 1960s and '70s, my mentors included firebrand Rev. Billy James Hargis, scholarly Dr. David Noebel, and the eloquent Dr. Stuart McBirnie, all of whom were progenitors to today's Christian neo-fundamentalist Right.

In the 1980s, I was a "rock star" of the Christian Right, cofounding the pugnacious *Christian Voice* while ever-present as a "talking head" on the evening news and programs like *Donahue* and *60 Minutes*.

A decade later, I helped to awaken the political consciousness of Pentecostals and Charismatics that birthed political leaders like Sarah Palin. In fact, I was part of an elite team that introduced Peter Wagner, the leader of Sarah Palin's scary brand of "spiritual warfare" theology, to the theocratic concept of "godly dominion."

By the dawn of the twenty-first century, I'd evolved as a leader of the small but influential group of hard line theocrats called Reconstructionists, who even now continue to provide the blueprint for Palin's Fundamentalist-Pentecostal-Christian

Right axis.

Yep. I'm one of those hotheaded know-it-alls who got us into this culture war quagmire. I'm a version of Sarah Palin from an older generation and I carried the torch of the same movement she does. If I hadn't left, I would probably be managing one of their presidential campaigns today. But I did a 180-degree turn. What happened? What did I see in the paradigm and worldview that made me jump ship?

In retrospect, my breaking away from neo-fundamentalism had all the earmarks of a failing paradigm. Paradigm shifts happen when our worldview can no longer provide us with the necessary answers. Specifically, as I was completing my ten-year labor critiquing the evolution of Evangelical orthopraxy in a work called *The Late Great Evangelical Church,* I realized that I was writing it from the typical neo-fundamentalist/modernist point of view. This meant that *my people* were objective—possessing as we did God's "objective word"—while the unenlightened (including most Christians) were hopelessly lost in a maze of subjectivity. So I began to ask myself a basic question: just how was it that *we* were privy to God's *objective* truth and everybody else was so pitifully *subjective* or just plain wrong? Annoyingly, the question kept cropping up and simply wouldn't go away. Then my pastor at the time, conservative theologian Andrew Sandlin, had the epiphany that "assuming that we have access to God's objective word, the problem is that we're going to *interpret it* subjectively."

My world was rocked. I had my answer. *There's no such thing as absolute objectivity on our part.* That's why there is precious little agreement, even in neo-fundamentalist circles, on many points, let alone in wider Evangelical circles. It dawned on me—this is why we have over 25,000 Christian denominations; looking at the same Bible or the same "facts," everybody has their own "take." As Nietzsche famously wrote, "Everything is interpretation." Very simply, we each have our own interpretation.

The founder of Christian Reconstructionism (the godfather of Sarah Palin's dominion theology, which we'll get to later), Rousas J. Rushdoony, died on February 8, 2001. I last spoke with him when he was in great pain on his deathbed. It was a good closure. With the death of my longtime mentor, it seemed that the neo-fundamentalist paradigm that had formed so much of my life was also dying. I could no longer believe that I could perfectly interpret "God's inerrant word."

Then, just seven months later on that fateful day of September 11, 2001, Islamic fundamentalists massacred thousands of innocent people in New York, Washington DC, and Pennsylvania, all the while bellowing "God is great." Talking with several of my colleagues, I realized that the main difference between "our people" and "their people" (Islamic fundamentalists) was that ours (with the notable exception of bombing abortion clinics and assassinating doctors) had not (yet) resorted to violence.

September 11 was my turning point. I was free to move on. I began to seek out wise men from other Christian traditions: one of my old mentors Bob Mumford, reformed theologian John Armstrong, emergent church leader Brian McLaren, postmodern theologians/thinkers Stanley Grenz, Leonard Sweet, and a few longtime pastor friends. These men helped me see the flaws of my "foundationalism." As I discuss chapter 3, foundationalism is the paradigm employed by almost all ideologies and religions to construct their worldviews. Supposedly, objective truths form a philosophical or theological foundation. A number of unassailable propositions (dogma) are then erected on that foundation.

For instance, the Bible as God's inerrant word, clearly understandable to all, is the neo-fundamentalist foundation, which in turn produces hundreds of propositions regarding abortion, homosexuality, spiritual warfare, and so on. The unstated, even unconscious presupposition involved in the construction of all such foundations, *including secular ones*, is that one can objectively verify the ultimate or eternal truth of one's foundation. Once I realized that my objectivity was nothing more than illusion, the consequences were clear—the necessity of granting others the benefit of the doubt, of striving for confidence rather than certainty, of embracing pluralism, and last but not least, following Jesus in loving people rather than condemning them. *I had been born again, this time as a post-conservative, post-fundamentalist, postmodern Christian.*

I share this with you not to demonize or perpetuate the culture war, but to heal the rifts and create a dialogue.

I can hear it now—the groans and sighs, "But why bother? Those people are so infuriatingly narrow-minded, there's no talking to them even if I wanted to!" I know. Believe me, I know. But we have arrived at a critical time in American history where we have to choose what kind of America we want to live in: a free, peaceful America where all worldviews, no matter how crazy, are free to join the banquet table of public discourse, or an America where the poles of thought are so far apart and radical that fear, demonization, and even violence are used to force everyone into the dominant worldview. The rise of neo-fundamentalists in current politics and presidential campaigns, with the accompanying rancor, are proof positive that the time we have to make this decision is growing short.

In order to guide us back to the peaceable path, we have a few questions to answer: How did we get here? What makes people like Sarah Palin, Rick Perry, and Michelle Bachmann possible? And how in the world can you talk with your neo-fundamentalist neighbors and family members without it quickly escalating into high-decibel conversation?

To answer these questions, we need to peer into the neo-fundamentalist mind and history. It could be a secular, Muslim, or Christian fundamentalist—it really doesn't matter because they all work in essentially the same way—but for our purposes, we'll hone in on the Christian version. We'll start by first getting a handle on the "culture war"—what that means and who's fighting. Then I'll tell my story to give you a firsthand, in-depth look into a neo-fundamentalist mind at a major turning point in the war. Then we'll pull out and analyze it, showing what neo-fundamentalists believe and why.

Along the way, we'll go on a whirlwind tour of (relatively) recent Western political, social, and religious history to discover how we finally ended up at a point in history that makes it possible for people like Sarah Palin and Rick Perry to run for presidential offices. In fact, we'll focus on Sarah Palin's rise to power, not to conduct a witch hunt, but because, just as she is the "Queen Esther" of her neo-fundamentalist tribe, she really has come to symbolize everything the Christian neo-fundamentalist stands for. Some of what you read will be bizarre, even frightening, but hang in there, because it will pay off in the end.

Finally, we'll look at why all of us are tempted to be both dogmatic and intolerant. I offer what I hope is a somewhat unique and helpful paradigm, as well as new strategies for us to begin a civil dialogue, both locally and nationally, that can lead us to a mutual understanding, if not reconciliation.

Time is short, so let's get started, shall we?

How the Culture War Started

"The First World War of religion is upon us." —Peter Kreeft, in *Reclaiming the Great Tradition*[1]

It's a dangerous time for the world and for America. Beset by fearsome challenges within and without, our country and our people need to be at their best—wise, resourceful, stronger, and more united than ever. Instead, dissension is rife within our borders: blue vs. red states, liberals vs. conservatives, Democrats vs. Republicans, the "politically correct" vs. the "biblically correct," the Tea Party vs. the Establishment, the Christian Right vs. the Christian Left, and many other permutations threaten to turn America into a cultural wasteland.

In this time of global crisis, America is polarized and paralyzed as never before. Our democracy is rapidly disintegrating into a vituperative partisanship fueled by visceral loathing between the faith community and the nonreligious, between left and right, "progressives" and "traditionalists." All sides are becoming more entrenched, launching fusillades of invective that favor demonization over civil dialogue, wedge issues and propaganda over honest debate. While many fear the Islamic fundamentalists' plot to place the world under Islamic Law, the Sharia, most Americans may not know that Christian conservatives, long the dominant wing of the Republican Party, are increasingly falling under the spell of theocratic utopianism with its goal of establishing "God's Law" as the law of the land.

Many of us are weary of being caught in this raging uncivil

war, euphemistically known as "the culture wars." Some even call it a second civil war. Concerned with and confused by the increasingly shrill discourse, toxic atmosphere, and complexity of the culture wars, many Americans from across the politico-religious spectrum are wondering, "What's all this brouhaha about anyway?" The answer is deceptively simple: Control of our culture. If we define culture as the sum of our shared beliefs and values, and the consequent norms, or expectations, of behavior flowing from them (such as laws to criminalize behavior deemed unacceptable), the stakes become much clearer. Culture is nothing less than defining our national identity—our values and purpose as a people.

Maybe you don't think it's *that* bad, but commentators from all sides have been trying to warn us of the conflict's gravitas. Bill Moyers compares our national distress to a "political holy war . . . guided by savvy partisan operatives"[2] who know how to use wedge issues to drive us apart. Mel White, former ghostwriter for Christian Right superstars like Jerry Falwell and Pat Robertson, charges that "Christian fundamentalism is a greater threat to this country than Muslim terrorists could ever be."[3] Progressive Evangelical spokesman Jim Wallis warns:

> We contend today with both religious and secular fundamentalists, neither of whom must have their way. One group would impose the doctrines of a political theocracy on their fellow citizens, while the other would deprive the public square of needed moral and spiritual values often shaped by faith.[4]

And why does Sarah Palin, the iconic symbol of the Christian Right/Tea Party Alliance, engender more polarization than Barack Obama, George Bush, or Bill Clinton? How did *that* happen?

America is changing rapidly, radically, and fundamentally. As late as the 1950s, over 90 percent of all voters identified themselves as Christians.[5] But now the United States is home to a pluralistic "rainbow" of colors, creeds, and faiths. And while secularists (nonreligious) are still numerically in the minority, their rapidly growing population, when combined with significant numbers of liberal-leaning "mainline" Protestants and Catholics, form the majority of those in the knowledge industry (education, media, think tanks, lobbyists)—an industry that has leveraged their rapidly growing influence over the last few decades to secularize American culture.

Christian fundamentalists seek to preserve biblical principles as a basis for law and culture, insisting that their version of Christianity is the only true religion. They feel increasingly aggrieved as they witness their hierarchy of cherished values concerning the traditional family, patriarchy, homosexuality, abortion, and a host of other issues, which were generally accepted by the culture of the 1950s, become vastly diminished or invalidated by the cultural revolution that took flight in the 1960s.

For us to get a sense of the magnitude of this revolution, consider the America of the mid-1800s, which was divided into two warring nations each seeking God's guidance and blessing. Lincoln himself noted the irony that both North and South "read the same Bible and pray to the same God, and each invokes His aid against the other."[6] Both sides were energized and mobilized by Christian activists and pastors. The abolitionists who successfully goaded the North into taking on the antislavery cause as a moral crusade saw themselves as doing God's work. Theological arguments also guided the South, where prominent Calvinist theologian Robert Lewis Dabney served not only as a chaplain for Robert E. Lee's army, but as Chief of Staff to confederate hero General Stonewall Jackson.

During this time, Americans honored the Bible (or at least paid it lip service), believing it to be God's infallible revelation of Himself as the creator of both humanity and the universe (i.e. the Genesis creation story). They wrapped themselves in Victorian morality, complete with floor-length dresses and bathing suits that covered them head to ankle. Washington Post columnist E. J. Dionne Jr. notes that during this period "our nation drew upon this shared Protestant spirit to connect people to one another and to the institutions of their common democracy."

Fast-forward almost one hundred years later to the mid-1960s. There is a sexual revolution in full swing, "sex, drugs, and rock 'n roll" seemed to capture the national zeitgeist more accurately than "In God we trust," and the new trinity of Darwin, Freud, and liberal theology reigned supreme. A whole way of living—of understanding God, life, and the world—had been turned upside down in the remarkably short span of just five generations.

But Christian fundamentalists are not taking this "culture shift" sitting down. They are fighting back, waging a war for the very soul of America, a "defensive" war as they see it, to return our culture to the more traditional moral consensus that held sway previous to the 1960s. As Pentecostal TV preacher and former presidential candidate Pat Robertson demands, "We want our nation back. . . . We want our rights and privileges back. We want our symbols back and our beliefs back."[8]

Following an essentially Orthodox or "traditional" Christian dominance of American culture for most of the seventeenth, eighteenth, and nineteenth centuries, which Dionne deems "the era of white Protestant hegemony,"[9] secularists (non or antireligious folks) and those of a more liberal spiritual persuasion, jumped in the driver's seat at the dawn of the twentieth century and pretty well kept control for the better part of a century. But in the waning decades of the last millennium, conservative Christians tired of their status as back seat drivers (especially since it seemed to them that all their driving instructions were met with stony silence or painful derision) and got their hands back on the steering wheel, attempting to redirect the vehicle and its passengers on a more "godly" road. Liberal or secular passengers felt carjacked, demanding "their car" back!

These two sets of passengers—let's label them, for convenience sake, progressive-liberal-secular vs. religious-traditional-conservative—now compose two very different nations within our United States. Actually, they more resemble two entirely different worlds. The problem is that these two worlds are mirror opposites of each other. What is up in one is down in the other; what is black in one is seen as white in the opposing world. Both worlds celebrate human and individual rights, proudly proclaiming a high standard of morality and integrity. In the progressive world, the right of adults to control and autonomously exercise sovereignty over their bodies (deciding on an abortion or whether to enter into a gay relationship, for example) is sacred. But in the traditional and conservative world these very same acts desecrate all that is holy and honorable.

In a similar vein, conservative insistence on protecting the rights and life of an unborn human being and reserving "holy matrimony" and the "God-ordained institution" of marriage strictly for heterosexuals is experienced as an oppressive violation of God-given or inalienable rights by many progressives.

Consequently, what one world celebrates as patriotism, the other condemns as treason. Each side views the other through a prism of perplexity, suspicion, fear, and sometimes it seems, pure loathing. As culture observer Morris Fiorina wrote, "Many of the activists in the political parties and the various cause groups do, in fact, hate each other and regard themselves as combatants in a war."[10]

Because each army sees itself as *the* champion against evil, neither side is willing to even consider a neutral zone. Why would fundamentalists who claim to represent God and who demand God's sovereignty over His creation give any ground to those "godless humanists" who would elevate man over God in order to pursue their humanistic agenda? They honestly wonder why anyone would reject this paradigm.

But secularists certainly have their reasons, a few of which might be articulated in the following ways:

1. An infinite God is too complex for finite beings to comprehensively and infallibly interpret, let alone accurately enforce His edicts. (This view is actually representative of most Christian theologians or thinkers, from Thomas Aquinas to C. S. Lewis.)

2. Those influenced by the reigning zeitgeist of postmodernism suggest all spiritual experience or sacred knowledge is filtered through personal bias, cultural conditioning, limitations, flaws, and ignorance, and is therefore highly subjective and unreliable as a standard

to which we can demand conformity.

3. For others, God (at least the "anthropomorphic" interventionist God ascribed to by fundamentalists) does not exist. At best, if there is a God, it is inaccessible or only sporadically accessible. This is the view held by many secularists as well as members of some non-Christian faith traditions.

Ironically, each side believes it has history on its side and can provide dozens of experts to verify that the United States was (a) founded by Christians as a "new Zion" or "city on a hill" to reflect God's values to the world, or (b) an enlightenment and deist-influenced experiment in freedom of thought and religion. Trying to find a balance, Jeff Sharlet, a secular author, writes: "Our refusal to recognize the theocratic strand running throughout American history is as self-deceiving as fundamentalism's insistence that the United States was created a Christian nation."[11]

And when it comes to "experts," each army fights its battles through proxies composed of highly specialized think tanks, public policy advocates, lobbyists, and political strategists—all of whom act as polarizers. In fact, these special-interest groups have expanded exponentially from a small handful in the 1950s to a major industry a half century later.

Believe me, this is something of which I have firsthand knowledge. During the rise of the Christian Right (1978-1988), I led two of the "Big Three" fundamentalist political organizations with a reputation for playing hardball. Literally dozens of books and hundreds of newspapers either documented or decried our power, influence, and tactics. One book, entitled *God's Bullies*, credited us with regularly intimidating members of Congress. *The Religious Right: A Reference Handbook*, a sort of who's who of the Christian Fundamentalist Right, noted that I was known for my combative style.[12] When we consider that the very *raison d'être* for these groups is not only to put forth policy proposals on every issue under the sun but also to prevail at all costs, the ferociousness of our civil warfare becomes understandable.

Each army believes it has a special duty to save America from the other. Consequently each side experiences anger, indignation, and a sense of profound betrayal of America's principles by the opposing force. Each side is ready to impeach the president (whether Bush, Clinton, or Obama) and to mete out punishment to its own leaders who deviate from the party line—as evidenced by the Tea Party defeat of numerous moderate GOP incumbents in their own primary elections in 2010.

Lastly, each army has millions of enraged, energized foot soldiers ready to do hand-to-hand combat in neighborhoods, school districts, and churches. Indeed, while the Tea Party uproots the GOP establishment and elects conservative Republicans to Democratic seats, the million strong "New Apostolic Reformation" movement, which counts Sarah Palin as its major contribution to American politics, is preparing for massive spiritual warfare. As we will see in chapter 5, even now Sarah Palin's "prayer warriors" are busily scouting out Satan's strongholds, where liberals and other dupes do his evil bidding, to prepare for their forthcoming "strategic spiritual warfare" campaign.

If you think my use of military metaphor is a bit exaggerated, a number of very credible observers of the culture war, perhaps mindful of the dictum of Carl von Clausewitz, old Europe's famous military genius, that "war is the extension of political struggle by different means," have speculated that in the words of Evangelical historian Joel Carpenter, we may be facing "the specter of religiously fueled civil war."[13] Catholic theologian Richard John Neuhaus agrees:

> We are headed for religious warfare . . . this society could unravel and we would have our own version of the wars of religion in the 17th century.[14]

And sociologist James Davison Hunter, one of America's leading experts on the culture war, offers this sobering analysis:

> There is little doubt that we are in the midst of a culture war of great social and historical consequence, and thus the possibility of conflict and violence should not surprise us.[15]

Hunter goes on to quote cultural commentator Andrew Sullivan, who adds this chilling thought: "The fracturing of our culture is too deep and too advanced to be resolved by anything but coercion; and coercion . . . is not a democratic option."[16] We do not have to look any further than modern-day Eastern Europe, specifically the former Yugoslavia, to see that when political dialogue polarizes, verbal warfare—the very sort we are now inundated with—can turn physical, even in the twenty-first century. When fundamentalists' fear of losing their world and their way of life is so threatening that violence becomes an option, it's time for an intervention.

A Timely Intervention

To intervene effectively, we need to understand the uniquely potent combination of fear and dogmatic certainty held by each side of the culture wars. To this end, I will draw from the three decades I spent within the leadership of the secular conservative (think Tea Party) fundamentalist, Pentecostal, and Christian Right axis to tease out the overarching fundamentalist paradigm common to *all* parties religious and secular. Hopefully you will better understand the motivation, rhetoric, and goals of all fundamentalist ideologies—Islamic or Christian, Secular or Religious, Left or Right.

Before we begin, you need to know that I define a fundamentalist as anyone who is absolutely certain that they possess the "truth" or have the "correct view." When confronted with an opposing view, their reflexive response is a defensive rejection or offensive attack rather than extending the benefit of the doubt and calmly considering the opposing view. They tend to dismiss, demean, or demonize—often all three.

Some of the questions we will explore are:

- What are fundamentalists' assumptions about themselves, God, and others?
- What are the dynamics of radicalization that drive the fundamentalist mindset from fear to hatred to demonization, leading in some cases to violence?
- Do young men just wake up one day and decide to be suicide bombers, or to kill abortion providers, or spew out hatred toward homosexuals or members of other religions? Or do they start out wanting to serve a loving God or protect the values of their community?

One of my motivations for spending all too many months writing this book is to expose how this subtle yet powerful mix is leading to a jihad mentality, which I fear, is escalating to an inexorable flashpoint. Further, I intend to unmask the

prime mover behind the radical transformation of a once benign secular conservative movement—a little-known dogma
called Dominionism. When mixed with neo-fundamentalism,
you get a perfect storm of Puritan "covenant" theology, manifest destiny, enlightenment rationalism, with a healthy dol-
lop of Old Testament style theocracy on top. It all adds up to a
warfare theology where Jesus is King (as opposed to the historical Christian model where Jesus is a servant or steward) and
his warriors are duty-bound to "bring all things into submission to King Jesus." Dominionism or "Reconstructionism," as
Evangelical author Randall Balmer notes in *Thy Kingdom Come*,
"is a social ethic popular among leaders of the religious right
that advocates restructuring civil society according to the laws
contained in the Hebrew Bible."[17] And the problem with this,
of course, is that as Charles Kimball, professor of religion at
Wake Forest University, notes, "When zealous and devout adherents elevate the teachings and beliefs of their tradition to
the level of absolute truth claims, they open a door to the possibility that their religion will become evil."[18]

Please understand that I'm not talking about the Tea Party
movement that began in earnest in 2010. While in some ways
the Tea Party could be described as fundamentalist in its approach to complex economic issues, and I suspect it is heavily populated by fundamentalists, I'm not writing about them.
Not because I agree or disagree with them, but simply because
the depth of my thirty years of leadership lies within the world
of Christian fundamentalists and neo-fundamentalists. These
movements are in my opinion much more dangerous. The Tea
Party, from what I understand, stands primarily for a reduc-
tion in the size and inefficiency of government and less taxes.
While their approach may be overly simplistic, I think most of

us can agree that less taxes and a leaner government is at least an admirable goal. The Tea Party also seems to sport a streak of Libertarianism that I rather like. I don't think they want to control anyone. In fact they want less control of everything, which represents quite a contrast to the morally correct agenda of neo-fundamentalist politicians like Sarah Palin, Rick Perry, and Michele Bachmann.

As an insider, indeed a cocreator, of the neo-fundamentalist juggernaut, I have slowly (too slowly!) come to realize how our prideful, overbearing, self-righteous sense of an almost infallible certainty regarding our ability to objectively discern God's position on any number of issues inevitably leads us first to demonizing our opponents (think Clinton and Obama), then to outright hate (of homosexuals, abortionists, secular humanists) and finally to a religiously-fueled jihad in the form of a political/religious agenda of theocracy and "dominion." Interestingly, both Islamic and neo-fundamentalist jihadists are in agreement that America's liberal elite unwittingly serve Satan's interests by endorsing evolution, abortion, gay rights, and sexual promiscuity (including immodest dress). This is why Islamic jihadists refer to the USA as the "Great Satan." What separates these two jihadist camps is that neo-fundamentalists haven't resorted to the use of violence to achieve their goals— yet. The danger is that the radical fringe represented by my former Reconstructionist colleagues, who inspired violence, including murder, against abortion providers will gain more influence if neo-fundamentalists feel they are playing a game that they can't win.

Of course the hubris of absolute certainty and its concomitant tendency to vilify all who resist their truth is not limited to fundamentalist religious traditions. The nonreligious, atheists, and secularists as well as the extremes of both left and right have in the twentieth century proved to be the most intolerant of all. Neither the Nazis nor the communists were known for promoting religion or pluralism. As historian Karen Armstrong comments, "reason can on occasion become demonic and commit crimes that are as great as, if not greater than, any of the atrocities perpetrated by fundamentalists."[19]

Indeed, secularists' assault on fundamentalist Christian values, particularly over the last half-century, have predictably galvanized neo-fundamentalist Christians into a defensive political reaction. Secularists forgot the first law of thermodynamics—that every action is met by an equal and opposing reaction. As Jim Wallis observes, "It was, in part, the assaults of secularism that helped turn fundamentalism into the right-wing force it has become today in the United States."[20] Gary McCuen, writing a history of the Religious Right agrees, citing "uncritical and insensitive radical-liberal changes in the 1960s and 1970s"[21] as provoking a fundamentalist backlash. E. J. Dionne speculates that 1960s liberals shifting their focus from economic justice, trade unionism, and racial equality to issues of "gender, sexuality, and personal choice" including "gay marriage and Hollywood culture" not only caused a "rupture between liberalism and those religious traditionalists who had once been allied to progressives," but also "accounts for the rise of the Religious Right."[22]

Ironically the combined effect of these dynamics, which we will explore in more detail later, gave neo-fundamentalist theorists the tools they needed to convince many moderate Evangelicals that their pietistic paradigm of a private, internal Christianity (favored since the early twentieth century) was inadequate to meet the challenges of aggressive secularism. A more robust response was required. Armstrong sums up the conflict this way:

> Fundamentalists did not have a monopoly on anger. Their movements had often evolved in a dialectical relationship with an aggressive secularism which showed scant respect for religion and its adherents. Secularists and fundamentalists sometimes seem trapped in an escalating spiral of hostility and recrimination.[23]

Demonization in Real Life

If you think I am exaggerating, consider when Jerry Falwell and some of my other former colleagues implicated Bill Clinton as a murderer in a video in the 1990s. Or when President George W. Bush was blamed for everything from blowing up the World Trade Center on 9/11 to sacrificing American lives in Iraq so he and Vice President Cheney could increase oil company revenues.

But the craziness didn't stop just with your average unsophisticated, placard-waving agitator. This unthinking knee-jerk demonization was also promoted by, in Palin's words, members of the "media elite." National Public Radio and MoveOn.org both propagated comparisons between President Bush and Adolf Hitler while MSNBC's Keith Olberman called Bush a fascist on national television.[24] On other occasions Olberman turned his role as news anchor into a bully pulpit to describe the duly elected president of the United States as a "pathological liar or idiot in chief . . . guilty of panoramic and murderous deceit."[25]

Unfortunately both sides don't stop at demonizing leaders of whom they disapprove, but extend their rant to entire people groups as aptly demonstrated by MSNBC's Ed Schultz when he declared during the health-care debate, "The Republicans want to see you dead. They'd rather make money off your dead corpse."[26] Really? All Republicans? Liberal, moderate, conservative, Catholic, and born-again Evangelical Republicans—all want us dead? It is this pattern of mass demonization that often precedes genocidal attacks. This type of hate speech does not belong in America. And neither does talk show host Michael Savage's inflammatory rhetoric that President Obama "is raping our democracy."[27] Of course President Obama fares no better than Bush did. Many neo-fundamentalists, including some ministers, believe he is the Antichrist and even more think he is a Muslim. Other people, like neo-fundamentalist Tom Delay, the former Republican majority leader of the U.S. Congress, also suspect the President is a closet communist, or at least a socialist.[28]

Hope for the Future

The great challenge I hope we will explore together is how to transcend this escalating spiral before the fabric of our national unity is torn apart so violently that we cannot be made whole again. In future chapters we will discover ways of identifying and dialoguing with emerging voices of goodwill—sane voices of reason who, while committed to and confident (as opposed to adamantly certain) of their positions, are at least aware of the possibility that they—in their humanness—may not have a 100 percent lock on absolute and objective truth.

To heal the wounds afflicting America's soul—the toxic polarization of the culture wars and the political stalemate of acrimonious partisanship—we must completely cease the mutual demonization of each other. We need to say "ENOUGH!"

We all need to stop attacking and start listening.

We must learn to understand, even empathize with, the fears that drive *both* sides of the culture wars. We must set aside our preconceived notions and judgments to get inside the mindset found on the extremes of our paralyzing national divide of liberal vs. conservative and religious vs. secular. *Only then can we begin a national dialogue of hope, healing, and reconciliation.*

Let there be no mistake—reconciliation is a necessity, not a luxury. As Wallis notes, "In a deeply polarized country, when half the people do feel crushed, the need for some kind of political healing and reconciliation becomes clear."[29]

Is it possible for sides so polarized to call a cease fire long enough to be able to hear, understand, and maybe—just maybe—empathize (not sympathize!) with the other side's fears and perceptions? Can we open a dialogue based on values from both sides: from the secular side, tolerance, civility, and mutual respect for humankind; and from the religious side, an approach that follows Jesus' great command of loving your neighbor as well as your enemy, turning the other cheek, and treating others as you would like to be treated?

Think of the possibilities if all the warring parties would call a time-out to their mindless exchange of epithets and mutual recriminations. Perhaps for the first time, they could listen long enough to understand each other—without having to agree! The good news is that this dialogue of hope, healing, and reconciliation, so imperative for our survival as a nation, is eminently possible. After all, "sides" are made up of individuals—people like you and me—*and I'm ready to listen if you are!*

2

My Journey from Idealist to Christian Jihadist

I WAS AT the top of my game. A Christian Right power bro-
ker comfortably ensconced in my penthouse office a stone's
throw from the Potomac River. I had good reason to be satisfied. I was the guy in charge of mobilizing Evangelicals to cast
their ballots to reelect Ronald Reagan as the fortieth president
of the United States of America, and we had just swept forty-
nine states. *Forty- nine!* It was the biggest electoral landslide in
recent history, and to sweeten the victory, the hapless losers,
former Vice President Walter Mondale and Congresswoman
Geraldine Ferraro, both had lashed out at my national multi-
media campaign to demonize them. My poisoned arrows had
hit their mark, just as they had four years previously against
Jimmy Carter and almost the entire liberal leadership of the
U.S. Senate. Sitting in my Washington command post, having
ensured the future freedom of the Republic from communism
abroad and socialism at home, I had for the first time in a decade the luxury to relish where I'd been and dream of where I
would head next.

I had accumulated everything needed to launch a new "crusade" against the next enemy. I had power, money, an enviable track record, and consequently, prestige. Along with a few partners like mega best-selling author Tim LaHaye, I had built a confederation of neo-fundamentalist organizations that included a lobby, political action committee, tax-exempt foundation, and the largest coalition of Evangelical leaders ever mobilized. It included 1980s era Christian TV goliaths like Jerry Falwell, Jim Bakker, and Jimmy Swaggart. In fact, *U.S. News and World Report* identified two of my organizations as part of the "Big Three" Christian Right powerhouses, the third being Jerry Falwell's Moral Majority. I also was working directly under Lyn Nofziger—Reagan's former press secretary, White House political director and then campaign manager. I chaired the Reagan-Bush Christian Voter Registration Task Force, charged with registering and mobilizing the millions of Evangelical voters who had been a vital part of Reagan's 1980 upset over the incumbent, born-again Southern Baptist Sunday school teacher Jimmy Carter.

When I wasn't strategizing the next move for one of the key players on the 1984 election chessboard, I could be found raging against child abuse, gay rights, abortion, and of course, liberals on my *Christian Voice Washington Report,* broadcast daily into key election states. In my spare time I published the *Presidential Biblical Scoreboard,* a glossy full-length color magazine awarding every candidate for federal office a morality score (ostensibly based on their voting record in public office). Walter Mondale reacted by waving the *Scoreboard* in front of a phalanx of TV cameramen, vehemently objecting to being demonized by the "new Ku Klux Klan." During the week of the 1984 GOP national convention, the media was starving for news with Reagan's renomination a foregone conclusion. While the country waited for official notice that Reagan had once again accepted the nomination, the feature story on the network news night after night was the *Presidential Scoreboard*, a copy of which I had provided to every delegate at the convention, and the full page ad I ran in the official GOP convention handbook that boldly threatened to crush any liberal trying to outrun our Christian Right juggernaut.

Requisite to the exercise of political influence is the perception of power. After foundation studies and several books (with titles like *God's Bullies*) concluded that our ground troops had played a major role in defeating three dozen liberal members of the House and Senate, the media smelled power.

Soon thereafter I was interviewed by CBS anchor Dan Rather on *60 Minutes*, who described my organization, Christian Voice, as "one of America's largest and most influential Christian Right groups." I was also on Phil Donahue's show, as well as on primetime network news for three consecutive evenings. The media liked me because I was, to say the least, provocative. In 2007, *The Religious Right: A Reference Handbook* observed, "Doner was noted for his combative style in his appearances on television programs."[30] A full-page interview in *The Washington Times* followed, then an avalanche of interview requests from every conceivable media—from Swedish television to the Baton Rouge, Louisiana *Advocate*, from radio and TV talk shows to local churches (where I usually received standing ovations). It wasn't long until the ink was splashing far and wide across national magazines ranging from a cover story in *Christian Life* to *Time Magazine*.

With extensive media coverage for results, both promised and delivered, came notoriety. I was a Christian Right rock star. When I attended conservative megachurches, pastors routinely noted my presence in the pews from their pulpits. I often wondered about this. Wasn't a holy service supposed to focus on Jesus and not political celebrities? Of course I didn't mind all that much! As I said, I was at the top of my game. I had fulfilled my childhood vision, a vision that had relentlessly propelled me forward for the last twenty years—my entire adult life. Like my peers who had been energized exactly two decades earlier by Barry Goldwater's quixotic quest for the presidency, I had dedicated myself to the victory of the free world over the godless, totalitarian "Evil Empire" of communism, as Ronald Reagan so famously termed it. Now at least theoretically, every inhabitant of Planet Earth could share the American dream of life, liberty, and the pursuit of happiness as well as justice for all.

But rather than feeling satisfied or elated, I found myself totally, devastatingly depleted. In place of my heart, I felt only a huge, aching void. It was as if serving as a commander in the culture wars had sucked out my very essence, leaving a hollowed out shell. I began to sense that in my quest to save America I had lost my soul. Jesus asked, "What good is it for a man to gain the whole world, yet forfeit his soul?" (Mark 8:36, NIV). I thought I knew what he meant. I hadn't lost my soul, but I had lost my way, which is what I think Jesus was talking about. My obsessive devotion to the culture wars had sidetracked me from the path I had embarked on as a child—to follow Jesus, whatever that meant.

Second Thoughts

As I contemplated my interrupted spiritual pilgrimage, I began to have second thoughts about the neo-fundamentalist agenda

I had helped to form. We were against a lot of things, but what were we *for*, other than empty clichés like "God and Country?" Specifically, we vehemently demonized the homosexual community and the pro-choicers, while ignoring the poor and sick in America and around the world. Where was Jesus' love and compassion for AIDS victims, for the rape victims, for unwed mothers who had nowhere to turn, for the downtrodden, the outcasts, and those "left behind"? In 1988, those doubts turned into a full-length book, *Second Thoughts*, which was eventually re-titled *The Samaritan Strategy: A New Agenda for Christian Activism*. Surprisingly the book garnered positive critical reviews from across the theological spectrum, from the liberal mainline protestant *Christian Century* to the centrist evangelical *Christianity Today* to the conservative Pentecostal *Charisma*. Unsurprisingly, it didn't become a bestseller. Serious "issue" books are a notoriously hard sell in the Evangelical book world, which is more oriented to personal growth, devotionals, celebrity testimonies, and of course, apocalyptic fiction like Tim LaHaye's *Left Behind* series.

From a different vantage point, the authoritative *The Religious Right* summed up my *Samaritan Strategy* this way:

Doner left Washington in 1986, having decided that the religious right had failed to achieve its objectives. After leaving Washington, Doner, reflecting on past political involvement, concluded that the religious right neglected to demonstrate sufficient concern for those in need, such as abused children and the homeless. Altering strategy, Doner began to seek contacts with more liberal evangelical Christians to try to work together in

achieving common service goals. He claimed that
Christians will merit the opportunity for leadership in their communities by caring for those in
need.[31]

As it turned out there was apparently one other significant
set of eyes combing through the pages of *The Samaritan Strategy*. In 1989 Pat Robertson, fresh from his abortive 1988 presidential run (which his campaign tried to recruit me to help
manage—I turned down their offer in order to write *The Samaritan Strategy*), and Ralph Reed were brainstorming their
next adventure, which would mark the launch of the second
wave of the Christian Right. At this auspicious moment, I sent
both Pat and Ralph autographed copies of *The Samaritan Strategy*. Christian Right watchdog and author Frederick Clarkson, in an intriguing report on Reed rolling out the "Samaritan Project" as the centerpiece of the Christian Coalition's
attempt to balance its hard-right agenda with a little compassion, wrote:

> A book by political strategist Colonel V. Doner
> drafted "a new agenda for Christian activism." Do-
> ner wrote, "What would a *Christian conservative co-
> alition* [emphasis added] in power really do about
> the economy, national defense, nuclear war, hun-
> ger, poverty, AIDS, etc?"

> Doner rejected the religious right's efforts to cap-
> ture the White House. Instead he described a
> bold new plan to bring the Christian Right into
> the next century. His 1988 book is called *The Sa-*

maritan Strategy. Then, exactly one year later, Pat Robertson launched the Christian Coalition with Ralph Reed at the helm. . . . The Christian Coalition and the Samaritan Project appear to mirror Colonel Doner's "Christian conservative coalition" and *The Samaritan Strategy.* Much of the Christian Coalition and Samaritan Project game plan appears in Doner's book.[32]

Like Pat Robertson and Ralph Reed, I was awakening to the realization that God expected more from us than just a long list of "antis." God required compassion as well as justice, and he wanted it for poor liberal Democrats as well as middle-class conservative Republicans. What I lacked was a cohesive framework, a way to put it all together. I needed a Christian worldview. So I determinedly set out on an arduous decade-long trek through the theological wastelands of Evangelicalism, searching for God's will for America and me. Along the way I became something of a Christian jihadist.

What in the world happened to me? How did I mutate from a young idealist on a "Jesus Quest" to a hardened Christian Right political operative and finally, to a Christian jihadist?

The journey from idealist to jihadist is not nearly as rare or unusual as you might think or hope. In fact, if you ponder the tens of thousands (millions?) of young Muslims who demonstrate a willingness to die for Allah as they anxiously volunteer to blow themselves and others to smithereens, you have to wonder what sort of insanity is at work.

Did these young men (and increasingly, women) just decide one fine morning they'd become suicide bombers rather than attend school or go off to work? Or did they start off as young

idealists seeking to serve God by defending justice, purity, traditional values, and truth, as they perceived it? Did their naive-
té, earnestness, and impressionability mark them as easy prey
for fundamentalist Imams to instill in them an *unshakeable
certainty* in Islam's claim to be the *exclusive voice of God*—and
a concomitant hatred of all those who oppose what's "good,
true and pure?" After teaching them it was their holy duty to
defend God against the encroaching infidels/pagans/rebels
against God, did their mentors point them in our direction?

Does the same thing happen within radical Christianity?
You bet it does! My hope is that I can shed some light on this
subtle yet insidious radicalization process by sharing how it
happened to me.

I'm in the Lord's Army . . . Yes, Sir!

I was raised a good Christian child by my loving parents in a
fundamentalist Baptist church in Orange County. Like most
kids raised in a fundamentalist home at that time, I made a
"born again decision" at a Billy Graham-style crusade when I
was twelve years old. I learned to love Jesus and to love others "as he loved me." But, like most kids, my sense of God's
love and justice was countered by how the world really works.
If evil and injustice were such a widespread problem, then I
wanted to do something about it! I started reading stories of
poverty and oppression, feeding my offended and outraged
idealism. By the highly impressionable and idealistic age of
fourteen, I had devoured thousands of pages chronicling the
horrific evils of Nazism and communism. I read about the
mind-boggling enormity of the millions of innocents (exclud-
ing military casualties) murdered by Nazi goons and the even
larger number of souls annihilated by Stalin, Mao Tse-tung,

and their crazed imitators in Mother Russia and China, Africa and Cuba, Afghanistan and Cambodia. The sheer monstrosity of the Holocaust, the gulags, the torture of millions of men, women, and even children appeared to me to be nothing less than evil incarnate.

So at fourteen, resolving to fight oppression and injustice and to "punish the evildoers," I sweet-talked my dear mother into typing up a paper outlining how I would stop the advance of communism, since Nazism (or "National Socialism") was no longer much of a target, at least in its official form. Throughout high school my idealism shifted loyalties from Jesus and was gradually wedded to an ideology, as idealism often is— an ideology based on strident anti-communism, fervent free-enterprise, American exceptionalism, and Christian preeminence.

My independent fundamentalist Baptist church, which was too independent to even be associated with any other Baptist churches, was captained by "Fighting Bob Wells." Orange County at that time in the 1960s and '70s was a hotbed of right-wing activism, so it shouldn't be too surprising that at the tender age of fifteen I was inducted into the John Birch Society and the hard-right California Republican Assembly. Before I was old enough to drive a car, my rabble-rousing talents were rewarded by an equal vote at a weekly strategy meeting of several dozen conservative leaders from around the county.

While membership in the conspiratorially minded John Birch Society may seem bizarre to a twenty-first-century perspective, in the mid-sixties it was considered by many conservatives to be America's premier patriotic anticommunist organization. Its admirers once included none other than Barry Goldwater and William F. Buckley. With the Soviets threatening nuclear war over the twin crises of Berlin and Cuba, with John F. Kennedy considering a first strike on Russian soil, with *Life* magazine declaring "The American people are willing to face nuclear war for Berlin," and with IBM awarding employees enough cash to build their very own nuclear fallout shelter, cold war anxiety was at its zenith.

Similar to the experience of many youths attending Islamic mosques, it was my religious authority, "Fighting Bob Wells," who initiated my radicalization by personally introducing me to the Reverend Dr. Billy James Hargis, the president of the "Christian Crusade," the '60s precursor to the Moral Majority. Hargis was recruiting students for the inaugural class of his Christian Anti-Communist Youth University called the Summit, located in idyllic Manitou Springs, Colorado, at the foot of the regal Pikes Peak. So in 1963, I signed up to be trained several weeks every summer for the next four years in the newly minted ideology of the neo-fundamentalist Christian Right. Basically it consisted of a Birchite agenda of rabid anticommunism, unrestrained nationalism, unfettered capitalism, and states' rights camouflaged underneath a Christian veneer.

Anxious to engage the enemy or anyone suspected of providing "aid and comfort" in my first year as class president, I garnered several days' worth of headlines as the controversial head of a "right-wing youth militia" by organizing a boycott of local merchants. Their offense? Subsidizing "slave labor" by selling exports from the Soviet bloc to unsuspecting Americans—in other words, handicrafts produced in Eastern Europe.

By my fourth year, at age eighteen, I was promoted to the faculty and marketed nationally as the first prototype of a new generation of leaders (send more money so we can train *more* young militants to save America!). When I wasn't training my peers to return home and organize (or disrupt) their local campuses, I served as *aide de camp* to Major General Edwin Walker who had just been personally terminated from his NATO command by the Kennedys. It seems Walker had, like many other senior officers, relied on "Birchite" educational materials, which questioned the loyalties of everyone from Presidents Truman and Eisenhower on down. Walker's dismissal was greeted by rage from conservatives in Congress and the media. In turn, liberals feared—as perhaps Kennedy himself did—a right-wing military coup. So while my buddies were off playing sports, I was meeting and greeting hundreds of adults amazed that General Walker's attaché, "Colonel" Doner, appeared so young!

One of my mentors during this time was the Summit's dean, the brilliant Dr. David A. Noebel. Noebel is arguably the intellectual progenitor of the Christian Right. He was the first to identify the major issues that the Christian Right would rally around, writing full-length books about the dangers of secular humanism, abortion, rock music (it led to premarital sex), and homosexuality (which, of course, was even worse!). He was also one of the first to write, along with Francis Schaeffer, a massive tome on the definitive Christian worldview, *Understanding the Times*. He followed that up by writing with Tim LaHaye a book called *Mind Siege*, which attacked secular humanism.

With the exception of his dislike of rock and roll, conservative Evangelicals have wholeheartedly adopted Noebel's agenda and his rationale for Christian activism. It's not a coincidence that to this day one of his most vocal backers is neo-fundamentalist powerhouse James Dobson.

In an interesting aside, Noebel's boss Hargis, as well as his colleague General Walker, were both toppled from power in gay scandals. The good General in a Texas men's room and The Reverend Hargis for seducing both male and female students on his American Christian College campus (where Noebel had served as dean).

As I reflect back on those early years when my worldview was formed, I now realize that it was then that I had become a Christian jihadist. A jihadist in the sense as it's explicitly understood in Islam (and implicitly understood in other fundamentalist traditions) as an eternal struggle—or revolution—against any force that usurps God's sovereign right to enforce His law over humanity. The jihadists' inability to admit any gray areas or neutral zones, or to acknowledge any uncertainty regarding their universal truth claims, inexorably concludes with demonizing any and all challengers. We'll explore this worldview in more depth in chapters 3 and 4.

And so it was in my teenage years, I committed my body and soul to defeating the satanic forces of communism, atheism, and secularism that threatened God's sovereignty over our Christian nation. I found my inspiration in the violent men of God I learned about in Sunday school—men like Gideon who, with only 300 godly warriors, annihilated over 135,000 men who served false gods. My personal favorite was Samson who, "filled by the spirit of the Lord," grabbed the jawbone of an ass and slew 1,000 unbelievers in a brief afternoon's work.

Decades later, as I led the legions of Christian leaders into battle armed with their election kits; my entourage decided I was a modern day Joshua. Joshua, as you may remember, was Moses' right-hand man who laid siege to the unfortunate city of Jericho "where the walls came a-tumbling down" (as a favorite fundamentalist hymn goes). Scriptures proudly report he wiped out the whole city including every man, woman, and child (with the exception of his spy, Rahab the prostitute and her family), as well as all the livestock. He was a take-no-prisoner type of guy, a perfect role model for me as a Christian Right political hit man! My legions would be more modern but no more merciful and certainly not less effective than Samson's jawbone.

What's Faith Got to Do With It?

When I entered the professional ranks of Christian Right strategists at age thirty, my entire motivation was to elect candidates to support Reagan in defeating the Evil Empire (mission accomplished!), scaling back the American bureaucracy, and safeguarding the rights and freedom of every American. Unlike many politicians, Reagan pretty much fulfilled these campaign promises, which is why he's loved by so many people, even retrospectively by people who never even voted for him— including more than a few Democrats.

While I'd given my life to Ronald Reagan, I had become more ambivalent about Jesus. I was still sorting through the maze of distortions about following Jesus that had been my fundamentalist heritage. I was spiritual, but not religious. I wanted Jesus, but not Christianity (can you relate to this?). I thought I might take the next decade to work it all through, but as I rose in the political ranks, I had to give more interviews to shows like *60 Minutes* and I realized that I could no longer avoid questions about my faith. I had purposely kept myself in the background because I really didn't consider myself to be a solid Evangelical, and I had the integrity to not want to misrepresent myself as something that I wasn't. Like many of my peers, I became an atheist in college, substituting Ayn Rand for Jesus—one fundamentalist paradigm for another. When both my parents died within a year of each other shortly after I graduated, I began to contemplate death and eternity. I cautiously edged back to Christianity as I began to wonder where was I going to end up—heaven or hell? Lost in thoughts of the afterlife, I happened to catch evangelist Billy Graham on TV. As always, the man's integrity and sincerity impressed me. I sat down and read his tome on being "born again" and decided to renew my childhood commitment. This time it was final. I joined up with the local mainline Presbyterian Church in town and began to study C. S. Lewis, the patron saint of Evangelicaldom, and of course, my Bible. I asked my live-in girlfriend to move out and I quit smoking. I was on the path. From then on, however, I would continue to make an important distinction: I was *not* a Christian leader and did not want to be regarded as such. Rather, I was a political leader who happened to be a Christian. But they still weren't mutually exclusive—my idealistic, fundamentalist roots were still offended by evil and that fueled my passion and sense of outrage.

In order to bring down the Evil Empire, I was ready to do whatever it took to replace communist-coddling liberals with militant cold "war-riors." It didn't take me long to become a hardened political pro, willing to exploit issues that I was personally ambivalent about (like gay rights and abortion) to win elections. As I explained to one of Reagan's top three confidantes, my good friend Lyn Nofziger, we would never be able to motivate Evangelicals to the polls based on the issues that he and I were most concerned about—economics, national defense, and foreign policy. I asked, "Lyn, do you really care if we defeat liberal senators like George McGovern, Frank Church, John Culver, and Birch Bayh on *our* issues or if we do it using prayer in school, abortion, and gay rights?" He paused for a moment, looked me in the eye, grinned, and offered his help. Personally, I had nothing against homosexuals. Several of my young Republican friends were gay. And I was mostly ambivalent about abortion, although it seemed to me that cutting up a baby that had already developed fingers and toes was a long stretch from zapping a formless embryo. Nevertheless, as a political strategist, these were efficacious wedge issues I could not afford to ignore.

It was tying these two issues around Carter's neck like the proverbial albatross that made a majority of Evangelicals switch their votes from Jimmy Carter, a born-again Southern Baptist Sunday school teacher, to a divorced, non-churchgoing movie actor with a weakness for astrology. When ABC News began to bombard me with questions about whether or not we were going to run TV commercials against Carter, I was a little slow on the uptake. It took me a few days to figure out that if we actually had a few commercials "in the can," ABC would probably give them free airtime—that's prime-time evening airtime! Necessity was clearly the mother of invention as I raced about producing the TV spots. I scrounged together some footage of the reliably "outrageous" annual gay rights parade in San Francisco, which ended up with a flamboyant gay couple making out in a park. We froze that particular scene into a frame and morphed it into a picture of President Carter with the overlaid message that President Carter and the Democratic Party were supporting the gay-rights agenda. Syndicated columnist Judy Bachrach wrote, "Doner's group has done far more than merely endorsing Reagan. In a TV commercial written by Doner himself, it managed to transform Jimmy Carter's character quite miraculously."[33]

I also hurriedly scratched out several additional commercials, hiring a local film crew to film my executive assistant, a matron with four children sitting on the porch of my West Coast headquarters, a Victorian office building in beautiful Monterey, California, ticking off the reasons why she, as a "Christian mother of four, could not vote for Jimmy Carter because of his pro-gay-pro-abortion-anti-prayer-in-school platform."

We couldn't have planned for (or prayed for!) what happened next. ABC immediately began running almost nonstop clips of the ads on the network news, soon followed by NBC and CBS. So we had all three networks running poor Jimmy Carter being morphed into a gay-rights advocate while reporting that we were going to spend over a million dollars (that's 1980 dollars) on our media buys.

That's all President Carter needed to see. He was apparently so stunned by the first wave of TV commercials presenting him as a gay-rights proponent that he called a national press conference. All that did, of course, was to guarantee my message was given front-page exposure across the country for every Evangelical to read. When I similarly demonized Vice President Walter Mondale four years later, he too couldn't resist taking the bait—and with similarly disastrous results.

1984—Riding the Reagan Wave

For George Orwell, 1984 was an ominous year, as well as, I suspect, for most liberal Democrats. For me it was an auspicious year beginning with Lyn Nofziger, now acting as Reagan's reelection campaign manager along with the notorious Lee Atwater, sanctioning me to form an Evangelical Task Force for the Reagan/Bush reelection campaign called the Reagan-

Bush Christian Liaison Committee. When I arrived at Reagan's headquarters for our first meeting it was like old-home week as I embraced a number of Reagan's regional campaign managers who I knew from my Young Republican days, or in the case of former Congressman John Rousselot, from my old John Birch days. Our assignment was to mobilize a massive effort to register Evangelical voters. The Reagan campaign was savvy enough to realize that Evangelicals, critical to Reagan's 1980 victory, would be needed once again. While many voters assumed Reagan would easily take the '84 election, the voter-registration gurus at Reagan/Bush were panicking over reports of Jesse Jackson's success in mobilizing black voters in the South. It was feared that these voters might cancel out the conservative blue-collar voters or "Reagan Democrats" that the Reagan campaign counted on. Our job was to be sure we offset Jackson's efforts. We were Reagan's insurance policy.

My first duty was to recommend to Lyn a high-profile Evangelical leader to serve as our public face to millions of not-yet-registered Evangelical voters. I had to think long and hard about whom would be the best candidate to chair our Liaison Committee. I knew that it couldn't be any of the so-called "TV ministers" like Robertson or Falwell, because they saw each other as competition—for "souls" as well as dollars and ratings. If I put one in charge, the others might not play ball. So it occurred to me that my good friend Tim LaHaye would be perfect. He was popular, not a TV preacher, and he was well liked by all the other major players.

I set up the first meeting of the Task Force at Reagan headquarters, hosted by none other than Reagan campaign manager Lyn Nofziger. The day of the meeting I had to act quickly to avert disaster: Lyn had no idea who LaHaye was, and LaHaye was having serious second thoughts about accepting the position because Reagan was too liberal! So minutes before our crucial inaugural meeting, I pulled Lyn aside and took a few minutes to brief him on LaHaye's background. I also pulled Lyn's large cigar out of his front jacket pocket and hid it in his inside pocket so as not to offend LaHaye's fundamentalist piety. Filing into the conference room, Lyn buttonholed Tim in a way that you would have thought he was his old lost army buddy. Once we were all seated Lyn greeted us "on behalf of the President of the United States" and asked LaHaye to lead. LaHaye, instantly mesmerized, eagerly accepted the chairmanship.

But it soon became apparent that something was missing, namely money, the "mother's milk" of politics. We needed a sophisticated network to run a massive voter-registration campaign that would be separate from the GOP apparatus in order to provide the GOP plausible deniability should someone want to make an issue of Reagan's closeness to the Christian Right. That size of an operation would demand money—and lots of it. Consequently, we came up with the idea of the American Coalition for Traditional Values (ACTV), which would do the real work of voter registration. The question I wrestled with was who would be most effective in enrolling as many of the nation's Evangelical leaders as possible? Once again, LaHaye seemed to be the most likely candidate. He accepted with relish when I suggested he would be the ideal spokesman. The only hitch to taking the position was that he had to relinquish his position as chairman of the Reagan Voter Registration Task Force, a problem he quickly solved by nominating me for the job.

I then found myself in the enviable position of serving as

liaison between the Reagan campaign and the Evangelical
community, being CEO for Christian Voice and the American
Christian Voice Foundation, and serving as one of the three
directors for the American Coalition for Traditional Values.
This also made me the "official link" between the GOP and
the Christian Right, which John Buchanan, a liberal Republican Evangelical member of Congress, loudly complained about
in his syndicated column:

> In another indication of the close ties between the
> Republican Party and the religious right, Colonel
> Donner [sic] the leader of the ultra-fundamentalist
> group Christian Voice, was appointed "chairman
> of the Christian Liaison Committee for the Rea-
> gan/Bush '84 campaign. ... His duties included the
> "responsibility to initiate, coordinate and monitor
> all Christian activity in support of President Rea-
> gan's campaign."[34]

The White House knew I would do anything it took to reelect the president. In fact, White House aide Carolyn Sunds-
eth wrote me a personal note of appreciation on behalf of the
President, remarking, "Your willingness to do whatever was in
your power, no matter what the sacrifice, were of real value to
the President and excellent help to us."

But as single-minded and committed as I was, I remained
concerned that I was not doing enough to reassure Reagan's
reelection. So I produced the nation's first one-hour Christian
Right TV special, "America Betrays Her Children" featuring a
number of Evangelical leaders and "talking heads." The program aired in all fifty states and lost massive amounts of mon-

ey, but it pumped up our voter-registration efforts.

The rest of the story, as they say, is history. We celebrated Reagan's Washington DC victory party and both Lee Atwater and Lyn Nofziger were particularly kind in their praise for my efforts. Lyn even took the time to write me a personal note congratulating me, "Your role in structuring the American Coalition for Traditional Values and its voter registration campaign was outstanding and certainly played a significant part in the president's overwhelming victory!"

But after two decades as a Washington operative and Christian Right leader, credited with helping elect Reagan in '80 and '84, and with playing a central role in the defeat of three dozen liberal members of Congress, I felt I was done. In fact, it was the very week the *Washington Times* featured *on the front page* a large full-color picture of me holding forth at a press conference on the steps of Congress that I decided to leave. Why not exit at the top of my game? Of course it also helped that I was burned out physically, spiritually, and emotionally. I was thirty-seven and experiencing a mid-life crisis. So I jumped into my turbo-charged "Z" car and raced west to northern California's rugged coast and lush vineyards, away from the spiritual vacuity of my political world. I was on a quest for the spiritual fulfillment I'd put on hold long enough to "save America."

I was looking for Jesus.

Instead I found the Coalition on Revival and Dennis Peacocke, one of Peter Wagner's 500 Pentecostal "Apostles," a battalion of nutty zealots who would "disciple" me, and eventually Sarah Palin. I also found R. J. Rushdoony, the prolific Calvinist theologian and patriarch of the theocratic Dominionist movement.

Joining the Jihadists: The Coalition on Revival

As a star of the Christian Right's Evangelical/Charismatic wing, I quickly came to the attention of the leaders of the Coalition on Revival (COR), a coalition of over 600 Evangelical theologians and neo-fundamentalist leaders who believed in "reconstructing" America into a biblically based society. COR included a raft of Evangelical college professors, respected academics, best-selling authors, a cohort of Christian Right leaders, and, most ominously, a platoon of Assembly of God (Sarah Palin's denomination) types, who would eventually combine their spirit-filled Pentecostalism with COR's Dominionism to create a novel theory of "spiritual warfare" that fueled an army of spiritual commandos (we'll dive into these waters in chapters 6 and 7). While the coalition was ostensibly a theological enterprise, its real mission was to hammer out twenty-two worldview documents showing how to "apply the word of God to every sphere of life." This meant applying the "Law of God" to everything from business (ethics) to medicine (no stem-cell research), from government (no abortion, gay marriage) to the arts (must honor God). In other words, COR was designing the intellectual and theological blueprints for a government based on biblical law.

COR was headed by the irrepressible and highly energetic Jay Grimstead, whose real passion was to spawn a never-ceasing stream of complex models to organize "Godly Warriors in every county for a Christian takeover." Grimstead's vision grew increasingly ambitious, from forming a "Shadow Government" during the "ungodly" Clinton years to establishing COR beachheads in eighty countries for the purpose of convening a global church conference in 2017. He wanted the conference to mirror the historic church councils, which refined and established Christian doctrine on such major topics as the essence of Christ and the nature of the Trinity, in order to establish a biblical law in every nation. Move over Taliban!

Before you could say "Ten Commandments," I found myself thrust into a dual role as chairman of COR's Government Policy Section as well as COR's corporate treasurer. As a senior COR leader, it wasn't long until I was introduced to the intellectual shepherds of COR's flock, Reconstructionism's founding father Dr. R. J. Rushdoony, the radical Theonomist intellectual Dr. Gary North, and prolific Dominionist author Gary DeMar, who would be the cochair of my Government Policy Task Force.

Many consider Rushdoony to be the intellectual godfather of the Christian Right. As one commentator on the Christian Right notes:

> Most, if not all, of the upper echelon of the radical religious right receive their marching orders in one way or another from Chalcedon, Inc. and its cadre of staff like the Rev. R. J. Rushdoony, Rev. Andrew Sandlin, and Colonel V. Doner. Doner is considered by many to be one of the master architects and central figures behind the radical religious right movement, while Rushdoony and Sandlin are considered its religious mentors.[35]

Rushdoony has over seventy books (some of them several inches thick) to his credit, and his network of intellectuals were theonomists. They believed God, as creator and ruler of the universe, was in charge of the world—an assertion that most Christians, in one fashion or another, could agree with.

Their "unique selling point," inherited from John Calvin and the Puritans, was that God had provided a clear set of laws for humanity to follow, mostly found in the Hebrew Bible—the Tanakh. Further, they believed God had established a chosen few known as the "elect" to serve as His Vice-Regents in administering His Law throughout the world.

I had finally found what politics had failed to provide—an intellectually rigorous, theologically coherent Christian worldview. Derived from a literal interpretation of an inerrant Bible, it offered a consistent fundamentalist paradigm based on a black-and-white view of the world. It was a worldview that taught me to view everything—and everyone—as part of the eternal war between God and Satan. This cosmic struggle was so real, so vital, and so imminent that it demanded its own legion of "spiritual special forces," as one of their leaders once explained to a hapless waiter (who looked at him like he'd just landed from Mars). God's Green Berets got their orders directly from the Big Man Himself, often in visions or dreams, but usually as prophetic words, like the ones spoken over Sarah Palin by an African Exorcist—a detail we'll get to later. Promising leaders like Sarah Palin and myself were routinely singled out for special "anointing" to protect us against "the enemy" and to enable us to effectively lead the troops invading Satan's strongholds. In this spiritual warfare, the mother of all wars, no one could be neutral, even if they tried. You were either on God's side or not. And if you weren't on God's side, you were demonized—something I was already adept at doing to people. Dominion theology offered me a unique opportunity to further hone and put to good use the divide and conquer "wedge issue" skills I had developed over three decades. But this time I would not be serving the kingdom of man or even the GOP—I would be serving the kingdom of God.

For the next decade in the 1990s, as I researched and wrote *The Late Great Evangelical Church*, my epic critique of Evangelical social theology—or rather the lack of it—R. J. Rushdoony was my guide and mentor. I learned eagerly and quickly. As Rush wrote about me, I was a "man after God's own heart" and his as well. He encouraged me to use my skill at "beating up Democrats" to now "concentrate on God's enemies." I did so with a vengeance. Within a year or two I was writing Reconstructionist books, headlining their movement's public policy journal and keynoting their conferences. My message was simple: The earth and everything in it belongs to God. He has given us his Law in the Bible. There are only two types of people: Those who obey God's Law (covenant keepers) and those who break God's Law (covenant breakers). It was the job of the former to deal with the latter.

While I've given you a glimpse of my journey to becoming a Christian jihadist, I haven't talked much about the beliefs that led me there, and those beliefs get to the heart of what motivates all neo-fundamentalists, whether religious or secular.

Part II

How to Win Converts
and Influence a Nation

3

The Five Pillars of Neo-Fundamentalism

It doesn't take a genius to figure out that all religions, political ideologies, and philosophies represent a belief system.
You buy into a belief system (become *a believer*) by embracing
its fundamental principles. I call these principles "pillars" because they support the platform on which subsequent ideas
or propositions may be placed and developed. In other words,
certain propositions—for instance that your opponents are
manipulated by Satan or that God is going to personally punish you if you violate the rules—rest on ideological or theological platforms, the individual pillars of which support those beliefs. Identifying the pillars of any belief system, whether the
five pillars of Islam or the five pillars of Christian neo-fundamentalism, is the gate to understanding why "true believers"
act the way they do. Seemingly irrational or inexplicable actions become understandable, even predictable, once the pillars are clearly visible.

Is your shovel ready? We're going to unearth the five pillars that support the neo-fundamentalist understanding of the
world.

Pillar One: The Divine Action Manual

So armed with the Bible, ordinary people were liberated from "staid ecclesiastical traditions" and could escape the control of "the respectable clergy." —Mark Noll[36]

The central pillar is the belief that the Bible is an error-free (inerrant), divinely dictated manual that can be applied to any issue of the twenty-first century. Without this pillar, all the others fall. And yet ironically, the neo-fundamentalist method of reading the Bible runs counter to many accepted norms of biblical interpretation.

This is an important point because many people, especially non-Christians, are unnecessarily put off from Christianity as a whole when a slick TV evangelist or an obnoxious next-door neighbor pulls some arcane verse out of context from the Old Testament or interprets some metaphorical or theological passage literally. When mega-bestsellers, like my old friend Tim LaHaye's *Left Behind* series, build entire fantasies on obscure apocalyptic passages from the book of Revelation that neither Luther nor even Calvin would bother commenting on, reasonable people shake their heads in bewilderment. When the Bible is mishandled in this way it can discredit the Scriptures, Christianity, even God.

Neo-fundamentalists don't realize that their particular literalistic method of reading an inerrant "God-dictated" Bible is a relatively recent approach practiced by a distinct minority of Christians. The early church fathers (the first Christian theologians) read the Bible in a number of different ways. To read every word of the Bible literally, according to them, was to make "nonsense" of Scripture. In the fourth century, Augustine, one of the Western church's greatest scholars, called the four most popular methods of understanding Scripture the *quadriga* (Four). The Four methods include: *allegorical*—drawing out a moral principle through metaphor; *anagogical*—finding hope or inspiration in a particular story; *tropological*—discovering guidelines for moral conduct; and lastly, *literal*—reading for the literal meaning of the text.

Most contemporary Christian scholars (Roman Catholic, Orthodox, and Protestant) view the Bible as the sacred record of God mysteriously inspiring His people to communicate *their experience* of God as the transcendent Creator of the Universe. Many of these theologians, pastors, and priests would also posit that those early writers of what later came to be understood as Scripture were limited by their flawed humanity as well as the cultural context in which they lived, thought, and wrote. The mindset of the first century Middle Eastern audience is crucial to understanding the ideas, idioms, metaphors, parables, and narrative the ancient writers originally intended to communicate.

Consequently, scholars insist that the Bible must be carefully interpreted through the lens of the first century's cultural context, which was heavily mythical as well as metaphorical, rather than through a twenty-first-century hypermodern and distinctly Western lens.

In contrast to the fundamentalist literal hermeneutic (the way one approaches and interprets the Bible), most biblical scholars, liberal *and* responsible conservatives alike, argue in some of the following ways:

First, the Scriptures themselves do not claim that God dictated every word, but they were rather "God breathed," a mysterious term usually taken to mean God "somehow" inspired them. If anything, Scripture specifically states that some pas-

sages are the opinions of their human authors, not of God, as
the apostle Paul wrote, "Here I want to add some suggestions
of my own. These are not direct commands from the Lord, but
they seem right to me."[37] C. S. Lewis, regarded as a modern-
day saint by many Evangelicals, believed that God gave "im-
pressions" to ancient sages who interpreted them as best they
could within their *historical* and *linguistic limits.* As such, they
recorded *their* experience of God, not God's pure word. In other words, God taught his children through simple metaphors
like the Genesis creation story, the sort of thing that one learns
as a child in Sunday school. John Calvin called it baby talk.[38]

Second, the New Testament is not one seamless volume
magically dropped from the heavens, but rather a collection
of letters from early Christian leaders and thinkers (apostles)
imparting encouragement, admonition, insight, guidance, and
even "organizational tips" to young Christian communities
who were trying to sort out various issues and problems that
were relevant to them——two thousand years ago. The problem, as megachurch pastor Rob Bell comments, is that:

> To take statements made in a letter from one per-
> son living in a real place at a moment in history
> writing to another person living in a real place out
> of their context and apply them to today without
> first understanding their original context sucks the
> life right out of them. They aren't isolated state-
> ments that float, unattached, out in space.[39]

Indeed, the challenge of mining ancient conversations
for relevance centuries later is why the Christian church employed Augustine's *quadriga* as its primary hermeneutical tool

for the first millennium. Evangelicals' penchant for applying the literal sense to contemporary issues didn't come into
vogue until the opening decade of the sixteenth century with
Martin Luther.[40]

The danger of interpreting every word of ancient Scripture as literally applicable to modern questions is clearly illustrated in literalism's contribution to the Civil War. In the
mid-nineteenth century, America was undeniably a Christian
nation, and when it came to the Bible, the North agreed with
the South (where Puritan theology was still dominant) that the
only acceptable method of interpretation was the literal one.
As slavery threatened to rip America asunder, Southern theologians handily employed widely scattered verses as "proof texts"
to show that the Bible sanctioned slavery (the apostle Paul told
slaves to obey their masters; many of the ancient patriarchs
owned slaves, etc.). Above the Mason-Dixon Line, the leading
literalist theologians in the North (Charles Hodge of Princeton,
for example) and border states (Robert Breckinridge of Ken-
tucky) vehemently opposed slavery. Both scholars insisted that
although God allowed slavery in biblical times, a first-century
institution and mindset should not be applied in modern times.
Sadly, they were trumped by their own literal hermeneutic. In
a churchwide national debate, they had to admit the validity
of the South's literal interpretation of Scripture and were ren-
dered impotent to enlist the massive moral authority of the
church to stop the war. In time, the literalists'—both Southern
and Northern—blatant failure to reach similar conclusions on
an issue as fundamental as slavery and human dignity proved
to be the beginning of the end for literalism as the dominant
hermeneutical method for interpreting Scripture.[41]

Third, much of what the apostles wrote was geared for a

first-century interpretation of Old Testament Scripture within a Greek philosophical matrix. Because they lived in a Hel-
lenic or Greek culture, Paul and the early-church fathers attempted to adapt the first Jewish Christians' understanding of
Jesus as Messiah into Greek neo-platonic terms. And since the
Gentiles (non-Jews) were not interested in some new version
of Judaism, the early church sought to explain Jesus to their
Hellenistic minds using familiar Greek concepts like *logos* (the
eternal power of creation, the eternal principal of truth, wisdom, and light), presenting him as savior of not just Israel, but
of the whole world.

Another reason it's problematic to interpret New Testament
passages without understanding the first-century Greek mindset is that the apostles at times wrote in the "shorthand" of
the day. This shorthand would be equivalent to someone humming a few bars of a familiar tune today and expecting the intended listener to fill in the words. Unfortunately, many of the
first-century tunes, their themes and idioms, were lost ages
ago; hence the necessity of scholarly research into their original meanings and context. For instance, the apostle Paul's admonition that it's better not to be married was couched in his
and other church leaders' expectation that Jesus was coming
back (as Jesus seemingly promised) within *their* generation. In
other words, why get married if the end of the world is at hand
(1 Corinthians 7)? A few other examples (out of hundreds) include Paul's prohibition of women speaking out in church (1
Corinthians 14:34—clearly a reflection of the prevailing pa-
triarchal culture which molded Paul's understanding of how
the sexes relate to each other), Jesus' prohibition of divorce
(which addresses a debate between competing schools of rab-
binic scholars[42]), and Jesus' use of the term "hell" (which was

translated from the Greek word *Gehenna* and actually referred to the local garbage dump). Thus it appears Jesus was warning people that if they didn't shape up, their lives would be filled with a lot of garbage!

Finally, while the Holy Scripture contains the Word of God, its written words are not necessarily synonymous with "God's Word." This was the view of many of the early Protestant reformers and was championed more recently by Karl Barth, widely recognized by Christian scholars, including many Evangelicals, to be the greatest theologian of the twentieth century. In fact, prominent Evangelical theologians from Clark Pinnock to Bernard Ramm agree with Barth about the Bible's "very human authorship" and "its frequent reliance on myth and metaphor." I hasten to add that these terms are not meant to be pejorative, but rather descriptive as Bernard Ramm, taught:

> The ancient Hebrew and early Christian cultures that produced the Bible saw no reason not to employ saga, legend, and pseudonymity in expressing God's word. Since they clearly did employ these literary forms in writing Holy Scripture, he argued, *Christians today are bound to accept these forms as vehicles of the Word*. Revelation is no less divine when it accommodates our natures and worldly conditions and literary forms that were current during Biblical times.[43]

The Use of Metaphor and True Myth in the Bible

Linguists and professional communicators understand metaphor as common currency of effective communication. Sharing stories and metaphors with people is often more effective than overwhelming them with a lot of complicated themes bursting with complex doctrinal propositions, data, and formulae. This is why people like to read books that are heavy on anecdotes that colorfully illustrate the moral of the story rather than wading into a densely technical philosophical/theological work.

Do you think God shares in this communication secret? Is it conceivable that God—who the Church (Catholic, Orthodox, and Protestant) has always asserted is mysterious, transcendent (meaning wholly other), and thus not fully comprehensible to finite man—would dumb down or anthropomorphize the unknowable (as C. S. Lewis and even John Calvin affirmed)?

In the ancient world, long before the development of the printing press, religious teaching had to be transmitted orally. The trick was to find a way to make the content simple enough that it could be faithfully retold for generations. The vehicle for the ancient transmission of truth was "true myth." Myth was regarded as neither fact nor fiction, but located somewhere in between. Like any good story that illustrates a moral, myth took what was regarded as an observable universal truth, for instance, the existence of evil, and wrapped it with the trappings of a memorable metaphor, like the Garden of Eden. A story like that could be passed along orally for thousands of years. According to Gary Dorrien, C. S. Lewis believed that:

> The question is not whether Christianity is fundamentally mythical, but whether Christ became and fulfilled the great myth. . . . He (Lewis) never tired of explaining the ultimate way that myths

are true. What myth communicates is not "truth" in the formal sense, he observed, but reality. . . . Myth is more like an isthmus, "which connects the peninsular world of thought with that vast continent we really belong to." . . . Christianity is true myth not in the sense of being a univocal description of Divine reality "but in the sense of being the way in which God chooses to appear to our faculties." Put differently, Christian myth works on us as the word of God formed so that limited human understanding can appropriate it.[44]

Barth thought that the Bible contained many "sagas" (myths) because they are "intuitive and poetic pictures" of reality that are nonhistorical. He noted that Scripture contains few examples of either pure saga or pure history. Rather, most of the Bible mixes together saga and history so thoroughly that it is impossible to definitely distinguish one of them from the other. According to Barth, as a true witness to God's Word, Scripture is obliged to speak in the form of saga, precisely because its object and origin are nonhistorical. Barth held that the Bible would not be Scripture if it did not absorb the nonhistorical element into its witness, "and if it did not usually do it by mingling the two elements."[45] Indeed, the evidence for biblical saga and myth is so overwhelming that Clark Pinnock, once *the* leading defender of an inerrant Bible, has come to the conclusion that "Evangelicals have been grievously wrong to commit themselves to the indefensible *claim* that Scripture contains no myths or legends."[46]

Why would the authors of Scripture tell stories (myths) rather than just relaying cold, hard facts? The answer lies in understanding how the apostles' first-century audience might interpret their message. The ancient mindset differed radically from our modern, rationalistic model, which accepts only supposedly objective facts. The ancients, obviously unaffected by enlightenment rationalism, understood that the limited language and conceptual ability of finite man was simply not capable of adequately describing an infinite being. In the words of Evangelical theologians Stanley Grenz and Roger Olson, "In the search for the transcendent, purely rational approaches are inadequate. The transcendent can be spoken of only by means of the use of myths, which serve as symbols of ultimate truth."[47] But the ancients' ability to perceive universal principles artfully embedded in narrative was shunned by the modern mind, as Karen Armstrong notes:

> The rational bias of the modern world now made it impossible for many Western Christians to understand the role and value of myth. Faith had to be rational, *mythos* had to be *logos*. It was now very difficult to see truth as anything other than factual or scientific.[48]

Consequently, neo-fundamentalists, enraptured with modernism's disdain for myth and metaphor and its preference for empirical data, *attempted to literalize the ancient myths incorporated into the Bible,* misconstruing the ancient narrative as a pseudo-scientific collection of "God facts." Ironically, the answer for both fundamentalists of either a religious or secular stripe is, as Armstrong suggests, to

> disabuse ourselves of the 19th century fallacy that

myth is false or that it represents an inferior mode of thought. We cannot completely recreate ourselves, cancel out the rational bias of our education, and return to a pre-modern sensibility. But we can acquire a more educated attitude to mythology.[49]

Lost in Translation

Even though only a small group of top-ranked Evangelical scholars and almost no mainline Protestants or Catholics still believe Scripture was directly dictated by God, most neofundamentalists still insist on promoting the inerrancy theory developed by three nineteenth-century Princeton scholars, Charles Hodge, A. A. Hodge, and Benjamin Warfield. Faithful to Calvin and the Puritans, they insisted that the original biblical autographs were *word for word* dictated by God and without error. The Princeton scholars asserted that,

> The Scriptures not only contain but *are* the word of God, and hence all their elements and all their affirmations are absolutely errorless and binding on the faith and obedience of man.[50]

How this theory of inerrancy could possibly be represented in each one of more than 700 English Bible versions currently in print is a mystery to me. Inerrantists would respond to my concern by stating that only the original copy of the Scriptures, which of course like the Holy Grail has yet to be discovered, is without error. They would admit at least minor errors and disagreements between the thousands of manuscripts in existence and consequently in the various English translations of

the Bible. These qualifications, however, remain closely guard-
ed in academic circles. The average fundamentalist is directed
to study the English language Bible, itself likely a flawed translation of a German translation of a Greek translation, with the
confidence that he is reading the pure, direct, undefiled Word
of God, even though it's incredibly difficult to translate Greek,
German, or Hebrew *directly* into English, let alone through
multiple languages.[51] As an example, one of Jesus' more incredible statements, translated in some Bibles as "be perfect as your
Heavenly Father is perfect" (Matthew 5:48) turns many Evangelicals into neurotic, performance-driven hypocrites. Others
give up even trying. A more accurate translation, however, is
to be "mature." Which is quite a difference from "perfect"—
witness the result of an imperfect translation. Nevertheless, in
1978 three hundred neo-fundamentalist leaders updated their
nineteenth-century brethren declaring:

> Holy Scripture, being God's own Word, writ-
> ten by men prepared and superintended by His
> Spirit, is of infallible divine authority in all mat-
> ters upon which it touches: it is to be believed, as
> God's instruction, in all that it affirms; obeyed, as
> God's command, in all that it requires; embraced,
> as God's pledge in all that it promises. . . . Being
> wholly and verbally God-given, Scripture is with-
> out error or fault in all its teaching, no less in what
> it states about God's acts in creation, about the
> events of world history, and about its own liter-
> ary origins under God, than in its witness to God's
> saving grace in individual lives. The authority of
> Scripture is inescapably impaired if this total di-

vine inerrancy is in any way limited or disregard-
ed.[52]

In contrast, Fuller Seminary, the Evangelical flagship, recently conceded that Fuller doesn't "deem inerrancy to be helpful in coming to terms with the phenomena of Scripture."[53]

In their rejection of mainstream orthodox hermeneutics
and modern scholarship, neo-fundamentalists essentially de-
faulted to the Puritan model. Every word of the Bible is a word
directly from the mouth of God for them personally in the
present moment. *Hence any principles inferred from "God's Word"
can be formed into rock-solid propositions to apply with gratifying
certitude to any and every aspect of life.* Pertinent to our theme,
even the civil law for Old Testament Israel, containing instruction on things like executing homosexuals, must somehow be
followed even if adapted for modern sensibilities where such
conduct is criminalized but not punishable by death. As we
shall see, the belief that one is in possession of God's Divine
Action Manual can both empower and encourage the abuse
of power, especially when combined with an almost infallible
belief in one's ability to plumb the depths of God's mind—or
at least to interpret His instructions with a high degree of certainty.

Pillar Two: Absolute Certainty

*The word of God, as soon as it shines upon an individ-
ual's understanding, illuminates it in such a way that
he understands it.* —Huldrych Zwingli, Protestant
reformer[54]

If you have God's literal, dictated, inerrant word in your very own hands, do you need God's permission to interpret the text for yourself? Martin Luther, who more than any single figure begat the Protestant Reformation, was the first to provide that permission. In 1517, he broke with 1500 years of Catholic tradition by asserting that "religious authority rested finally and solely in each individual Christian, reading and interpreting the Bible according to his own private conscience in the context of his personal relationship to God."[55] Luther's revolutionary principle of "Sola Scriptura" ("Scripture alone") meant that Holy Scripture itself—not the Catholic Church—would be the final authority in settling theological disputes. The conundrum was to determine just *how* Scripture would interpret itself. The answer: through the Holy Spirit guiding each believer.

With the Reformation overthrowing the Catholic Church as the historic mediator between man and God, each individual was now free to interpret the Bible on his or her own. But Luther wasn't blind to the potential chaos of this theological Pandora's box, asking, "is every fanatic to have the right to teach whatever he pleases?"[56] Consequently, while the founders of Protestantism used Sola Scriptura to break the Pope's "stranglehold" on Scripture, they quickly sought to substitute their own interpretive standard. If you were a good Protestant, you were still not free to interpret Scripture on your own to end up with "nonsense," proving as Luther complained, that "beer is better than wine." Rather you read Scripture through the lens of John Calvin or Martin Luther. As my friend John Armstrong, a conservative theologian notes, "The ordinary Christian is lost in confusion of multiple interpretation."[57]

In fact, the Protestant founders were only slightly less adamant about protecting *their* interpretation than the Vatican had been. Luther aggressively attacked anyone deviating from his view and even called for the death of some of his opponents. Calvin went one step further by actually agreeing to the execution of a troublesome theological opponent who refused to repent of his "erroneous teaching." But the hierarchical ground rules and borders Luther and Calvin laid down in Europe came completely undone in the maelstrom of American democracy.

By the time the early nineteenth-century American revivals, called "The Second Great Awakening," rolled into town, the newborn Evangelicals had effectively reinterpreted Sola Scriptura in their own image. They began to regard the Bible as not just the *final* authority on matters of doctrine, but *sans* church and Orthodox tradition, the *only* authority. Better adapted to America's visceral democratic spirit, "the Bible alone" became the Evangelical creed, the sole authority on faith and practice. The big question of course is who then, if not the Pope, Calvin, or Luther, is competent to interpret God's holy Word? According to the new corps of revivalist preachers, *every "true believer" could interpret the Bible with certainty for themselves.*

Church historian Mark Noll comments:

They also held that the Bible was the only reliable source of religious authority and that personally appropriated understanding of Scripture was the only reliable means of interpretation. American theologians remained traditionally Christian in beliefs about divine providence. They were, however, less likely to stand in awe of God's mysterious powers and more likely to assume that they could know and adapt themselves clearly, simply, and directly to the ways of God.[58]

In the decades of violent warfare between the Roman Catholic Church and those who protested their authority (the Protestants), the locus of the struggle for power was which group
had the authority to interpret Scripture. But now the golden
key, the key to understanding God, the universe, and life itself,
was handed to whoever asked for it. Historian Alister McGrath
notes that this development "placed the private judgment of
the individual above the corporate judgment of the Christian
Church concerning the interpretation of Scripture. It was a
recipe for anarchy."[59] Every believer would now stand alone before God as the arbiter of his own Biblical truth, the clarity of
God's Word taken as a given.

Updating this concept for moderns in the early 20th century, fundamentalists developed the theory of "Soul Competency," a term coined by E. Y. Mullins, one of the founding theologians of the Southern Baptist denomination, which adopted
Rene Descartes' dictum that if we use our intellect responsibly,
God will not allow us to be led astray.[60] Fundamentalists held
that God, or the Holy Spirit, would personally guide each believer to correctly interpret and apply God's word. What many
Protestant scholars today derisively regard as "Private Interpretation", as opposed to interpreting Scripture within the historical guidelines of church or Orthodox tradition, was embraced as Soul Competency. Every individual believer, even if
they lacked formal education or had been a Christian for less
than a week, was capable of plumbing the depths of God's will.
As Sarah Grimke, an activist in the anti-slavery movement, explained in 1837, "I claim to judge for myself what is the meaning of the inspired writers, because I believe it to be the solemn

duty of every individual to search the Scriptures for themselves with the aid of the Holy Spirit and not be governed by
the views of any man, or set of men."[61]

One hundred and thirty years later, I was taught as a teenager that God's "special revelation" is open to everyone. So
naturally, after immersing myself in "The Word" for several
weeks, I felt confident enough to challenge a professor of theology's Christianity during a public lecture since his lecture
didn't correspond with my understanding of Scripture.

Essentially, fundamentalists created their own individual-
istic hermeneutical model, ripping the Bible out of its historical context and jettisoning a 2000-year-old Orthodox model of
consulting church authorities and tradition before attempting
one's own interpretation. [62]

In the hands of fundamentalists, the church's historic Scriptures
were transformed into a magical book no longer tied to tradition,
church authority, or even historical context. The Bible was now a
veritable genie in a book ready to do the bidding of a crazy array of
free agents.

The litany of abuses—just watch "Christian" TV for a day—
has become such a sore point even within Evangelical circles that scholars, authors, and pastors have kept up a steady
stream of protest culminating in this surprising assertion from
maverick theologian Stanley Hauerwas:

> Most North American Christians assume that they
> have a right, if not an obligation, to read the Bi-
> ble. I challenge that assumption. No task is more
> important than for the Church to take the Bible
> out of the hands of individual Christians in North
> America. . . . They read the Bible not as Chris-

tians, not as a people set apart, but as democratic citizens who think their "common sense" is sufficient to "understanding" the Scripture. They feel no need to stand under a truthful community to be told how to read. Instead they assume that they have all the "religious experience" necessary to know what the Bible is about.[63]

I can identify with Hauerwas' sentiment, having attended literally hundreds of Bible studies and small-group sessions, as well as large Bible conferences, where each teacher, pastor, or believer concocted any number of contradictory, bizarre, and nonsensical—in other words, unorthodox—interpretations. It gave cognitive dissonance a whole new meaning.

An Unquestioning Certainty

One of the things people seem to find most irritating about neo-fundamentalists is their almost unbearable smugness on any given topic. Of course right-wing Christians are not the only example of unrestrained hubris. Many names, beginning with Bill Maher, could be cited on the left. But since I am writing primarily about Christian neo-fundamentalists, the question is where do they derive their supreme confidence in all matters religious or political? Having confidence in one's ability to read Scripture is one thing. Knowing with *certainty* that you correctly understand the message demands more than the mere permission granted by Luther and Calvin. As I mentioned before, the promise of absolute certainty came from an unlikely source—Enlightenment philosopher René Descartes. Descartes inaugurated the modern mindset by making the heretofore-heretical claim that humans could reason their way to ultimate truth by using their God-given objective reason, unaffected by bias or subjectivity:

> Descartes enthroned human reason as the su-
> preme authority in matters of knowledge, capable
> of distinguishing certain metaphysical truth and
> of achieving certain scientific understanding of the
> material world. Infallibility, once ascribed only to
> Holy Scripture or the supreme pontiff, was now
> transferred to human reason itself.[64]

Reinforcing the power of Luther's claims a century earlier, Descartes and other Enlightenment thinkers assured readers that, due to the supreme ability of their rational mind to accurately grasp objective reality, they could find absolute certainty on any issue that they carefully analyzed. In time, average believers came to think that, through the efficacy of their own reasoning, they could interpret the intentions of the Ruler of the Universe as expressed on any number of topics in Holy Scripture. As Harvard trained theologian Carl Raschke observed, "The Reformers replaced the authority of the church with the authority of Scripture . . . the Enlightenment exchanged the authority of Scripture for the sovereignty of reason."[65]

Neo-fundamentalists ingeniously wedded these two concepts to-
gether—their sovereign reason could objectively interpret God's sov-
ereign Word, allowing them to clearly see "the truth." As Raschke adds, "The rule of sovereign reason was the irrepressible outcome of the Reformation exaltation of personal conscience."[66]

This unprecedented confidence in the power of human reason was solidified in the eighteenth century thanks to Thomas Reid and his Scottish common sense school of philosophy, which uniquely appealed to American self-reliance and pragmatism. Simply by exercising our common sense we could, *with certainty*, understand both God and His revelation to man in the Bible. In this, Reid echoed Descartes' assertion that men of good sense, using simple reasoning, could discover the truth of any situation. It is somewhat ironic that Reid, perhaps the Enlightenment's most forceful advocate of the efficacy of pure reason was also an influential factor in spawning American fundamentalism:

> It was the marriage of Reid's common sense philosophy with evangelical Methodism and Calvinism along the American frontier during the 19th century that gave rise to what a century later came to be labeled by critics of Christian evangelicalism, usually disparagingly, as fundamentalism.[67]

In America this new confidence resulted in replacing the past deference to church authorities on matters of interpretation with the literalistic hubris expressed in an 1843 issue of *The Methodist Quarterly Review:* "We claim to be not only rigid literalists, but unsparing iconoclasts—ruthless demolishers of all theories."[68] And because they so rigorously "demolished" the interpretive theories or models of the past, "attempting to understand the Bible literally became the only possible goal."[69]

One reason fundamentalists, whether Christian or Islamic, are difficult to dialogue with is their default setting in any argument: "How can I yield or compromise on what God has clearly said?" Their culturally mandated buy-in to Cartesian rationalization blinds them to the possibility that what is clear to them may not be so clear to others.

The end result for fundamentalists—other than the rapid proliferation of over 25,000 Protestant sects all claiming to practice "what God has clearly said"—was an unshakable belief that God was directly and clearly communicating with *them.* As a popular fundamentalist bumper sticker declares: *"God said it, I believe it, that settles it."* Notice how this one slogan sums up the first two pillars: "God said it" implies an inerrant, God-dictated Bible. "I believe it" demonstrates one's competence to fully comprehend God's mind. "That settles it" is indicative of the naïve certainty that brooks no disagreement. The fact that the most eminent Evangelical of the twentieth century, Billy Graham, admits "there are many things in the Bible I don't understand" and that he no longer believes every word of the Bible to be divinely dictated[70] has had little impact on neo-fundamentalist certainties. It only proved Graham had become "liberal."

Practically, Pillar Two allows people like me and Sarah Palin to be certain not only about God's purpose for our own lives, but also for the world and everyone in it—certain about how to save their soul, your soul, and the soul of America. In my case, I was certain God wanted me to defend Godly righteousness and destroy evil. That meant defeating liberal members of congress who supported abortion, gay rights, and anything opposed to the Christian Right agenda.

This sense of certainty also encouraged us to see the world in overly simplistic, black-and-white terms—a tendency encouraged by Pillar Three.

Pillar Three: The Great War Between God and Satan

The world is the battleground between good and evil,

God and Satan. —Colonel Doner[71]

We have learned thus far that "when we become Christians, we are automatically involved in a vast spiritual war that spans both heaven and earth."[72] Did you ever wonder why religious fundamentalists seem obsessed with Satan? It's because Satan is at war with them. And if you don't believe as they do, then you may be a hapless tool of Satan and must be brought down with him!

In his authoritative work, *Terror in the Mind of God*, Mark Juergensmeyer lists three indicators of when a confrontation between worldviews, like the culture wars, is apt to turn into cosmic war:

1. *The struggle is perceived as a defense of basic identity and dignity.* If the struggle is thought to be of ultimate significance, a defense not only of lives but also of entire cultures, such as Sikhism or Islam, the possibility is greater that it will be seen as a cultural war with spiritual implications.

2. *Losing the struggle would be unthinkable.* If a negative outcome to the struggle is perceived as beyond human conception, the struggle may be viewed as taking place on a transhistorical plane.

3. *The struggle is blocked and cannot be won in real time or in real terms.* Perhaps most important, if the struggle is seen as hopeless in human terms, it is likely that it may be reconceived on a sacred plane, where the possibilities of victory are in God's hands.[73]

As we shall see, the culture war meets all three standards. It should not surprise us then that neo-fundamentalists, particularly Sarah Palin and her neo-fundamentalists, find themselves involved in a war of cosmic proportions.

Every Christian or Islamic fundamentalist knows that from the very beginning of history when Lucifer, cleverly disguised as a snake, caused Eve to lead Adam astray in the Garden of Eden, God and Satan have been waging a war for the "hearts and minds" of mankind. This seminal event, known as the "fall of man," doomed us all to perpetual sin and a state of depravity, as St. Augustine theorized. Augustine's thoughts on this, as well as a myriad of other issues, have been concretized into Roman Catholic and Protestant church doctrine for over 1,000 years. Eastern Orthodox Christianity on the other hand, thought he was basically nuts and branded him a heretic.

This historical battle between God and Satan is the only war of its kind in the history of humanity—a war that is refought every century. It's a war against spiritual powers that manifest themselves as human beings. As we shall see in later chapters, Sarah Palin's spiritual mentors believe Satan has appointed "demonic princes" over various nations. Peter Wagner, the leader of five hundred neo-fundamentalist "apostles" of the New Apostolic Reformation (NAR) asserts that "Satan delegates high-ranking members of the hierarchy of evil spirits to control nations, regions, cities, tribes, peoples, groups, neighborhoods, and other significant networks of human beings throughout the world." [74]

Recently I watched Jack Hayford, pastor of a 20,000-member NAR-type congregation in Los Angeles, introduce Wagner on video. Wagner proceeded to explain why the Japanese economy had stalled, the yen was down, and real estate was in a freefall. Shintoism, Japan's national religion, reveres a sun goddess (note the rising sun in their national flag). It seems that during their annual religious festivities, the Emperor had

intercourse (Wagner wasn't sure if it was physical or just sym-
bolic) with the Goddess—which of course was just another demon. Wagner's inevitable conclusion? Japan was controlled by
Satan, which was why things were going badly.

Medieval crusaders sought the defeat of the satanic forces
of Islam abroad while the inquisition rooted them out at home.
Martin Luther admonished his followers to defeat the devil. In
England's seventeenth-century civil war, the Puritan forces
of Oliver Cromwell, Lord Protector of England, defeated the
"anti-Christ" armies of Roman Catholic King Charles I, whom
Cromwell had executed. Meanwhile in the colonies, the Puritans were quite literally burning the devil out of their villages.
In the American War of Independence, the Presidents of Yale
and Harvard urged their compatriots to wage war against the
"satanic forces" of Britain's King George III. As America grew,
so did the list of Satan's tools and henchmen as alert fundamentalists identified—and then reidentified—the Antichrist
as the Pope, then the League of Nations following World War
I, then Hitler and Mussolini, and finally, following World War
II, the United Nations. Of course everyone, from Billy Graham
to my mentor Billy James Hargis, saw "Godless atheistic communism" as an extension of Satan's hellish empire. Popular
Evangelical author Arno C. Gaebelein included in his classic
The Conflict of the Ages, everything from the Illuminati and the
French revolution to Roman Catholics and Jews as satanic con-
spiracies against Christian civilization.[75]

In the nineteenth century, C. I. Scofield, a convicted felon
and disbarred lawyer, created the *Scofield Reference Bible,* which
featured more of his notes on some pages than actual verses of
Scripture. Selling millions of copies, it became *the* Bible of reference for every fundamentalist. I still have my mother's well-

worn and heavily underlined copy. Many readers understood his commentary notes as "God's truth" since after all, they were printed right there in the Bible! Laying the foundation for how generations of fundamentalists would interact with their neighbors as well as their political system, Scofield boldly proclaims in his commentary on Revelation 13:8, "The present world-system, organized upon the principles of force, greed, selfishness, ambition, and sinful pleasure is Satan's work."[76] One of the primary progenitors of modern Evangelicalism, the revivalist Charles Finney agreed, confidently asserting that Satan himself "has usurped the government of this world."[77]

Updating Scofield and Finney, whom he ironically regarded as heretics of the worst sort, Reconstructionist theologian R. J. Rushdoony believed that *every* secular expression of "humanistic" belief—Republican or Democrat, conservative or liberal— served Satan. His logic was simple—if you're not part of God's team (acknowledging his sovereignty over all of life), you are *de facto* on the *other* team. In other words, if you're not for us, you're against us. *By this definition all non-Christian-fundamentalist religions, including liberal mainline Christian denominations, are somehow directed by Satan.*

Unfortunately, Rushdoony was simply drawing the logical conclusion held by many Evangelicals that "all human beings, without exception, regardless of how clever or educated or cultured they may be, if without Christ, are helpless victims of satanic control . . . completely unable to escape by any wisdom or power of their own."[78] When we ponder why the culture war is so polarizing, the conviction that one's opponents are foils of the devil is surely a contributing factor. As one fundamentalist housewife summed up, "We're surrounded by demons."

This war is as unrelenting as it is total, and it's being fought 24/7 in real time. And as popularized in the best-selling spiritual warfare novels of Frank Peretti, it's being fought in *your* neighborhood. Peretti casts a spellbinding tale of Satan's demonic hordes taking over a small town, using New Agers and secularists to do their dirty work. Then the "prayer warriors" kick into gear and an angelic cavalry comes to the rescue, vanquishing the bad guys. As fiction, this makes for good entertainment. But it is another matter when millions of Evangelicals are convinced that satanic princes control entire countries, cities, and political parties. As we will soon see, the New Apostolic Reformation has refined a novel process for mapping demonically held territories and then colonizing them that is as bizarre as it is frightening. Seminars abound teaching the faithful how to dispatch demons from their communities and to ward off Satan's temptations.

About the same time that Sarah Palin was probably being trained in trench warfare against demonic forces by her mentor "Apostle" Mary Glazier (whose official biography informs us that she is a powerful leader "on the subject of spiritual warfare"), my Christian Right staff and I were very excited to attend similar seminars led by the late Milton Green and sponsored by televangelist James Robison. It didn't take us long to put what we learned into action. After a spiritual warfare seminar led us to realize that physical objects representing false religions were infected by demonic power, I heard that my very wealthy friend had dutifully smashed his exquisitely carved collection of jade Buddhist artifacts to smithereens. Meanwhile I returned to California and burned all my books on yoga, meditation, philosophy, and Eastern religions. Years later, when he lost his fortune, I wondered if my friend wanted his jade Buddhas back. I sure wanted my books.

Whether it's Christians smashing Buddhas in Texas or the Taliban dynamiting them in Afghanistan, it's all part of the epic struggle between the forces of good and evil and the stakes couldn't be higher. In this all-out war between Satan and God, the prize is you, your children, and the future of all mankind. Pastor and author Ray Stedman explains:

> Battling against these forces of darkness is what makes human life possible on this earth. If Christians, who are the salt of the earth, were not giving themselves to an intelligent battle with Satan and satanic forces, fighting along these lines which Paul suggests—being "strong in the Lord and in the power of his might," it would be absolutely impossible for human life to exist on this planet.[79]

As a relatively new Christian, I took these exhortations very seriously. The constancy of daily (hourly!) spiritual warfare was quite literally a normal part of my vocabulary, as demonstrated in a cover interview I gave *Christian Life* magazine:

> God has shown us that before our people battle the forces of evil they had better be wearing the armor of God and be praying unceasingly (Ephesians 6). . . . We can defeat Satan only by successfully casting down all speculations or lofty things raised up against God. Such things might be idolatrous philosophies, which deny God and elevate mankind, or an elite group of men—things like humanism.[80]

Of course this last comment about an "elite group of men" and "things like humanism" was code to my Evangelical audience. Decoded, the message read: We can only do God's bidding to defeat Satan by "casting down" (eliminating) liberals and secular humanists.

Like Sarah Palin, it was simply how I saw the world and its inhabitants—everyone is either a demon or angel, or at least a demonic agent or saint. While this way of viewing one's world may seem strange to say the least, to me it felt increasingly natural as it was reinforced by a constant deluge of sermons, lectures, and Evangelical books I eagerly devoured on Christian living. As former Christian Right leader and bestselling author Frank Schaeffer observes, about 90 percent of all Evangelical books seem in some way oriented to helping readers resist the wiles of Satan. The most powerful influence of all, of course, was my church friends and ministry colleagues. They were hypervigilant against "Satan's snares," the evil one's attempts to corrupt and enslave each and every human being. As one of our most respected local pastors taught, "The aim, the goal of Satan in all this clever stratagem, by which he has kept the human race in bondage through these hundreds of centuries, is to destroy, to ruin, to make waste. That is his purpose toward you and me."[81]

Spiritual warfare is also the preferred lens to understand world affairs or current events. Why is Africa poor? Simple. Because many countries are at least partially animist or pagan. They worship the devil, who consequently has established a stranglehold over the entire continent. Why is there an uptick in crime, pornography, child abuse, abortion, or homosexual activity in your community? Easy. With the increase of secularism, the satanic principality over your town is growing

stronger. Through this lens, one's opponents are easily suspected of being in league with Satan. This is the primary reason Sarah Palin's "prayer warriors" pray curses on their opponents and, as we shall see in subsequent chapters, rejoice over
their prayer targets' misfortunes. It's not a coincidence that in
her 2011 book "America By Heart," Sarah Palin offers thanks
to her "prayer warriors" whose prayers have presumably paved
the way for her meteoric rise in the body politic.

The Spiritual War Becomes the Cultural War

Naturally, it is the duty of every good neo-fundamentalist warrior to "take back the earth." Just as our God is a "man of war"
(Exodus 15:3, KJV), we are to follow Him into battle. The front
lines, of course, are our culture. As LaHaye never tired of telling me, the culture war is nothing more than a thinly disguised battle between the forces of God and Satan. His mantra
was repeated by every Evangelical leader worth their salt, as
demonstrated by the late Bill Bright, my former colleague and
founder of America's largest college campus ministry, Campus
Crusade for Christ, who wrote:

> We believe we are engaged in a war—not a con-
> ventional war fought with guns and bombs, but
> an ideological war, a battle for the mind of every
> American, old and young alike....It is time to get
> back onto warfare footing. That means life *not* as
> usual. It means "tearing down the fortresses" of
> Satan. It means boldness, commitment, sacrifice
> and penetration. It means victory.[82]

I learned the lesson well as I proclaimed in the same *Chris-*

tian Life interview quoted earlier:

> Obviously the world is the battleground between good and evil, God and Satan. . . . I believe that Satan knows he must destroy this nation as a bastion of godliness, as a missionary nation, before he can wreak havoc freely throughout the world.[83]

The status of Satan's conquest of God's own country has caused a bitter divide within neo-fundamentalist ranks. "Premillennial dispensationalists" like Hal Lindsey, whose books have sold well over 30 million copies, argue that Satan's victory is imminent and therefore the only strategy is to escape by praying for Jesus' early return (the rapture). On the other side of the eschatological coin is the New Apostolic Reformation. They act on the assumption, which in many cases contradicts their eschatology, that the godless liberal secularist legions of Satan can be defeated, or at least delayed, in order to allow more time for "soul winning," if they work hard enough to motivate enough Americans to repent of their evil ways and turn back to God. In other words, if neo-fundamentalists will only be faithful to God's special covenant with them, He will protect them from Satan.

Pillar Four: The Eternal Contract

If we serve God faithfully, by defeating the godless forces of liberalism and humanism, God will reward us. If we fail, we deserve God's judgment. —Colonel Doner in a public address, 1998

In the beginning, according to Hebrew Scripture, God made

a covenant, or a divine contract, with his chosen people, the Jews: "Honor my laws [the Ten Commandments] and I'll bless you. Disobey my laws and you'll inherit a rash of blood-curdling curses." Being a wrathful and terrible as well as a loving and forgiving God, He provided an escape route for transgressors. If they got God's people to repent, all would be well: "If my people, who are called by my name, will humble themselves and pray and seek my face and turn from their wicked ways, then I will hear from heaven and will forgive their sin and will heal their land" (2 Chronicles 7:14, NIV). Fail to repent and you're toast. As Calvinist theologian Gary North ominously warns, "The judgment of God can come upon a nation swiftly."[84]

"Covenant" theologians, from John Calvin through America's Puritan founders to today's neo-fundamentalists, believe the true church (theirs) replaced ancient Israel as God's covenant partner. The import of this belief is that they are the exclusive heirs of *all* God's promises, expectations, and consequent blessings or curses as originally given to the Hebrew people. As a neo-fundamentalist, I understood that God's covenant of promises and threats given to Jews in the Old Testament were now in force with "The Replacements"—the Faithful Remnant of American neo-fundamentalists in twenty-first-century America and myself. Exegeting the book of Deuteronomy, Calvin taught that God set up a nonnegotiable covenant with His people, one that He rigorously enforces throughout all eternity. Talk about performance anxiety! To make matters worse, as Gary North explains, the "logic" of the covenant is that "similar sins result in similar judgments."[85] Translation: sexual sins like homosexuality reap the curse of sexually transmitted diseases, particularly AIDS. I wonder what hubris, arrogance, and lack of compassion are rewarded with?

God's Divine Covenant is a good news/bad news kind of contract. The good news? God blesses His people, those that follow His ways or His "law." They and their children and grandchildren will lead long healthy and peaceful lives, enjoying God's many blessings. The bad news? God also curses His people, especially the Church as a special representative of His people, if they fall away from strict observance to Jehovah's ways. As the prophet Hosea ominously warned, "They sow the wind and reap the whirlwind."[86] What does God's whirlwind look like? Not pretty, according to the book of Deuteronomy:

> But if you will not obey the voice of the Lord your God, being watchful to do *all* His commandments and His statutes (laws) which I command you this day, then *all* these curses shall come upon you and overtake you: Cursed shall you be in the city, and cursed shall you be in the field . . . Cursed shall be the fruit of your body, of your land, of the increase of your cattle and the young of your sheep. Cursed shall you be when you come in and cursed shall you be when you go out. The Lord shall send you curses, confusion, and rebuke in every enterprise to which you set your hand, until you are destroyed, perishing quickly because of the evil of your doings by which you have forsaken me. The Lord will make the pestilence cling to you until He has consumed you from the land into which you go to possess. The Lord will smite you with consumption, with fever, and inflammation, fi-

ery heat, sword and drought, blasting and mildew; they shall pursue you until you perish. . . . The Lord will smite you with the boils of Egypt and the tumors, the scurvy and the itch, from which you cannot be healed. The Lord will smite you with madness and blindness and dismay of mind and heart. And you shall grope at noonday as the blind grope in darkness. And you shall not prosper in your ways; and you shall be only oppressed and robbed continually, and there shall be no one to save you.[87]

But God's curses on those who walk away from Him (Leviticus 26:23) aren't meant strictly for them. God's chosen nation, America, the new Zion, also faces calamity as God's wrath is often threatened against an entire people:

The Lord shall cause you to be struck down before your enemies; you shall go out one way against them and flee seven ways before them, and you shall be tossed to and fro *and* be a terror among all the kingdoms of the earth. And your dead body shall be food for all birds of the air and the beasts of the earth, and there shall be no one to frighten them away.[88]

The Old Testament book of Judges tells of some of God's faithful who failed to heed His warnings, "provoked the Lord to anger," so that God "handed them over to raiders who plundered them [and] sold them to their enemies."[89] But the litany of horrors doesn't end here. There's more to come including watching your significant other being "ravaged" and your children sold into slavery—whew! To be faithful to God's holy contract, neo-fundamentalists have no choice but to win the culture war. They *have* to save America and themselves before it's too late!

As fundamentalist recruits and heirs of God's promised blessing, my colleagues and I were sometimes curious as to why God had seemingly left us, His faithful and righteous remnant, at the mercy of a virulently unchristian culture. What's up with that? We found our solace in the Old Testament's prophetic books. As Bible scholar Bart Ehrman notes:

> What were the ancient prophets to think, then, when in later times the people of Israel suffered but God did not intervene? Much of the Hebrew Bible is taken up with this question. The standard answer comes in the writings of Hebrew prophets, such as Isaiah, Jeremiah, Ezekiel, Hosea, and Amos. For these writers, Israel suffers military, political, economic and social setbacks because the people have sinned against God and he is punishing them for it. But when they return to his ways, following the directions for communal life and worship that he had given to Moses in the Law, he would relent and return them to their happy and prosperous lives.[90]

Perhaps now you can understand the sense of urgency and the ferocity that drove my fellow culture warriors and me to prevail over those who dared to tempt God's wrath by ignoring "His statutes." Our sense of desperation can be seen in a letter entitled, "An Urgent Message to a Few Christian Leaders" from Dr. Jay Grimstead, director of the Coalition on Revival. He wrote,

> We believe that America is now under God's "remedial judgment" and that if we do not repent and change our ways, God has every right to judge and devastate His Church and the people in America as He did in Jerusalem on 587 BC and AD 70.[91]

Just a few years before, I had told an interviewer, "I believe that Satan is successfully leading Americans to destroy themselves."[92] I went on to explain in a later speech to a megachurch that God was judging us for our disobedience to His biblical commandments.

Rebuilding the Walls

We can see that for neo-fundamentalists the choices available are painfully clear—enjoy God's riches and blessings in peace and health for the rest of our days or see our children and grandchildren cursed by living in a pagan culture that practices child sacrifice (abortion), sexual perversion (homosexuality), and all manner of degeneracy while worshipping "false gods" (human intellect, scientific materialism, and consumerism). *The catch is that to save ourselves we have to save all of America.* After all, America was, as the Puritans imagined, the new Zion—"One nation under God," a once Christ-honoring, Bible-believing nation that has displeased God with its moral laxity and lack of deference. And it is now paying the price. To avert a total meltdown we have to act quickly and decisively—"If we want to recover our culture from ruin, we must return to biblical principles of life and to the God of the Covenant."[93]

Pillar Five: The Fear of God's Wrath

His wrath towards you burns like fire. —Jonathan Edwards

At this point I think it's fair to say that neo-fundamentalists' prime motivation is in truth neither about politics or power, but rather the most powerful motivation of all—fear. The fear that as the United States is "de-Christianized," we risk sliding down the slippery slope of unrestrained godlessness and heathen debauchery of the type described and severely punished in the Old Testament. It was fear that God's wrath was being visited upon us that motivated Pat Robertson and Jerry Falwell to attribute the terrorist attack on September 11, 2001, to God's judgment on America for liberals and secularists coddling gays and abortionists. That same week several neo-fundamentalist leaders expressed this same sentiment to me personally.

You might be wondering why these poor souls seem so petrified if God is supposed to be the very essence of love. The answer is simply because the neo-fundamentalist God is *not* the forgiving God of love and peace that mainstream Protestants claim ("But you are a forgiving God, gracious and compassionate, slow to anger and abounding in love." Nehemiah 9:17). He isn't the God of mystery wanting to have a loving union with his creation that the Eastern Orthodox and Catholic mystics seek ("Everyone who loves has been born of God and knows God." John 4:7, NIV). Nor is He the God of blessing, celebration, and joy of many charismatics ("The Lord is good to those whose hope is in him." Lamentations 3:25, NIV). He is certainly not the God of nurture and kindness that motivates a wide swath of Christianity from liberal and progressive Evangelicals to the servants of the Church like Mother Teresa ("The faithful love of the Lord never ends! His mercies never cease." Lamentations 3:22).

Rather, the fundamentalist God is *Yahweh*—the God of wrath. He is the war God of the ancient Hebrew prophets delivering to Joshua the pagan city of Jericho with instructions to "devote the city to the Lord." Here's what their devotion looked like: "They devoted the city to the LORD and destroyed with the sword every living thing in it—men and women, young and old, cattle, sheep and donkeys."[94] He is the God who taught the hapless leaders of the village of Succoth a lesson they would remember for refusing to resupply Gideon's 300 super warriors. After Gideon's men vanquished an army almost 500 times their size, according to Scripture, they celebrated their victory by returning to torture the town's seventy-seven elders with "thorns and briers."[95] Then they slaughtered every man in town. He's the God whose warriors, after annihilating a godless army of ten thousand, sliced off the thumbs and toes of their king to emphasize who's in charge.[96] He's also the God of the Patriarchs who condemned adulterers and homosexuals to death.

He's the God of the Crusades, the Inquisition, the Puritans, the Calvinists, and American Revivalists like Jonathan Edwards, who was "both the last of the Puritans and the first of the Evangelicals."[97] Edwards, the eighteenth-century Calvinist theologian whom many historians regard as America's foremost theological thinker, is perhaps best known for his infamous sermon "Sinners in the Hands of an Angry God," wherein he cogently distills the classic Puritan view:

> The God that holds you over the pit of hell, much
> as one holds a spider or some loathsome insect
> over the fire, abhors you and is dreadfully pro-
> voked: his wrath towards you burns like fire; he
> looks upon you as worthy of nothing else but to be
> cast into the fire.[98]

While neo-fundamentalists have since adapted Edward's
harshness to modern sensibilities, this is in essence the sermon
I and millions of others around the globe endured, rehashed,
and reframed in myriad ways each and every Sunday. The bottom line is if you're not a born-again Christian and you die in a
car accident on the way to Sunday brunch, God's going to toss
you into the fiery pit for forever and ever. The incredible stay-
ing power of this view of God prompted postmodern Evangelical thinker Brian McLaren to write:

> The conventional doctrine of hell has too often
> engendered a view of a deity who suffers from
> borderline personality disorder or some worse
> sociopathic diagnosis. God loves you and has a
> wonderful plan for your life, and if you don't love
> God back and cooperate with God's plans in exact-
> ly the prescribed way, God will torture you with
> unimaginable abuse, forever.[99]

The God McLaren describes has doomed to hell everyone
except for a very few of the "elect" or the faithful remnants
(perhaps only one out of every 17,456, according to one pastor![100]) who, of course, always turn out to share exactly the
same faith as neo-fundamentalists.

Commentators on religion have long speculated that your view of God significantly impacts how you approach life, culture, and politics. A 2006 survey by Baylor University verified their speculation. The study identified four views of God: *authoritarian, benevolent, distant,* and *critical.* The authoritarian God, God as king and judge, is "angry at humanity's sins . . . He is ready to hurl the thunderbolt of judgment down on the unfaithful or ungodly." Interestingly enough, the survey found that almost a third (31 percent) of Americans see God in this mode. Not surprisingly, these are mostly the folks who make up the base of the neo-fundamentalist Christian Right.[101] The survey clearly showed those worshiping this "authoritarian God" were the most rigidly conservative on culture war issues, from abortion to gay rights to prayer in school.[102]

Another factor contributing to the neo-fundamentalists' fear of a wrathful God is their literal interpretation of John's apocalypse found in the book of Revelation. As I mentioned before, this is a book that Protestantism's founders apparently held in low regard. Calvin, claiming it was incomprehensible, refused to do a commentary on it, and Luther publicly mused whether the early church erred in even including it in the biblical canon. However, for those Evangelicals who take Revelation literally, God's wrath toward those who fail to meet His litmus test is sobering indeed, "as Jesus, His garments dipped in blood, sheds the blood of unbelievers."[103]

One of Jerry Falwell's associates estimated that 1.5 *billion* souls, including 130 million Americans, would perish during "the Great Tribulation," when God wraps things up. "This is not pessimism . . . These are cold, hard facts."[104] (Wow—thanks for the clarification!) Falwell himself wrote, "There will come a day when God will unleash His wrath and judgment upon unbelievers. He will crush them beneath His thumb."[105] Unfortunately Falwell and his associate were simply stating what every neo-fundamentalist knows to be true. An interesting question is whether or not pastors like Mike Ross of Junean Christian Center ("We are living in the last days.") and David Pepper of Church on the Rock ("God will not be mocked—judgment day is coming.") passed on this dooms-day scenario to Sarah Palin. The answer is apparently "yes" ac-cording to a well-known Alaskan blogger, who asked Palin what she thought about the "end times." Palin reportedly re-plied that not only did she believe the world would end dur-ing her lifetime (which would mean Christ and the Antichrist would duke it out in a world war), but that this expectation of Christ's imminent return "guided her every day." If someone like Palin became president, would they feel it was their duty to hasten Christ's return by moving toward the global conflict neo-fundamentalist theorists predict would trigger the apoca-lypse? After all, if God had once already been so angry with humankind that He wiped out the planet, then what's keeping him from doing it again?

Literally interpreting the Hebrew sagas, neo-fundamental-ists believe that God was so unhappy with the human race that he purposefully drowned every baby, toddler, and child who couldn't squeeze into Noah's Ark. Then there's the Old Testa-ment book of Amos, where God punishes His sinful children by bringing drought, crop failure, and starvation. And who can forget the hapless citizens of Sodom and Gomorrah, deci-mated to the last child for immorality. In fact, God was said to be so mad that He turned Lot's wife into a pillar of salt for disobeying His instruction to not to look back at the carnage. This is the same God that the Old Testament prophet Nahum rhetorically asked:

> Who can stand before His indignation?
> And who can endure the fierceness of His anger?
> His fury is poured out like fire,
> And the rocks are thrown down by Him. (Nahum
> 1:6)[106]

By literally interpreting ancient metaphors and sagas, neo-fundamentalists have created a God whose "wrath against sin is real and terrifying."[107] The relevant question for them becomes, as Gary North, America's most radical neo-fundamentalist theologian, asked:

> How long do we expect God to withhold His
> wrath, if by crushing the humanists who promote
> mass abortion (including certain faculty members
> in supposedly orthodox seminaries), He might
> spare the lives of literally millions of innocents?
> Will God hesitate to bring us low, just because we
> have grown accustomed to indoor plumbing and
> central air conditioning, in the face of mass mur-
> der?"[108]

In other words, God might just curse us all with disaster—like flying passenger jets into our financial and military nerve centers—in order to destroy the "humanists" who presumably control America (and apparently teach in Evangelical seminaries) and who are responsible for the mass murder of the unborn.

Exactly how this apocalyptic scenario might play out debuted in a 2006 *full-page* ad in *USA Today,* placed by my former Christian Right compatriot and Southern Baptist television evangelist, James Robison. The headline announced that "We have a choice—humility or humiliation." [109] Robison then predicted that Americans soon "will cry out to God on our faces." Why? Because a wrathful God is going to judge His people with "unparalleled, indescribable devastation," which Robison believes will consist of terrorist-launched nuclear or bio-technological strikes on America's major cities, which he describes as "truly the sum of all fears." The only way for America to avoid this terror is, in the spirit of 2 Chronicles 7:14, for our nation to repent of "its current practice of abortion on demand, selfish indulgences revealed through sexual excesses and perversion."

With language straight out of the Old Testament, God has apparently assured Robison that Americans "can choose whom and what they serve. They can eat of the fruit of their ways or receive liberating truth and life-changing love." Of course "liberating truth" is a result of "real repentance" *a la* 2 Chronicles. What will this repentance look like? According to Robison, "The family will once again be defined properly—husband, wife and children [and]…a major part of the entertainment community will forsake the promotion of adulterous and perverse lifestyles."

Can it be any clearer what drives the neo-fundamentalist agenda? It is fear of God's terrible wrath for our national moral lapses and the consequent destruction of nation, church, and family. Even one wrong move, according to popular author and TV preacher John Hagee—a one-time McCain advisor—might cause God to punish us using terrorists to execute His wrath.[110]

The fundamentalist message is as simple as it is timeless—whether Pastor John Straton sermonizing in 1918 on "Will New York Be Destroyed If It Does Not Repent?" or New York Evangelist David Wilkerson prophesying in 1985 that:

> God is going to judge America for its violence, its crimes, its backslidings, its murdering of millions of babies, its flaunting of homosexuality and sado-masochism, its corruption, its drunkenness and drug abuse, its lukewarmness toward Christ, its rampant divorce and adultery, its lewd pornography, its child molestation, its cheatings, its robbings, its dirty movies and its occult practices.[111]

Or whether myself throughout the '80s declaring daily over the airwaves of my national radio program that God was judging our land for our lack of repentance and godly legislation. Or Jerry Falwell and Pat Robertson blaming gays, abortionists, and liberals for September 11th in 2001. Or James Robison in 2006. Or John Hagee in 2008, pronouncing that Hurricane Katrina was God's way of punishing New Orleans for immorality.[112] The way out of the dilemma, according to Robison, is national repentance, a change of heart that will be demonstrated by legislating morality since "our laws will reflect the condition of our hearts." In other words, if God is judging "our hearts," we'd better be sure that we get the right laws in place to avoid judgment.

Remarkably, you may have noticed the issues neo-fundamentalists like Robison focus on seem to be exclusively sexually oriented. Their agenda clearly reflects the concerns of the Christian Right as opposed to, perhaps, an agenda that might be proposed by progressive Evangelicals, mainline Protestants, or Roman Catholics. For instance, isn't God going to judge us for our neglect of the poor,[113] as the prophet Isaiah warned as he spoke on God's behalf?

> The kind of fast I want is that you stop oppress-
> ing those who work for you and treat them fair-
> ly and give them what they earn. I want you to
> share your food with the hungry and bring right
> into your own homes those who are helpless, poor
> and destitute. Clothe those who are cold and don't
> hide from relatives who need your help.[114]

We have unearthed the five pillars that the neo-fundamentalist "platform" rests upon. Now the question is, what kind of worldview are these pillars propping up? Is there a shared mindset that we can identify?

4

Understanding the Christian Fundamentalist Worldview

*The tragedy of Fundamentalism in any context is its
capacity to freeze life into a solid cube of meaning.*
—Thomas More[115]

How do the five pillars of neo-fundamentalism come together to form a coherent worldview? What sort of mindset develops as a result? To help you grasp the utter weirdness
and the inherent danger of *my* former jihadist mindset, I'd like
to use the analogy of a computer game. Let's call it *God's Prayer
Warriors vs. The Infidels.*

In this game, 90 percent of the world population is under
the influence of the Dark One, knowingly or unknowingly
serving him in his Evil Empire. Worse, his agents are controlling *your* culture with the intent of subjecting every person—
especially you and your family—to their depraved, godless,
bent-for-hell lifestyle.

Worse yet, the Dark Prince has been wily enough to create false religions like Hinduism, Buddhism, Islam, even Roman Catholicism and Liberal Protestantism, which at best distract their unfortunate victims from serving the one and only true *concept* of God, or at worst are so demonic in nature that they provide a direct chute to hell.

But not you. You are a keeper of God's covenant, part of the faithful remnant, and a warrior-regent made in your Creator's image. Millions will be lost to hell if you don't "save" them by converting them to born-again Evangelical Christianity. Your mission is to keep the United States of America—God's own land, the modern Zion—free of demonic influences by winning souls for Christ and destroying the enemy liberal humanist base. Your ultimate goal is to take dominion over the whole world until all people and institutions bow before "King Jesus." But you don't have eternity to do it—you have to win as many souls as you can before the Creator dismantles His creation in righteous rage with his "Heavenly Host" of killer-angels.

The *good news* is that you are well-armed for this epic cosmic battle:

In a regally bound, calfskin cover, you carry the inerrant word of Almighty God (a.k.a. the Bible) for immediate consultation on and application to a vast array of possible situations.

You have the security of knowing that God's enforcer, the Holy Spirit, is guiding and protecting you 24/7.

If for some reason the Creator is unavailable in an emergency, you have a two-way prayer intercom linked directly with his one and only Son.

Remember: you are a specially chosen member of God's faithful remnant, the sole guardian of God's truth serving on the front lines of a war that threatens to destroy all mankind.

Be courageous and obedient, and God will guide and protect you.

You might think this description of my former mentality is overly simplistic and melodramatic. It isn't. Just watch the documentary *Jesus Camp*. Or play the very real, and violent, video game "Left Behind: Eternal Forces" and its sequels.[116] You also might think that, with a few minor word changes, this game analogy could be a description of an Islamic extremist mentality. You would be right. Unfortunately, however, we don't have to look overseas for the worldview this description implies; it's right here—the worldview of many, thankfully not all, of my former neo-fundamentalist colleagues.

What Is a Worldview?

Worldviews are something we will talk a lot about throughout this book. For now let's just say that a worldview is a way—your way—of viewing the world, of deciding what or who is right or wrong, moral or immoral. It is the process or paradigm by which we reject, accept, categorize, and interpret all information that comes our way. Our worldview helps us sort out and fit a complex world into a simplified and understandable context. It helps us make sense of life and frames answers to questions like "why do so many bad things happen?"

We've all heard the expression "looking at the world through rose-colored glasses," meaning that you have a "rosy" or optimistic view of life. Similarly, the color of our worldview lens affects how we interpret reality. In essence, our worldview *becomes* our reality!

To paraphrase Immanuel Kant, it's impossible for us to have direct, objective knowledge of the world because we are invariably stuck with imperfect or incomplete knowledge that is filtered through our unique worldview. In the case of neo-fundamentalists, they view the world through prescription-made "Scripture" lenses, which focus on how a literal interpretation of the Bible applies to each idea, situation, or person they have contact with.

Where do worldviews come from? You can't just go out and buy one, although purchasing a college education may help color your lens conservative or liberal, religious or secular, depending on the institution. Rather, worldviews are built on presuppositions—principles that we presuppose or unquestioningly assume are true. We may have picked up our presuppositions in kindergarten or graduate school, at home or in Sunday school, in front of the television or on the streets, or most likely from all these sources—and many more. We usually don't consciously choose our presuppositions, we just absorb them. Consequently, most of us don't even recognize that we *have* a worldview. And the worldviews most of us have are amazingly eclectic. Knowingly or not, we borrow concepts or principles from various religions and political philosophies, blending them all together into our own unique worldview. Often cobbling together contradictory notions, our worldview can induce a severe case of cognitive dissonance. In fact, it can disincline us to identify with those who have a consistent and less contradictory worldview. And of course the religious and secular fundamentalists, the ideologues of both the left and right, disdain the average American's ambivalence toward them. Both sides deplore the "apathetic middle," disparaging them with clichés like "those middle of the roaders" who "want to have their cake and eat it too" (whatever *that* means).

So while the average American's worldview may be relatively simple and somewhat inconsistent, those of a more ideological bent are possessed by the certainty that flows from their presuppositions or beliefs. Atheists presuppose there is no God, therefore all religions are nonsense. Christians presuppose that God exactly matches the Bible's description of Him since, after all, the Bible "tells me so." Neo-fundamentalists presuppose the truths of the Five Pillars we discussed in the last chapter, and these truths provide the framework for their worldview.

The Neo-Fundamentalist Worldview

If there is one consistent theme running through Western Christianity from Augustine to Luther, from Calvin to Jonathan Edwards, it is a fear of eternal damnation and torment. As we saw in Pillar Five, Augustine's theory of the Adamic fall of man teaches that we are all sinners, doomed for destruction unless we are saved by Jesus Christ. But how are we to obtain salvation? For Roman Catholics the answer is relatively easy— the church as the "Body of Christ" on earth grants salvation to its faithful.

But for the Protestants, who reject the church's role as sole mediator between God and man, it's not so simple. The downside to their theology of salvation is that we all stand entirely alone before God Almighty. How could one small, sinful person feel assured of their salvation? How could they know they were on God's side, and more importantly, that God was on their side?

Convinced of their competence to interpret an inerrant Bible correctly (Pillars One and Two), fundamentalists constructed doctrines that provide reassurance, even certainty, that not only did God love them "with a father's heart," but that He had a "perfect plan" for their lives. This certainty, based on the belief that they possess absolute truth, provided what Eric Hoffer defined as "a net of familiarity spread over the whole of eternity. There are no surprises and no unknowns."[117]

As reassuring as this may be for some, others feel that an intellectual creed or dogma asserting God's love for us is not sufficient. Particularly in a stressful, dangerous world where we often feel threatened, inadequate, lonely, and meaningless, something more is required—we need intimacy. So neo-fundamentalists filled the modern void of alienation, for example the secular notion of man as a biological accident, forever adrift in a meaningless universe, with an intimacy far surpassing the fickleness of human love—the love of Almighty God Himself, the sovereign ruler of the universe who keeps an ever-vigilant watch over His creation.

Imagine a world where the need for an intimate relationship that offered acceptance, safety, and love in an alienating world was available for the asking—a world where God's only son, Jesus, is both your best friend and trusted confidante, imparting a divine sense of purpose and certainty. For many Evangelicals, Jesus *is* their best—and sometimes only—friend, as expressed in the old fundamentalist hymn *In the Garden,* which I sang every Sunday as a child:

> I come to the garden alone
> And He walks with me, and He talks with me,
> And He tells me I am His own;
> And the joy we share as we tarry there,
> None other has ever known.

Consider another love ballad to Jesus, sung in many neo-fundamentalist churches:

You are my strength and my shield.
You are my heart's desire
And I long to worship thee.
You are my lover from the start.
You are my sun.
The highway to your city runs through my heart.

Here Jesus is portrayed as much more than a friend—he is their hearts' first desire, their true love. I always wondered what husbands thought as they stood beside their wives rapturously belting out these lyrics. Maybe that's why so many Evangelicals get divorced. Praying nonstop for hours a day (instead of for just a half hour like her husband), bestselling neo-fundamentalist author Edith Schaeffer told her son Frank, "I really want to talk to the Lord. [Why] would you only want to have half an hour of conversation with your best friend?"[118] For most neo-fundamentalists, even if Jesus is not their best friend, they at least keep up a running conversation with him as they go about their day.

Investigative reporter and author Jeff Sharlet managed to get himself embedded in "The Family," the secretive bipartisan neo-fundamentalist power network that operates out of The Cedars, a colonial mansion in the leafy suburbs of Washington D.C. He provides a tantalizing glimpse of their perceived connection to God:

They believe God is present, as in here, now. Interventionist, as some theologians would describe their conception of the deity, is too wonky a word for the Jesus they believe is simultaneously sitting right next to them and possessing them, guiding

every breath, every thought, every flicker of their
eyes."[119] This close "personal relationship with Jesus" is one of the unique selling points of modern
Evangelicalism. Of course this relationship is also
very exclusive. In fact, God doesn't even listen to
anyone else but Fundamentalist Christians as Bai-
ley Smith, formerly the president of America's largest Fundamentalist denomination, Southern Baptist, suggested when the he infamously declared,
"God does not hear the prayers of a Jew."[120]

He could have added, "Or the prayers of a Muslim, Hindu,
Buddhist or, for that matter, Roman Catholic."

For these fundamentalists, God is also their true "Father in
heaven" with a "perfect plan" for their life. This reassuring belief works quite well for many middle- and upper-class Americans who lead stressful but relatively secure lives. Why God's
life plan turns out less than perfect for the millions of Christians massacred in the Sudan or Rwanda, or the millions of
Christians dying from AIDS, starvation, and malnutrition on
the African continent as a whole is never questioned. Neither
are the tragedies of loneliness, despair, poverty, and disease
that afflict Christians here at home. Such thoughts might dark-
en one's rose-colored lenses!

Imagine a world where you *spoke directly to God—and He* spoke
back*!* This is the world inhabited by "charismatic" Christians,
the fastest-growing segment of neo-fundamentalism. It's really not as mysterious as it sounds. One "talks" or communicates with God by praying, or by meditating perhaps as the
Christian monks and mystics did. Hearing God's response is,
of course, the trick. Charismatics, and many non-charismatic

Evangelicals as well, rely on different factors to indicate God has talked to them. Having a certain thought enter your mind or a general "sense" or impression, stumbling upon a particular Scripture, even receiving some well-timed advice from a friend, can all be construed as hearing from God. The subjective nature of these indicators, as well as the obvious danger of mistaking "God's voice" for our own thoughts, has drawn unrelenting criticism from Catholics, the Orthodox, mainline Protestants, and even—perhaps especially—other non-charismatic Evangelicals. But for those who "hear" from God in this way, subjectivity is not a concern. Nothing can dent their confidence in "being led by the Spirit."

Imagine There's No Heaven . . . But There Is a Hell

Imagine a world where God wrote you a personal life-instruction manual covering every conceivable area of life, right up to and including the end of the world. As we saw in our exploration of Pillar One, neo-fundamentalists treat the Bible as a personal word from God for them as individuals versus a corporate message for the universal church. Given the neo-fundamentalist presupposition that the Bible is in fact God's personal revelation to them, shouldn't every word be obeyed? Who are we to argue with God's Word? As one fundamentalist friend told me, "Mine is to hear, believe, and act."

Another problem we saw with Pillar Two is neo-fundamentalists' overconfidence in their ability to interpret Scripture without subjectivity, bias, or distortion, compelling them to believe they have a direct pipeline into the "truth that God has made clear." The Rev. Dr. John MacArthur, president of a fundamentalist seminary, megachurch pastor, and popular author of 150 books clearly demonstrates the fundamentalist conundrum: "What is truth? Truth is not any individual's opinion or imagination. *Truth is what God decrees.* And He has given us an infallible source of saving truth in His revealed Word."[121]

Here, one of neo-fundamentalism's leading spokesmen acknowledges that opinion or imagination do not equal objective truth. So far, so good. Then he asserts that what God decrees in "His revealed Word" is truth. But the missing link of the equation is how are we to accurately apprehend that truth? Thousands of MacArthur's students or readers will leap to the assumption that when they read their infallible Bible containing "God's truth," their subjective processing of the words plays no role whatsoever. They are not interpreting Scripture; they are channeling truth directly from God. Conservative theologian P. Andrew Sandlin warns fellow conservatives that this approach borders on idolatry:

> To vest one's own interpretations with the divine warrant that inheres in the Triune God alone and (subordinately) in the Bible as the condescension of His revelation is to border on epistemic idolatry. This is to say that, in the final analysis, only God can speak for God. It is to say that man can know but that he cannot know as God knows, that man can know but not comprehensively or definitively or finally. We can know the truth, but not the *Truth*. We can know as a creature knows—prospectively, tentatively and provisionally.[122]

Imagine a world where you are in effect responsible for keeping God on His throne. A world where God's enemies—atheists, humanists, and liberals—are winning the battle for the soul of

Zion and attempting to shift our nation's locus of authority from the God of the Bible to the unregenerate mind of non-believers.

Imagine a world where one stands in imminent danger of God's terrible wrath (Pillar Five) if one's neighbors continue to tempt God by legalizing the evil God hates (homosexuality, abortion, sexual immorality), and worst of all, "whoring after other Gods"[123] (promoting pluralism).What's one to do but wage an eternal spiritual war (jihad) against God's enemies?

The Fundamentalist Mindset

> *My definition of fundamentalism, religious or otherwise, is the impulse to find the answer a way to shut down the question-asking part of one's brain. Fundamentalists don't like question marks. Fundamentalists reject both Christian humility and postmodern paradox. In that sense an atheist too may be a fundamentalist. And a fundamentalist wants to convince others to convert to what fundamentalists are sure they know.* —
> Frank Schaeffer[124]

How do you describe the mindset of a movement motivated primarily by the fear of eternal damnation from a wrathful God combined with a messianic vision of saving the world via Jesus or Allah? Whether addressing my own mindset, Sarah Palin's, or my former colleagues', I would describe us as angry, rigid, insecure, inflexible, and doctrinaire—a mirror image of fundamentalists around the world. Fearful of losing "our way," or even our salvation, ever vigilant against Satan's constant temptation, we had no room for error. Consequently we had a lot of rules. Anything that might have remotely caused us—or anyone else for that matter—to sin was taboo. For instance, illicit sex or sex before marriage was strictly *verboten*. To guard against sexual temptation, dancing was forbidden because it might lead to physical intimacy. So was drinking adult beverages. When people smoke, they often like to drink, so we banned smoking too.

What's all this got to do with you? Simply this: If God's rules are good for God's chosen, then they're good for America, God's chosen land, and that means you.

The tendency to be doctrinaire also meant not challenging the rules or the rule makers. To do so revealed a lack of faith, which in itself suggested that you were on the verge of backsliding. If you allowed Satan to lead you astray by doubting the inerrancy of the Bible or even questioning the propositions and rules that resulted from the fundamentalist hermeneutic and exegetical models of interpreting Scripture, you might lose your salvation, as one concerned friend warned me. To guard against this sum of all fears, you must diligently protect the integrity of the fundamentalist worldview by discrediting, demeaning, or demonizing any challengers (a.k.a. tools of Satan). In this way, the fundamentalist paradigm is a self-reinforcing, closed system that is impervious to outside challenges or influence.

As you might have already guessed, an important part of insulating ourselves from satanic attack, as well as pursuing our mission to reestablish Zion, involved establishing boundaries. We needed to be clear about who was on our side and who wasn't. We had to keep ourselves pure and keep out the forces of contamination, which of course led to an "us against them" mindset.

The hypervigilance of following the rules and avoiding people who don't, the constant concern about being seduced or deceived by Satan, the ungodly suspicions about who's *really* on our side, creates both paranoia and hostility as neatly exemplified by Dr. MacArthur:

> Satan employs every agent he can dupe into being a shill for him—demons, unbelievers, and (most effectively) people who are in some way actually associated with the truth or (even worse) who merely *pretend* to be agents of the truth and angels of light.[125]

In other words, Dr. MacArthur's theological opponents, even fellow-Evangelicals "actually associated with the truth," could be shills for Satan if they interpret the Bible differently than MacArthur.

Then there are those who are obviously employed by the Dark Prince. As an ardent fan of my daily Christian Voice radio program wrote me, "Satan is taking over this country through those sick people who abort babies." Pastor Ock Soo Park warned in a full page ad in the New York Times that "no matter how much good we [humans] do, we can only be destroyed."[126] Rev. John Hagee (infamously ejected from John McCain's 2008 presidential campaign) stated that Catholics are members of "a false cult system."[127] In the neo-fundamentalist mindset, the "nice" lost people are to be pitied and hopefully converted as soon as possible so they can join the redeemed and be saved. The "not-so-nice" lost—the liberals, sexually promiscuous, homosexuals, pro-choicers—are Satan's oblivious, disguised henchmen. Since the unredeemed person and the unrepentant heart are evil, if they can't be converted, they must be somehow brought under the dominion of Christian values.

Notice how easily you can slip into a jihadist mindset from here when you consider yourself one of God's chosen on a mission to save the world from evil, that you are a "warrior for God" and privy to His will, and that your role is to simply "see and do"—that is, to impose His will on everyone else.

In the interest of fairness and accuracy, and to set some uneasy readers' minds at rest, let me issue the following disclosure: The vast majority of Christians—including Evangelicals—are *not* neo-fundamentalists—thank God! While some will embrace a few of the five pillars, many will vehemently reject all five, and the consequent neo-fundamentalist mindset.

It is a common mistake to lump all Christians, Evangelicals, or even all neo-fundamentalists together. Our tendency is to blur their distinctions and confuse one for the other, as if neo-fundamentalists, fundamentalists, and Evangelicals are really no different from each other. One might ask the same question about Republicans—don't they all believe the same thing? The answer is yes...and no. While most Republicans may share a distaste for big government or high taxes, the distinction between social and economic conservatives, not to mention libertarians, can be quite drastic, as demonstrated by the Christian Right's lack of passion for Senator John McCain's candidacy in the 2008 elections.

So just who are the neo-fundamentalists and how do they differ from other Christian subcultures? And where in the world do they come from?

5

The Rise of Religious and Secular Neo-Fundamentalists

FOLLOWING THE REVOLUTIONARY War of 1776, Americans declared their independence from *all* authoritarian hierarchies, political as well as religious. "The Spirit of 1776" was a celebration of individual autonomy against autocratic authority, including the authority of ministers, church tradition, and dogma. The revolution provided fertile ground to incubate a distinctly American version of Christianity—a constellation of beliefs virtually unrecognizable to any Christian born before 1800. As Evangelical historian Nathan Hatch notes,

> As preachers from the periphery of American culture came to *reconstruct* Christianity, three distinct tendencies became evident. First, they mingled diverse, even contradictory sources, erasing distinctions that polite culture of the 18th century had struggled to keep separate. The crucible of popular theology combined odd mixtures of high and popular culture, of renewed supernaturalism and

Enlightenment rationalism, of mystical experiences and biblical literalism, of Evangelical and *Jeffersonian rhetoric.* At the same time, this environment accelerated this splintering of Christianity, what George Rawlyk calls a fragmenting Evangelical ethos. As increased numbers of these theological neophytes attempted to explicate religious matters for themselves, the overall range of religious options multiplied (emphasis added).[128]

The "Great Awakening," the period following the revolution, marked the explosion of American sectarianism: sects like your local independent community church, Bible church, or Independent Baptist Church that broke away from historic European Churches like Catholic, Anglican, Lutheran, and Presbyterian.

This reconstruction of American Christianity eventually became known as Evangelicalism, which blended four distinct and somewhat contradictory paradigms—Calvinistic Puritanism, American individualism, Anabaptist pietism, and Enlightenment epistemology—with two novel nineteenth-century innovations that soon became the tail that wagged the dog. The first innovation, *dispensationalism*, was invented by British pastor John Nelson Darby and legitimized by C. I. Scofield's extraordinary Bible. It focused on the end time's return of the Lord of the Universe and the horrific annihilation of every nonbeliever following a unique eschatological event commonly referred to as the "rapture."

This apocalyptic theme was popularized in such books as Hal Lindsey's *Late Great Planet Earth,* which sold thirty million copies in the 1970s—enough for every Evangelical in America to have one handy. At the turn of the second millennium, my former ministry partner Tim LaHaye updated this genre through his immensely popular *Left Behind* fiction series.

The second innovation was the debut of *born-again revivalism* first promoted by evangelist Charles Finney. Until Finney, Christians didn't think of themselves as born-again Evangelicals or fundamentalists, but as Methodists, Baptists, Presbyterians, or perhaps simply as Christians. Then Finney decided that to be a real Christian you had to have a born-again experience identifiable in time and space. He facilitated this experience through another innovation—the "altar call"—where he would boldly call people to come before the altar to receive Christ. Historically, serious Christians had considered themselves to be born again in the sense of laying aside old ways of thinking and beginning a new life. But now Finney and his revivalists insisted you had to have a specific born-again moment. It simply wasn't enough to grow up in the church, spending your life trying to follow Jesus' teachings. *This new born-again elite, much to the irritation of more traditional Christians, began to distinguish itself by introducing the term "Evangelical."*

The Debut of American Fundamentalism

In the early twentieth century, a new movement called fundamentalism offered conservative Christians a nonambiguous refuge from the assault of modernity in all its horrifying forms—Darwinism, scientific materialism, secularism, the Industrial Revolution, urbanization, and perhaps most importantly, biblical "higher criticism" and liberal theology. Terrified by the liberal and neo-orthodox blitzkrieg on an inerrant, literalistic God-dictated canon, confused and conflicted by the complexities and contradictions of modernity, and craving an island of certainty amidst a sea of change and ambiguity, conservative Christians morphed themselves into what we recognize today as fundamentalists. Fundamentalists sought to defend and preserve the "Rock of the Gospel," at least in its American form, by clearly defining the "fundamentals" of their view of Christianity. And it was no coincidence that the dawning of the twentieth century spawned religious fundamentalist movements in other parts of the world, most notably the fundamentalist Islamic Brotherhood, in reaction to modernism's perceived secular profaneness.

The moniker of "fundamentalism" came about in the early decades of the twentieth century (1910–1915) due to the mass distribution of millions of "fundamentals," a series of twelve small booklets designed as ammunition for the faithful to fend off the wiles of the ascending "liberal theology" that was rapidly capturing the leadership of the big Protestant denominations. Then the World Christian Fundamentals Association was founded in 1919. The fundamental beliefs they chose to defend were a literal interpretation of Christ's virgin birth, bodily resurrection, and miracles; the inerrancy of the Bible; and the belief that Christ had to sacrifice himself to redeem the sins of those who would choose to accept him as Lord and Savior.

Fundamentals that didn't make the cut included like God's unconditional love for mankind, caring for our earth, Jesus' dictums that his followers would be known by their unsurpassed love, helping their enemies, forgiveness, and helping the poor.

Thereafter, conservative Protestants used their selected fundamentals as a litmus test for the "true Christian," while liberals and progressive Christians concentrated mostly on the principles the fundamentals did not address.

After exhausting their quiver of fundamentals, conservative Protestants adopted a "circle the wagons" approach to preserve their faith handed down by their nineteenth-century forebears. The goal was to protect their system of biblical and cultural values from the contamination of contradicting data or tough questions. To keep themselves pure before the Lord and unsullied by modern (satanic) culture, fundamentalists separated themselves not only from the "ungodly" secular culture and liberal churches, but ironically from the historic Christian church of 2000 years as well. They considered the historic church to be "apostate," meaning fallen away from the true faith according to the dictates of their new dispensational paradigm that predicted the historic churches would grow increasingly impure.

Earning their reputation as separatists, they created their own subculture—duplicating key secular institutions, establishing their own publishing houses, books, and magazines, hundreds of "Bible Colleges," seminaries, and missionary training institutes, as well as four-year educational institutions, elementary through secondary schools, and radio and TV stations featuring a 24/7 combination of Christian music and exhortation to the faithful to stay faithful—and of course to send money.

But even this was not enough as the pressure from the surrounding culture threatened to overwhelm the fundamental fortress. For good measure, they decided to withdraw from those who were reluctant to separate, such as "compromisers" like Billy Graham who continued to associate with people who weren't fundamentalists. In the fundamentalists' view, these appeasers and traitors were likely to have their thinking and theology contaminated, so they had to be shunned as well, before they spread the contagion. For, as the apostle Paul warned the Corinthians, "Do not be deceived, 'Bad company corrupts good morals'" (1 Corinthians 15:33, NASB).

The Rise of the New Evangelicals and Charismatics

Following World War II, fundamentalism was distinguished by its Bible-thumping, hellfire-and-brimstone negativism, anti-intellectualism, narrowness, and eschewal of earthly pleasures—or by what Leonard Sweet calls its "crabbed and crabby view of the future." [129] This obscurantism wore thin on some of the movement's leaders, especially young, handsome, and charismatic "Youth for Christ" evangelist Billy Graham, as well as on several of their preeminent theologians like Carl Henry and Ed Carnell. Carnell, who eventually became president of Fuller Seminary, complained that the movement had become cult-like:

> Fundamentalism had become like a cult in that it was bounded and operated according to "mores and symbols of its own devising'" rather than by the gospel and Christ's commandments for the church—especially to live in love and unity.

The gospel had been warped, Carnell complained, into "Believe on the Lord Jesus Christ, don't smoke, don't go to movies, . . . and you will be saved."[130]

Fed up with a movement they found "intellectually lame, provincial, mean-spirited, stultifying and manipulative," these leaders birthed a new Evangelical movement reclaiming the term from its earlier prefundamentalist usage. In Henry's 1947 "resignation letter" to the fundamentalist movement, a small book entitled *The Uneasy Conscience of Fundamentalism*, he accused fellow fundamentalists of "cultural irrelevance, a harsh temperament and a spirit of lovelessness and strife." Graham and a slew of others followed him out of the fundamentalist-separatist camp. [131]

Meanwhile a similar sea of change was occurring among the Pentecostals who were basically fundamentalists who also believed they had the "gifts of the Spirit," like speaking in tongues, healing, and prophecy. Influenced in the 1970s by the "charismatic renewal" led by Pat Robertson and Bob Mumford (one of my mentors), millions of Pentecostals made a similar decision to jettison much of their fundamentalist-tinged "legalistic" tradition in favor of a more flexible, love-based theology. Just as the term Evangelical distinguished soft-liners from the old hard-line fundamentalists, Charismatics can be considered Pentecostal-lite.

One of the main distinctions of the new Evangelicals and Charismatics was a desire to integrate into mainstream denominations and culture with the purpose of converting them as disciples for Christ. This was at odds with the fundamentalist refusal to even talk to "those people!" Their approach was also more loving than that of the fundamentalists, meaning less confrontational with a greater emphasis on God's love as opposed to His wrath, and a little more humility about their certainty. For example, Billy Graham admitted "there are many things I don't understand [about Scripture]".[132]

Facing what they perceived as an increasingly adversarial culture during the 1960s and '70s, Evangelicals and their Holy Spirit-filled Pentecostal and Charismatic brethren began to evolve three distinct worldviews stemming from the three very different wellsprings of American Christianity midwifed during the Great Awakening: Puritan covenantalism, rapture-obsessed Dispensationalism, and Anabaptist-revivalist Pietism.

Claiming the broad middle ground, the revivalist-dispensational-rapture spring flowed into the ocean that became mainstream Pentecostalism and Evangelicalism with their emphasis on "soul winning"—converting someone and then getting them to "win others to Christ" (also known as evangelism)—and of course, waiting for Jesus' imminent return. This cohort of Evangelicals is by far the largest, representing 70 to 80 percent of the Evangelical-Charismatic community—a body of 40 to 50 million of our fellow citizens. For the most part, they were happy campers, content to lead the purpose-driven life and focus on the family while avoiding being left behind.

To the left of these, the Anabaptist-pietest impulse with its commitment to pacifism and compassion, aversion to dogma, openness to spiritual experience, and its perception of Jesus as a lover and not a fighter, evolved into Evangelicalism's "progressive" wing. This stream displays a distinctly more liberal approach to both politics and theology—often modifying or altogether jettisoning conservatives' paradigm of an infallible text, as well as literal representations of hell fire and damnation. Progressives are mostly found in Evangelical colleges and universities, as evidenced by the academic background of some of its main voices—Tony Campolo, Ron Sider, and Jim Wallis.

Meanwhile, on the right, the Calvinistic-Puritan spirit was beginning to percolate anew. God's "stewardship mandate"—that Christians are to serve as stewards or vice-regents under God in taking care of his world—also meant regaining control of the nation's political and educational institutions. The stewardship mandate was updated and expanded into a covenantal worldview by nineteenth-century pastor and theologian Abraham Kuyper, who later became Prime Minister of the Netherlands and founded the University of Free Amsterdam. Kuyper originated the concept of a "Christian worldview" and urged believers to rigorously apply scripture to every area of their lives, not only personally but in economics and government—especially government. Kuyper divided human activity into different spheres—business, cultural, political, religious—and developed a system to bring them all under God's authority. Interestingly, in its practice of religion as an all-absorbing "life system" that pervades and permeates every aspect of daily life, this covenantalism shares the same orthopraxy (practice of faith) as Islam.

Francis Schaeffer, the fundamentalist pastor, missionary, evangelist, and philosopher, popularized Kuyper's concept for a new generation in the 1960s–1980s. "Worldview" became the new catchphrase amongst politically motivated Evangelicals. This new hybrid of religious-political activist accepted the primary spiritual tenets of fundamentalism, but gradually replaced the pessimistic and somewhat unconscious defeatist presuppositions of "premillennial dispensationalism" with an implicit "postmillennial" eschatology of victory. In the postmillennial's optimistic end-time scheme, Jesus Christ would not come back to rescue a cowering people from a malevolent antichrist, as the dominant premillennial view proposed. Rather, Christ's covenant keepers—the Chosen—would essentially win the world for Christ who would then come back to reign for a thousand years (the millennium) of bliss. Unlike their separatist fundamentalist forbearers or their proselytizing brothers and sisters in the Evangelical center, these conservative Evangelicals believed in interacting with secular culture primarily so they could export Christian moral values and eventually "disciple" the majority of the world's citizens.

Meet the New (Neo) Fundamentalists

Of significant importance for their future political and cultural agendas, these right-wing neo-fundamentalists were more consistent in their fundamentalism than even the old school dispensational fundamentalists and their belief that the Old Testament was no longer relevant. These new Puritans would insist that the *whole* Bible, including the Old Testament, since it was part of the seamless word of God, was applicable to today's issues.

Thus, by the beginning of the third millennium, a new group of fundamentalists, still holding to the fundamentals but now motivated to achieve dominion over every nation, emerged on the world scene.

Meet the neo-fundamentalists.

I say "world scene" because, as I've hinted before, their emergence isn't limited to neo-fundamentalist Christians. As if an ominous harbinger of the times, Pope Benedict XVI suggests that radical elements of Islam bent on achieving submission of every nation to Koranic justice—Sharia law—are also neo-fundamentalists: "Islamism has been transformed into a *neo-fundamentalism* that cares only about reestablishing Islamic law, the *Sharia*, without inventing new political forms."[133] Jihadist expert Fawaz Gerges adds: "Conservative 'neo-fundamentalism' (which aims primarily at Islamizing society from the bottom up through what is called *da'wa,* 'the call') has generally replaced revolutionary jihadism, whose goal is to Islamize society by simply seizing state power."[134]

So now we have Christian neo-fundamentalists *and* Islamic neo-fundamentalists, both committed to world dominion, which sets us up for a potential—some will say inevitable—clash that may make our current culture war look like child's play. Unfortunately, that possibility is beyond the scope of what we can discuss in this book. But I would be remiss not to address the *other* antagonists of the culture war—secular fundamentalists.

Before I do that, let's talk about you and me and the average American who doesn't identify with either extreme. Ninety percent of us believe in God and most identify ourselves—if only somewhat loosely—with various faith traditions. Many of us consider ourselves "spiritual but not religious," and we are blazing a path to God without the aid of organized religion, which is increasingly experienced more as hindrance than help. And many people devoid of any religious or spiritual impulse, who could technically be classified as "secularists," hold no ill will toward their religiously minded neighbors. They may be secular (not religious) but they don't identify with secular*ism* as a belief system, which Webster's defines as "a system of doctrines and practices that disregards or rejects any form of religious faith and worship" and as "the belief that religious and ecclesiastical affairs should not enter into the functions of the state."[135]

Yet most of us still find ourselves caught in the withering crossfire of those pushing their neo-fundamentalist agenda and those who are self-consciously intent on a humanist or antireligious vision. *I'm tempted to call it the War of the Palinites vs. the Infidel Secularlists.*

So what about those secularists who have made an ideology out of their nonbelief by adding that extra "ism?"

Secular Fundamentalists—an Oxymoron?

All too often secular fundamentalists are those advocates of tolerance, diversity, and pluralism who react in a typically fundamentalist manner when their worldview or politically-correct code of conduct is challenged. In other words, they default at best to a defensively dismissive or demeaning mode, or at worst to offensive assault and demonization (sound familiar?).

You may be wondering who exactly *are* these warriors of secular culture. For the legions of neo-fundamentalists, they are the ultimate bogey man—the "secular humanists," secular because they deny the existence of God (or at a least the validity of religion) and humanist because they replace the sovereignty of God with that of humans. As Curtis Reese, a humanist minister, wrote in 1927, "There is a large element of faith in all religion. Christianity has faith in the love of God; and Humanism in man as the measure of values."[136] From a very different vantage point, postmodern philosopher Leonard Sweet makes the fascinating observation that one of the distinguishing characteristics of secular humanists is their fundamentalist style of zealotry and intolerance:

> Secular humanism is best described as one form of religious humanism, since it can be as fundamentalist and zealous as any right-wing religious or political fundamentalism. In its arrogance, secular humanism sees all religious faith as an irrational burp, something to be hushed at best and suppressed at worst.[137]

Similarly, Greg Epstein, Harvard's humanist chaplain, charges popular antireligious writers like Sam Harris and

Richard Dawkins with being "atheist fundamentalists."[138]

But what about Sweet's charge that secular humanists are "one form of religious humanism?" How can *secular* humanism be construed as a religion? Quite easily, according to famous humanist thinker Julian Huxley, who wrote in 1957:

> It is often stated that the essential of religion is belief in God, meaning by that in a personal or super personal Divine being, or at least a belief in supernatural beings of some kind. This, however, is manifestly not true. There are whole religions which make no mention of God.[139]

The first generation of American humanists, writing in the early twentieth century, clearly saw secular humanism as a religion to replace what they saw as a tired and outdated Christianity. As early as 1918, the author of *The Humanist Manifesto*, Roy Wood Sellars, observed: "[Humanity is] on the march towards a new religious faith which I dare to believe will provide us with a religion greater than Christianity."[140]

Perhaps America's foremost humanist philosopher, John Dewey, the primary architect of the modern public school system, cast the role of public education in a religious context, celebrating public schools as "performing an infinitely significant religious work"[141] by serving the cause of a secular religion. Not to be outdone by the most enthusiastic evangelist, Dewey ecstatically proclaimed, "in this way the teacher always is the prophet of the true God and the usherer in of the true kingdom of God."[142] Of course Dewey's religion was the very definition of a secular humanism, based as it was on the verities of "Science and democracy."[143] To make himself unmistakably clear, he added, "If we have any ground to be religious about anything, we may take education religiously. . . . Faith in education signifies nothing less than belief in the possibility of deliberate direction of the formation of human disposition and intelligence."[144] No doubt inspired by Dewey's ambitious vision, Sellars waxes prophetic while getting to the heart of the matter: "The religion of human possibilities needs prophets who will grip men's souls with their description of a society in which righteousness, wisdom, and beauty will reign together. . . . Loyalty to such an ideal will surely constitute the heart of the humanist's religion."[145]

Unsurprisingly, as American culture increasingly loses its taste for formal religion, so too have secular humanists, according to an early 2007 article in the humanist magazine *Free Inquiry,* which mollifies its more ardent secular readers by assuring them that even though *"Manifesto I* was drafted by philosopher Roy Wood Sellars for the explicit purpose of proclaiming humanism as a new religion, *Manifestos II* and *2000* were drafted by Paul Kurtz reflecting a wholly secular agenda."[146] Nevertheless, Paul "Mr. Humanist" Kurtz, writing in *Humanist Manifesto II* admitted, "Humanism is a philosophical, religious, and moral point of view . . . "[147] while opining that "traditional theism . . . is an outmoded faith."[148]

Do some humanists still consider their beliefs to be a religion, at least in some context? The answer oddly enough, may lie in the databanks of the Internal Revenue Service, which, at the request of the American Humanist Association, classified them as a church with all the tax-exemptions and legal benefits of your local fundamentalist church. Fortunately, we don't have to rely solely on the judgment of the IRS to determine the religious context of today's secularists. While many (probably most) self-conscious humanists would no more classify themselves as religious than Christian fundamentalists would see themselves as secular, a number of indicators may help us answer the question for ourselves. As we shall soon see, this question is important for us to fully grasp the intensely religious nature and fervor of the culture wars.

Telltale Signs of a Religion

But it is the "transcendental pretense," the attempt to project one's own subjectivity onto the world and other people—as "The Truth" Central—that is the most dangerous arrogance of all. —Robert Solomon[149]

Central to all religions is the necessity of dealing with big picture metaphysical questions. Why are we here? What is the nature of reality? What is the purpose of our existence? Of the universe? Where did it all come from and where is it all headed? Are we no more than a mere chemical accident? Are we devolving or evolving? What are the primary components of life—matter, consciousness, spirit?

Where do secular humanists turn for answers to life's major questions? According to progressive intellectual Michael Lerner, "They are captivated by a belief that has been called scientism. . . . science can answer every question that can be answered."[150] Contrasting his own metaphysical paradigm with his secular colleagues, Lerner concisely sums up secularists' attachment to scientism: "I don't rely on science to tell me what is right and wrong or what love means or why my life is important. I understand that such questions fundamentally cannot be answered through empirical observation."[151] Postmodern philosopher Ken Wilber adds, "There is a well-known term for what science becomes when it is absolutized: *scientism*. And the liberal Enlightenment, for all its enormous good and all its extra-ordinary intelligence in other lines, began with science and ended with scientism."[152]

If scientism provides the metaphysical foundation for humanism, what about the faith component? *After all, even those who reject all religious faiths are doing so on the strength of faith in their objectivity or the validity of their own presuppositions.* Rejecting all spiritual paradigms, secularists place their faith in what historians call scientific rationalism. Simply put, it replaces faith in God or spirit with Descartesian faith in our rationality—that we can determine truth by employing scientific methodology. Lerner explains:

> Once you understand that the Left really operates on faith—faith in their values—you unlock the secret as to why so many people are angry at what they see as an arrogant elitism coming from people on the secular Left. The secular Left often presents itself as if it is operating on a higher moral plane than everyone else, precisely because it imagines that its worldview has been sanctioned by science and rationality. . . . The truth is, they have no better foundation for their ethical views than I for my spiritual views if *foundation* means "rooted in science, objective empirical observation, or universally accepted truth."[153]

Wilber concurs, noting that scientific materialism is "a worldview now taken on absolute faith by its adherents."[154]

Former MIT philosophy professor and world religions expert, Huston Smith, adds that scientism "carries the marks of a religion—a secular religion."[155] Do terms like "operating on a higher moral plane" or "a worldview now taken on absolute faith" sound eerily familiar? I think they do. In fact they sound a lot like Sarah Palin and her fellow neo-fundamentalists! Now we begin to understand why these two extremes can't communicate—they both know that they're right!

While humanists in the early twentieth century may have had ample reason to feel their faith was well placed in the objective certainty of the scientific method, time has intervened to deliver a somewhat less optimistic assessment, as Richard Tarnas observes in his comprehensive history of Western knowledge:

> The knowledge science rendered was relative to the observer, to his physical context, to his science's prevailing paradigm and his own theoretical assumptions. It was relative to his culture's prevailing belief system, to his social context and psychological predispositions, to his very act of observation. And science's first principles might be overturned at any point in the face of new evidence. Moreover, by the later twentieth century, the conventional paradigm structures of other sciences, including the Darwinian theory of evolution, were coming under increasing pressure from conflicting data and alternative theories. . . . All human knowledge is mediated by signs and symbols of uncertain provenance, constituted by historically and culturally variable predispositions,

and influenced by often unconscious human interests. Hence the nature of truth and reality, in science no less than in philosophy, religion, or art, is
radically ambiguous. The subject can never pre-
sume to transcend the manifold predispositions of
his or her subjectivity.[156]

If we can reasonably conclude that secular humanism holds
both a metaphysical system and a reliance on faith in common
with religion, what about the other telltale signs of a religion?
What about, for instance, an offer of salvation and a moral
agenda?

Not all religions offer a blissful afterlife as a reward for following "the path." Some, like Buddhism and Gnosticism, offer
the promise of enlightenment. Similarly, secularists like John
Dewey see education combined with the evolutionary process
as the best hope of humanity to reach the level of enlightenment necessary to save itself and the planet. When it comes
to a moral agenda, based on ideological or religious presuppositions (dogma), what could be a clearer example than the
secularist politically-correct agenda with its narrowly defined
and rigorously enforced moral codes that mandate "the correct
stance" on a myriad of issues from racism to sexism, ageism
to vegetarianism, from its focus on rights for various groups it
sees as victimized (including animals) to its defining what kind
of public speech is acceptable?

Secular Intolerance

Politically correct "true believers" all too often seem to share
another characteristic with religious fundamentalists: a smug
assurance that they and only they have a corner on the truth.

According to James Davison Hunter, a leading authority on the culture wars, the very concept of political correctness implies

> a position so "obviously superior," so "obviously correct," and its opposite is so "obviously out of bounds" that they are beyond serious discussion and debate. Indeed, to hold the "wrong" opinion, one must be either mentally imbalanced (phobic— as in *homophobic*—irrational, codependent, or similarly afflicted) or more likely, evil.[157]

Similar to religious fundamentalists, secular fundamentalists' unmitigated need to be right about their beliefs leads to a codified, rigid worldview as narrowly doctrinaire as any religious dogma. This sense of elitist superiority stems in part from scientism's pervasive intolerance to any nonmodernist, nonmaterialist paradigms as Huston Smith notes:

> Whereas science is positive, contenting itself with reporting what it discovers, scientism is negative. It goes beyond the actual findings of science to deny that other approaches to knowledge are valid and other truths true. In doing so it deserts science in favor of metaphysics—bad metaphysics, as it happens, for as the contention that there are no truths save those of science is not itself a scientific truth, in affirming it scientism contradicts itself.[158]

In a doctrinaire system, challenges to the prevailing orthodoxy are either summarily rejected or, in the case of internal dissent, ruthlessly stifled. Senator Joseph Lieberman, a liberal

Democrat regarded so highly by his party that he was selected as Al Gore's vice-presidential running mate in 2000, was
abandoned by the party just a few years later during his reelection campaign. His crime? Breaking with the left on just one
issue—the war in Iraq. Similarly, popular Pennsylvania Democrat Governor Ed Casey was denied a speaking role in the 1992
Democratic convention that nominated Bill Clinton because
he broke with liberal orthodoxy on just one issue—abortion.

Secularist Marcello Pera, a respected academic and former
president of the Italian senate, has this warning for fellow intellectuals who dare to violate politically correct sensibilities:

> A warrant will be sworn out for your cultural ar-
> rest. You will be banished from the literary salons,
> clubs, and academies. You can forget about win-
> ning any book prizes or being invited to speak at a
> conference or symposium[159]

Even Christopher Hitchens, the prominent atheist author of
God Is Not Great, was not immune from the "politically correct
orthodoxy police," who seem more like their Taliban counterparts roaming the intellectual landscape looking for moral offenders, when he dared to call Bill Clinton's character in
question during impeachment proceedings. David Horowitz,
formerly editor of *Ramparts*, once the avant-garde magazine of
the New Left, reported on the public shunning of Hitchens by
his liberal colleagues:

> In a brutal display of comradely betrayal, they
> publicly shunned him in an attempt to cut him
> off socially from his community. One after anoth-

er, they rushed into print to tell the world at large how repulsed they were by a man whom only yesterday they still called "friend" and whom they no longer wish to know.[160]

Secularists can also display an equal amount of intolerance to those outside their camp. In fact, the level of intolerance from the secular left has reached such an intensity that Pope Benedict XVI recently warned that a dogmatic intolerant political correctness "seeks to establish the domain of a single way of thinking and speaking . . . which threatens freedom of thought as well as freedom of religion."[161]

Jim Wallis, a leading critic of the Christian Right also complains: "Today there are new fundamentalists in the land. These are the 'secular fundamentalists,' many of whom attack all political figures who dare to speak from their religious convictions."[162] Stephen Carter, a liberal scholar and author of *The Culture of Disbelief,* offers an insider perspective on Liberals' tendency to not be all that liberal when it comes to opposing views:

Rather than envisioning a public square in which all are welcome, the contemporary liberal philosophers insist on finding a set of conversational rules that require the individual whose religious tradition makes demands on his or her moral conscience to reformulate that conscience—to destroy a vital aspect of the self—in order to gain the right to participate in the dialogue alongside other citizens. And such a requirement is possible only in a liberal world that regards religious knowledge

as being of a decidedly inferior sort. Thus liberalism, as a theory of politics, is moving in an unsettling direction. According to the philosopher Richard Rorty, "logical" positivism got a bad name by
calling religion and metaphysics nonsense and by
seeming to dismiss the Age of Faith as a matter of
incautious use of language. Liberal dialogue seems
to be headed down the same road, and in a nation
where so many citizens are centrally moved by
religious conviction, the consequences for liberal
theory are likely to prove disastrous—unless there
is a change of course. [163]

Stanley Fish, former dean of Liberal Arts and Sciences at
the University of Illinois, offers a similar but more concise perspective on the reason for liberal intolerance: "Liberalism is
tolerant only within the space demarcated by the operation of
reason; anyone who steps outside that space will not be toler-
ated, will not be regarded as a fully enfranchised participant in
the marketplace (of ideas) over which reason presides."[164]
Whether secular humanism meets the litmus test of a bona
fide religion or not isn't the point. The issue is that many of
them evidence the black-and-white thinking that typifies the
fundamentalist mindset. As Lerner advises, "It would be far
more honest for those on the Left to acknowledge that they
have a worldview and that it is not any less partisan than the
worldview of the Right."[165] Wilber, as a non-Christian philosopher, believes rabid scientism's "spiritual burden," its tendency to "dominate" and "repress" other belief systems, is a "prescription for cultural catastrophe."[166] What sort of catastrophe
concerns Wilber? The type where neo-fundamentalists think

"the modern world makes no room for my . . . religious beliefs and therefore I will blow up the modern world in the name of God."[167] As Jim Wallis noted, it is these same "assaults of secularism that helped turn fundamentalism into the right-wing force it has become today."[168]

Given the absolute certainty and self-righteousness with which each side has maintained its position, making it the only legitimate spokesman for America's future, cultural conflict has been unavoidable. The question is this: where is it headed? Historically, when two people groups are this polarized, the tendency is to repress and control the opposition if not wipe them out altogether. Noting the "anti-democratic impulse" of the culture war's conflicting parties, Hunter is also concerned with "the possibility of conflict and violence."[169] Should we be too?

Part III

Enter the Theocrats
(or, "She Seemed Like Such a Nice Girl")

6

How the Kingdom of God
Was Lost—and Found Again

Now THAT WE have a basic understanding of where religious and secular neo-fundamentalists come from and
of the fear that motivates them, let's narrow our focus back in
on American Christian neo-fundamentalists and explore their
strategy for national, and eventual world, dominion.

In order to reclaim America for God, neo-fundamentalists
needed to find a precedent for "godly government." Fortunately for them, it was in their own backyard in the form of America's Christian heritage and its dominance from the seventeenth
through the nineteenth centuries. As historian George Marsden notes, this was an America where:

> From the time of the Puritans until about the mid-
> dle of the 19th century, American evangelicalism
> was dominated by a Calvinistic vision of a Chris-
> tian culture. Old Testament Israel, a nation com-
> mitted to God's law, was the model for political in-
> stitutions.[170]

Noted liberal scholar Stephen Carter adds:

> Thousands, perhaps tens of thousands, of laws
> currently on the books were enacted in direct re-
> sponse to the efforts of Christian churches. Indeed,
> as recently as the 1950s, there was a major effort to
> amend the Constitution to provide that the laws of
> the United States were subject to the word of God,
> and to the rule of God's Son Jesus Christ. And in
> 1892, a unanimous Supreme Court made reference
> to "a volume of unofficial declarations" that added
> weight to "the mass of organic utterances that this
> is a Christian nation.[171]

And so the Puritans both in the USA and England, where
they took over the government by force, are the inspiration
for today's Christian neo-fundamentalists whose battle cry of
"traditional values" harkens back to a much, much earlier time.

It's 1860. God was securely on his throne in Protestant
America—the new Zion. God's special country was set apart
to be an example to the world. Puritan leader John Winthrop
proclaimed it to be, "a new Israel, a city set on a hill," to borrow a biblical metaphor, existing to disciple every nation for Jesus Christ. Then came the devastating Civil War, which ended
the Protestant hegemony. Then a massive invasion of "antichrist" forces—otherwise known as the Roman Catholic im-
migration—arrived followed by the unspeakable horror of history's first World War, launched by the "antichrist" German
Kaiser. These were culture shocks of epic proportions, but the
trauma inflicted on God's people didn't end there.

After 1500 years of Christendom's unrivaled cultural dominance, the seventeenth-century Enlightenment spawned a new menace more dangerous than all previous threats combined— modernism. This paradigm slowly spread through Western society until it cemented the Enlightenment's secular disregard of a religious or spiritual worldview. *The Menace of Modernism*, which fundamentalist leader William Bell Riley published in 1917, clearly shows that by that date the growing concern about the modern zeitgeist, reflected in both liberal theology and evolutionary naturalism, had turned to genuine alarm. Riley observed that modernism had gained substantial cultural power particularly among the educated classes, menacing the authority of the Bible, the moral foundation of American culture. Because of the modernists' subversive work, Riley warned, a whole generation of educated Americans was on the brink of moral suicide.[172]

The veracity of the fundamentalist Bible as a work of 100 percent historic fact, as opposed to a mix of fact, true myth, and metanarrative or metaphor, was being challenged by both modern theologians and science. In response, fundamentalists—represented by William Jennings Bryan, thrice the *Democratic* nominee for president—put teaching evolution on trial in the infamous "Scopes" case in July 1925 and were widely ridiculed in the press for their efforts. So fundamentalists began a tortured retreat from the public arena. Eventually the rest of America forgot about them, other than as an occasional object of contempt. The eclipse of their formidable cultural and political relevance was hastened by their defensive strategy of separatism—separating from a sinful culture—and premillenial dispensationalism, which predicted the world, as well as mainline churches, would continue to fall under the influence of the devil until Jesus returned. There was little left for the

"saints" to do other than pray, evangelize, and disappear under-
ground where they managed to build an extensive subculture,
which emerged with a surprising ferocity a half-century later
in the 1970s and '80s.

The 1930s and '40s were dominated by the Great Depression, Franklin D. Roosevelt's New Deal and, of course, World
War II. The 1950s were more benign—June and Ward Cleav-
er from the TV show *Leave It to Beaver* were the model family, kids like me prayed in school, saluted the flag, and pledged
their allegiance to one nation under God. But just as fundamentalists had begun to once again feel relatively secure in
Zion, they were deluged by the unprecedented chaos of the
"sex, drugs, and rock 'n roll" revolution of the '60s—a frontal
assault on family values and Christian morality if ever there
was one. This new zeitgeist that tore the culture from its traditional values moorings also enveloped the Supreme Court in
the '60s. According to neo-fundamentalists, God and the Bible
were kicked out of public school when school-sponsored prayer
and Bible reading were outlawed.

Something was going terribly awry in God's country. A vocal minority of fundamentalists were outraged. How could
a few men in long black robes outlaw God and His Word?
How dare they offend God and risk His terrible and righteous
wrath? A few fundamentalist thinkers were also beginning to
realize, as sociologist Steve Bruce observed, that "Modernity
does not challenge religion. Instead it subtly undermines it and
corrodes it."[173] But most conservative Christians still hoped the
secular offensive would be held at bay. Maybe it wouldn't affect
their local communities and families as long as they were pro-
tected by geographical (rural) and legal (i.e., states' rights) barriers, which provided the structural insulation needed for suffi-

cient autonomy in conducting their lives, raising their children, and expressing their beliefs toward immorality, abortion, and so on. But in the '60s, the barriers began to crumble. Just as many Islamists felt their safe haven in the Middle East violated psychically—with western immorality invading their fundamentalist cocoon through mass media and the Internet—and physically—via western troops (crusaders' boots on sacred ground). American fundamentalists felt similarly assaulted with the intrusion of an increasingly aggressive bureaucracy and its secularist, pluralistic agenda. As Bruce observes:

> Increasing secularity and liberalism could have been ignored by fundamentalists so long as they were permitted the social space in which to create and maintain their separate social institutions. Unfortunately for them, it is in the nature of modern industrial societies to reduce that social space.[174]

Historian Karen Armstrong vividly expresses the reactions of fundamentalists to their perceived lack of "social space" to practice their beliefs:

> Increasingly, during the late 1960s and 1970s, as the state expanded its notion of what constituted the public arena, very conservative Christians on the margins of modern society experienced these interventions as a secularist offensive. They felt "colonized" by the world of Manhattan, Washington, and Harvard. Their experience was not entirely dissimilar to that of the Middle Eastern countries who had so bitterly resented being taken over by

an alien power. The government seemed to have
invaded the inner sanctum of the family: a Con-
stitutional amendment giving women equal rights
of employment seemed to fly in the face of biblical
injunctions that a woman's place was in the home.
Legislation limited the physical chastisement of
children, even though the Bible made it clear that
a father had a duty to discipline his children in this
way. Civil rights and freedom of expression were
granted to homosexuals, and abortion was legalized. Reforms that seemed just and moral to liberals in San Francisco, Boston or Yale seemed sinful
to religious conservatives in Arkansas and Ala-
bama, who believed that the inspired word of God
must be interpreted and obeyed to the letter. They
did not feel liberated by the permissive society.[175]

The Rise of the Theocrats

In 1973, the Supreme Court legalized abortion, which laid the
groundwork for transforming Richard Nixon's *Silent* Majority into Jerry Falwell's *Moral* Majority. That was bad enough,
but then came the proverbial straw that broke the camel's
back. What happened next handed Christian Right field marshals like myself the very weapon we needed to mobilize both
the fundamentalists and the Evangelicals (who by the 1970s
far outnumbered their fundamentalist brethren) and reverse
the 65 to 35 percent margin they had awarded born-again candidate Jimmy Carter over the incumbent Republican, Gerald
Ford.

Jimmy Carter's Internal Revenue Service in 1978 issued

guidelines that would have revoked the tax exemption of thousands of private schools, including Christian, Buddhist, and Islamic. This assault by the IRS was perceived as an attempt to annihilate Christian education and to literally wipe out future generations of believers. As Armstrong notes, "It seemed an act of war on the part of liberal society. Only fundamentalists, it appeared, were not allowed 'free exercise' of the principles of their faith."[176] The liberal establishment and the media were caught totally off guard when Carter's actions, coming on top of the other provocations just mentioned, galvanized neo-fundamentalists to defend their most solemn and cherished values. The Christian Right was born.

Its first few spawnlings were my organization, Christian Voice, and Falwell's Moral Majority, which energized neo-fundamentalists to defeat Jimmy Carter and three dozen of the most liberal members of Congress, including almost every prominent Senate liberal just two years later. While "this sudden eruption of religion seemed shocking and perverse to the secularist establishment,"[177] the fact is, secularists and liberals simply weren't paying attention. As we've seen, the neo-fundamentalists were there all the time, just beneath the radar of America's secular elite. As Bruce explains:

> Liberals had simply forgotten that large numbers of people did not share their beliefs and values. The cosmopolitans and intellectuals who supervised the media and ran the bureaucracies of the major denominations had concentrated on the struggles for the rights of women and blacks, on the student movement, and on the protests against the Vietnam War, and neglected the American

conservative Protestant. It is not so much fundamentalism but *public awareness* of fundamentalism
which has been born again.[178]

In this perfect cultural storm, two elements began a col-
lision that would radically alter the face of American politics,
leading to the culture wars. The first was the just-discussed
unintentional provocation by secularists and progressives. The
second and perhaps more salient factor was the gradual replacement of fundamentalism's dispensationally driven defeat-
ism and separation from the wider culture with an aggressive
Calvinistic Dominionist worldview. As Historian Bruce Barron observed, "To the degree that they are exchanging their
former posture of cultural accommodation for one of resistance, one can say that there is a Dominionist trend within
Evangelical thought."[179] Calvin's theological dictums on godly government provided a ready-made platform for Dominionism, to adapt and update the Puritans' intention to secure
God's rule in the original colonies. As I gloated in a mid-90s
lecture to a room full of Christian Right pastors, "The rapidly
diminishing influence of premillenial dispensationalism (as in
'there's nothing we can do but retreat and wait for the rapture')
on many Evangelicals has opened the floodgates for victorious
Christian activism," by which I meant the Dominionist plan
for victory.

This metamorphosis is perfectly illustrated by none other
than my former colleague Jerry Falwell—the Jerry Falwell of
the 1960s—reacting to challenges by leaders of the old Right
like the Rev. Billy James Hargis. At first, Falwell argued:

Believing the Bible as I do, I would find it impossible to stop preaching the pure saving gospel of Jesus Christ and begin doing anything else—including the fighting of communism, or participating in the civil rights reform....Preachers are not called to be politicians, but to be soul winners.[180]

But after Falwell pondered the secular assault on long-cherished Christian values, he began preaching that for fundamentalists *not* to vote in the election was a "major sin." Something had to be done, as Armstrong notes: "because they had experienced modernity as an assault that threatened their most sacred values and seemed to put their very existence in jeopardy. By the end of the 1970s, Jewish, Christian, and Muslim traditionalists were poised to fight back."[181]

All they lacked was a biblical blueprint, which Dominionists (who will settle for a broadly defined Christian America), and their more radical brothers the Reconstructionists (who want to replace American civil law with Old Testament Law), were only too happy to provide. As Rushdoony prophesized, "The church of the 20th century must be roused out of its polytheism and surrender."

Building the Kingdom of God

Twenty-five years ago, the thought of reclaiming the Puritan vision of America as the new Zion, a theocracy directly governed by God, was not on anyone's radar screen other than a few hardcore Reconstructionists. These hardliners were churning out volumes of theological justification for Dominionism or theonomy (Taliban-style governance by Old Testament Hebrew law), that were read by a relatively few Christian scholars, pastors, and activists. What they lacked was a marketing arm, a distribution network reaching directly into neo-fundamentalist churches in every community. Enter Jay Grimstead, who had spent a decade honing his skills organizing college students for Jesus through an Evangelical youth ministry called Young Life. Growing restless with the limiting scope of youth ministry, Grimstead began to dream—and dream big! Concerned that Evangelicals were straying from the old fundamentalist model of interpreting an inerrant Bible literally, he envisioned bringing together leading Evangelical scholars to stop the whole subculture from sliding down further on the slippery slope of theological liberalism. Making his dream a reality, he organized the first International Council on Biblical Inerrancy, invited a veritable who's who of sixty-two neo-fundamentalist scholars, and together they reaffirmed the total inerrancy and infallibility of Holy Scripture. There he connected with neo-fundamentalist heroes like R. C. Sproul, J. I. Packer, and James Kennedy, all of whom would play a prominent role in his future endeavors.

Grimstead, a devoted student of Francis Schaeffer, was concerned the church was losing the battle for America's soul, as well as its own. Determined to "make one last ditch effort to stop the Anti-Christ, to go out in a blaze of glory rather than a whimper," he founded the Coalition on Revival (COR), explaining:

> In 1984 God led me, I believe, to call together 112 national Christian leaders to form a united, spiritual army willing to help mobilize the Body of Christ around several tasks, two of which were:
>
> To rally around the mainstream basics and create 17 Biblical Worldview Documents which would

outline the Church's biblical tasks in various areas of life such as law, government, economics, education, the media, science, the arts, and outline a biblical view of evangelism, discipleship, helping the hurting, pastoral renewal, and so on...

To offer the Church-at-large models, pathways, plans and documents from our consensus wisdom about how to impact every area of life with the Biblical Worldview as stated in these consensus documents. We can thus begin rebuilding our civilization on the principles of the Bible as a united, spiritual "Allied Army" of Christian leaders from every denomination and organization which cares to unite in such an effort.[182]

Combining his formidable organizational skills with his nationwide network of contacts from the Counsel, he created a transdenominational movement that surpassed even his most grandiose expectations, attracting over one hundred of the most respected neo-fundamentalist theologians, seminary professors, and pastors. The Coalition on Revival's inner circle included prominent TV evangelists James Kennedy and Jack Van Impe, Dee Jepson (Ronald Reagan's Director of Public Liaison), J. I. Packer (Evangelicalism's foremost scholar), Tim LaHaye (its number-one selling author), and Robert Dugan (the Executive Director for the National Association of Evangelicals). Especially enthusiastic was the cohort of charismatic neo-Pentecostal leaders who would later form the New Apostolic Reformation, which we will turn to shortly.

Grimstead also recruited stars of the Reconstructionist/Dominionist movement and the "Discipleship-Shepherding" cult dedicated to training a new generation of highly disciplined spiritual warriors. Ironically, Grimstead understood very little about either movement's agenda or theology. He was simply impressed that Reconstructionists "had a plan" and the shepherds were "men of action." Due to precisely these traits, these movements very quickly dominated Grimstead as well as the entire COR network. Forceful men with a clearly defined plan were exactly what COR members were looking for. Even Grimstead was susceptible, diving deep into Reconstructionist theology and taking shepherding leader Dennis Peacocke as his personal pastor, as well as making him one of the corporate officers of COR.

Here is where all this history reconnects with my story. Shortly after bringing in Peacocke, Grimstead recruited me as corporate treasurer for COR whereupon I promptly submitted myself to Peacocke's "spiritual authority" (which is something you do in neo-fundamentalist circles—you place yourself under someone's spiritual authority, like an imam or a Reconstructionist crackpot, from whom you learn and receive your holy marching orders).

Eventually the discipleship and Dominion movement blended together to form the basis for the New Apostolic Reformation that Sarah Palin (as well as Katherine Harris, the controversial Florida Secretary of State who certified George Bush's disputed election in 2000) is associated with. But I'm getting ahead of our story.

A few years later, in 1984, Grimstead issued a call to the nation's neo-fundamentalist leaders to come together for a week in Denver to the nation's first "Continental Congress on Christian Worldview" to discuss how the church should sort out the seventeen major challenges God's people were facing. And come they did! Over 500 delegates from every stream of Protestantism—Pentecostals, Independents, Charismatics, Fundamentalists, mainstream Evangelicals, and even a few old-line fundamentalists. They were drawn from the nation's most respected Evangelical seminaries, leading churches, and the biggest parachurch organizations like Bill Bright's mammoth Campus Crusade for Christ, the National Association of Evangelicals, the Moral Majority, and of course, my own Christian Voice.

Delegates signed up for workshops in the seventeen "spheres of influence" to hammer out position papers on topics that would eventually be released as authoritative directives to the church at large, similar to the early church councils of the first several centuries. Because the Reconstructionists and Dominionists were the only ones with a coherent agenda, they were paired with a leading neo-fundamentalist figure in each field. For instance, Jay selected me to chair the government policy section, pairing me with Gary Demar, a well-known Reconstructionist author (and later a client of mine). As in the other workshops, attendees came to get the perspective of a well-known leader (in my case, I was the dominant Christian Right leader at the event).

But what really happened solves the riddle of how a handful of Reconstructionist and Dominionist theologians managed to spread their ideas to millions of neo-fundamentalists in just the last three decades.

Like most of my peers who were supposedly leading the other sections, I knew I had only a sketchy idea of how the Bible applied to either politics or government. Therefore I deferred to my Dominionist cochair. In fact, it was so obvious to

me who would actually be controlling the agenda and writing the resultant position papers, I insisted Gary and I reverse
our titles (with me acting as cochair to his chairmanship). And
of course Gary wrote the entire document. I suspect much
the same thing happened in the sixteen other policy spheres
as hundreds of neo-fundamentalist leaders were baptized, full
immersion-style, in the Dominionist agenda. The delegates
took the next year to study and refine our position papers even
further so we could reconvene in Dallas and issue our final
product. That product was COR's *17 Worldview Documents* series, each providing a blueprint on how the church could dominate culture in "17 spheres" including the government sphere
I worked on, which pronounced: "The Lord God is the universal governor of all nations. Humans are unable to govern justly
without Scripture as their governing authority, the Bible is the
only standard by which to run a government, there is no absolute separation of church and state."

The law section was headed by attorney Michael Farris,
founder and president of Patrick Henry College, known as
God's Harvard and a major source of interns for the George W.
Bush White House. Farris's working group proclaimed:

We affirm that . . . God is the ultimate source of
law.

We affirm that God's standards of truth, morality,
and justice, and other transcendent legal standards,
by which civil law is to be promulgated, enforced,
and evaluated, are absolute.

We deny that the legal standards by which civil law ought to be promulgated and enforced are relative, allowing for subjective, cultural, or other factors contrary to Scripture.[183]

Other topics included economics, education, medical ethics, science, and psychology.

The final documents were signed and approved by neo-fundamentalist leaders like Adrian Rogers, president of the Southern Baptists (Evangelicalism's largest denomination), Luder Whitlock, president of a leading neo-fundamentalist seminary, and Ted Engstrom, then-president of America's largest overseas relief and development organization, World Vision. Another signator, a well-respected and at that time moderate Evangelical scholar was Dr. Peter Wagner of Fuller Seminary. As we shall soon see, after being influenced by his participation in COR, he was at least indirectly responsible for constructing much of Sarah Palin's worldview.

To maximize efficient distribution, the unwieldy seventeen documents were summarized in a briefer piece entitled "42 Articles of the Christian Worldview." The Dominionist agenda was now ready to be distributed to thousands of pastors, seminarians, and Christian Right leaders, complete with the "Good Housekeeping Seal of Approval" from the highly-respected Ecumenical leadership of the Coalition on Revival. None too subtly, COR informed its readers that they had "determined that it is mandatory for all Christians to implement this worldview in society."

The COR documents were officially released at an event staged to garner optimal fanfare. On July 4, (of course) 1986, over 700 delegates, including senior members of Ronald Reagan's White House staff, gathered under the sweltering sun at the Lincoln Memorial in Washington DC to officially sign yet another COR document, the *Manifesto for the Christian Church*, which essentially reminded readers of the terms of God's covenant: obey God and inherit blessings, ignore God and reap His curses. Fifty leaders, including myself, signed a "blood oath," a solemn covenant with Almighty God that we were willing to be martyred in order to do God's will. If you think this sounds a bit like the guys who blew up the Twin Towers, I would have to agree.

To help me with the writing of this chapter, I watched a video recording of the event and was amused to see that the first two delegates to boldly step forward and sign the oath were my "shepherd," Dennis Peacocke, today one of the lead "Apostles" of the New Apostolic Reformation and Reconstructionist *l'enfant terrible* Gary North. North immediately announced that the document represented "the new Christian agenda." As a member of COR's steering committee, I was asked to join theonomic leaders like North, Demar, Rushdoony—who warned God would destroy the delegates unless the church got about the business of saving America—and of course, Grimstead himself—who called the nation to repent and acknowledge Jesus as King of the Universe—in addressing the seven hundred warriors assembled at the Lincoln Memorial. I declined, thinking even back then that the whole document was over the top. Contributing to my discomfort was my increasing unease with Jay's manic and often disconcerting trumpet outbursts. After a particularly successful meeting Jay was known to grab his ever present trumpet and belt out a tune no matter where he was. When he did it on Capitol Hill in Washington DC in front of one of my favorite congressional watering holes, it was, to say the least, embarrassing.

My reservations aside, The *Washington Times* referred to the COR confab as one of the most important of the year. The keynote speaker, Dr. James Kennedy, who had just been voted Clergyman of the Year, said it had the historical significance of the Magna Carta or Declaration of Independence. In contrast, the irreverent *San Francisco Examiner* columnist and editor Warren Hinckle, who had once publicly decried my moving into his fair neighborhood, had a take a little closer to my own: "700 preachers shepherding 60 million born-again Christians gathered here not so much to celebrate America as to plot to take it over. The funny thing, if you have a bizarre sense of humor, is that they have a heck of a chance of succeeding."[184]

While COR is still a going concern, ginning up a myriad of ambitious strategies to do everything from closing down Planned Parenthood to establishing a "shadow government" and issuing an unending stream of proclamations likening the election of Barack Obama, "a socialist who is committed to black liberation theology," to be "part of God's continuing judgment upon America for tolerating over 50,000,000 murders of innocent, helpless little human beings,"[185] its power is dwarfed by the movements it helped to spawn.

In the aftermath of the COR convergence, a few Pentecostals wandered off to seek the Holy Spirit's guidance on what they had learned from their COR experience, but most of the neo-fundamentalist activists returned to their churches, parachurch organizations, seminaries, and Christian colleges to cobble together their own version of a softer, more compassionate form of Dominionism. A minority joined up with the hardcore Reconstructionists, as I would eventually do, to persuade their soft-core Dominionist cousins that at the end of the day, after successfully colonizing America for Jesus, the

logical next step was to institute strict biblical law. But the real
action was within the newly politically-sensitized (thanks to
COR and Christian Voice) neo-Pentecostals that make up Sarah Palin's world. As investigative journalist Fred Clarkson noted, "Perhaps Reconstructionism's most important role within
the Christian Right can be traced to the formation of COR....
nowhere...is Reconstructionism...having a more dramatic impact than in Pentecostal and Charismatic churches."[186] The
popularity of "dominion theology" in the rapidly growing
Charismatic, neo-Pentecostal denominations was no accident.
Even though Reconstructionists thought Charismatic distinctions—especially the spiritual gifts of prophecy, healing, and
"speaking in tongues" (glossolalia) practiced in the New Testament and believed by Charismatics to be available to "spirit-
filled" Christians today—were at best nonsense, if not hereti-
cal, they knew a soft target when they saw one. For their part,
Charismatics realized they were strong on spiritual experience
but weak on theology and doctrine, so they looked to Reconstructionists to fill the theological void. They wanted to know
how should tens of millions of spirit-filled believers, desperate
to please God, apply God's Old Testament Law in contemporary society? They found the answer in Rushdoony's *God's Plan
for Victory,* distributed by the thousands to carefully targeted
Charismatic churches, which said, "Christian political action
is necessary towards making the state again a Christian state,
and its actions conform with the law of God."[187]

With Charismatics and Reconstructionists in bed together,
the next thing they needed to begin reclaiming the country for
Jesus was a national, grassroots network and an inspirational
leader—a modern-day Joan of Arc.

7

Palin's Grassroots Network:
New Apostolic Reformation

WHILE DOMINIONISTS CONTINUE to provide the intellectual blueprints for various neo-fundamentalist tribes, the New Apostolic Reformation (NAR) is by far the largest, most energetic—and the most threatening. With an estimated following of several millions in the United States alone, Dr. Peter Wagner, a world missions expert claims, "It's the most rapidly growing segment of Christianity in every continent of the world." Bruce Wilson, in a Huffington Post article, describes NAR activists as "radical Christians with some Pentecostal/Charismatic parallels."[188] It is to this stream that *all four* of the churches Sarah Palin attended over the past thirty years are connected. It is the NAR movement that provided both Sarah Palin and myself with our very own personal apostles to disciple us.

In contrast to the neo-Pentecostal charismatics, the other Dominionist schools are fairly predictable. Using a strict Calvinist lens, Reconstructionists simply apply Old Testament law to every issue. Softer core neo-fundamentalist Dominionists seek to apply biblical "principles" rather than the letter of the law. The challenge for both groups, as we saw in the Second Pillar of neo-fundamentalism, is that each individual is free to interpret the Bible in his or her own way, potentially generating a thousand shades of interpretation. Thankfully, most people in the Christian Right are content to settle for a return to traditional values and godly government as loosely defined by their leaders.

But forecasting the augmentations and permutations of the NAR's worldview presents another conundrum altogether. While sharing their neo-fundamentalist cousins' penchant for "private interpretation" of Scripture, these believers take the process to its logical extreme—requiring no hermeneutic, no exegesis, and no tradition of interpretation. In fact they don't even require a Bible. And they certainly don't need trained theologians to interpret God's Word for them—they are "spirit-filled, tongue-talking children of the King" and fully competent to hear directly from their Father in heaven. Unsurprisingly, this hyper-individualistic method of determining God's will has bred thousands of freelance prophets traversing the land, prophesying "Thus sayeth the Lord" in a myriad of bizarre and contradictory contexts. Peter Wagner's New Apostolic Reformation is a prime example of this.

Just several years after signing the COR documents, Dr. Peter Wagner, a tenured professor at Evangelicalism's intellectual flagship Fuller Seminary, began to make a name for himself as a prolific writer and one of the world's top experts on missions and Evangelicalism. In his bestseller *The Third Wave of the Holy Spirit,* Wagner asserts that the first wave of the Holy Spirit's outpouring had been the Pentecostal movement itself, which had kicked into gear in the early 1900s. He continues,

"The second major wave of the Holy Spirit in the 20th century was the Charismatic movement emerging around the middle of the century."[189] Charismatics are basically Pentecostal-lite in the same way Evangelicals are fundamentalist-lite: The newer permutations kept the core tenets, but jettisoned "old fashion legalism," culturally-bound traditions like prohibiting drinking, dancing, the theater, and so on. Most importantly, Wagner calls the third wave "a new moving among Evangelicals" who didn't identify with the other Pentecostals or even the newer charismatics.[190] According to Wagner, "The major distinguishing point of the Third Wave is not the final result of the ministry of the Holy Spirit. Within it the sick are being healed, the lame are walking, demons are being cast out, and other New Testament manifestations of supernatural power are seen."[191]

As powerful as the third wave had been, Wagner began pondering why so much of the world, particularly Asia, was so uniformly resistant to miracles or receiving Christ as their personal Lord and Savior. He fastened on the concept of spiritual warfare. After all, what else could account for Hindus turning down Jesus' offer of eternal salvation but demonic interference? As megachurch pastor Harold Caballeros writes in Wagner's spiritual warfare manifesto *Breaking Strongholds in Your City,* "Any reasonable person to whom light is shown will prefer light against darkness."[192] So why do so many people resist the light? Demons, of course. And demons are everywhere. Wagner's expertise in world missions included studying pagan or animistic peoples whose belief in spirits convinced Wagner "that animistic cultural information on the unseen reality *can* be accurate."[193] Critics from within the Evangelical movement have argued that many missionaries and missiologists, like Wagner, have ironically been heavily influenced by the very

magical beliefs held by the animist religions they seek to con-
vert. Indeed, Wagner found evil spirits in his home attached
to everything from a stone puma to native masks and even
imported exotic lamps. All had been contaminated by indig-
enous, in his case Indian, demons. The spirits grew so strong
that Wagner reported "seeing a spirit in our bedroom." [194] He
attributed falling off a ladder "to the direct work of an evil spirit." His wife, Doris, awoke "to see a luminous green outline of
some being" (could it be Slimer from *Ghostbusters*?). Demons
also gave Doris "a horrible piercing cramp in her foot" and
cursed Peter with unrelenting migraine headaches.[195] Wagner and crew are convinced they are not delusional. In fact,
it's the rest of us who are delusional and regularly misappre-
hending reality. As George Otis Jr., one of Wagner associates,
writes, "We can see what is beneath the surface of the material world."[196] And that is, of course, a legion of demons who, according to Doris, author of the ever popular book *How to Cast
Out Demons*, are responsible for almost every ill afflicting mankind, including:

> manipulation and control...poverty, shame, greed,
> materialism...lying, deceit, kleptomania, stealing...
> loneliness, grief, abandonment...emotional cold-
> ness...perfectionism, rejection, stress...pride...arro-
> gance...anxiety, worry or depression...confusion...
> mental fantasy, escapism...fear...lust...fear of: wom-
> en...the opinions of people...or grocery stores...[sex-
> ual] resentment, bitterness, frigidity, emotional
> coldness.[197]

What is the source of this demonic invasion? According to

Doris, they seem almost infinite:

> Hypnosis...advanced education...Christian Sci-
> ence...Jehovah's Witnesses, Mormonism...Hindu-
> ism, Buddhism...Islam...Freemason[ry]...Shriner[s],
> Elk[s], Masonic regalia or memorabilia...Ouija
> boards...astrology...lucky charms...crystals...New
> Age movement...yoga...meditation...ESP...symbols
> of idols or spirit worship, such as Buddhas, totem
> poles, painted face masks, idol carvings, fetishes,
> pagan symbols, native art...music: rock and roll,
> punk rock, New Age, rap, heavy metal...martial
> arts...oral sex...anal sex...abortion...massage par-
> lors.[198]

But even this extensive litany could not explain Satan's iron grip over entire nations, where billions of souls are kept in "demonic bondage." Meanwhile, Wagner and Otis were hot on the scent of "the underlying explanation for the darkness that seems to engulf so many of the world's cities."[199] They found their answer in an obscure line the apostle Paul wrote to a few followers in the ancient city of Ephesus several millennia ago, warning them that they must contend with invisible principalities and powers (Ephesians 6:12). From Paul, they extrapolated the concept of "territorial strongholds" which, according to Wagner's associate Cindy Jacobs, one of "God's generals" who introduced the concept of spiritual mapping to the neo-Pentecostal women's movement, is:

> A fortified place that Satan builds to exalt himself
> against the knowledge and plans of God. An im-

portant thing to keep in mind is that Satan tries to
conceal the fact that these strongholds exist. He
cleverly cloaks them under the guise of "culture."...
Territorial strongholds are inherently defensive
and offensive in nature. While their dark ramparts
ward off divine arrows of truth, demonic archers
are busy launching fiery darts in the direction of
unprotected targets abroad. While their spiritual
prison camps retain thousands of enchanted captives, evil command and control centers are re-
leasing manifold deceptions through the spiritual
hosts of wickedness in their employ.[200]

What Jacobs, Wagner, and their fellow warriors failed to
recognize was that rather than following in Paul's footsteps,
they were actually much closer to the ancient Druidist, Wic-
can, and Pagan cults who believed certain forests, trees, ponds,
or other landmarks were reigned over by "territorial spirits"
and thus represented areas of magical or spiritual power. Accepting what might appear to be a fantastical metaphor for
the struggle between good and evil reminiscent of the *Lord
of the Rings* trilogy as reality, Wagner and his camp of followers developed a unique four-part strategy for employing spiritual warfare to clear the way for Christianity's global triumph
against the demonic strongholds of humanistic culture.

First Stage: Spiritual Mapping

Since these demonic territorial strongholds are the main im-
pediment to Christians "colonizing" (one of Wagner's favorite terms) the earth, military-style reconnaissance in the form
of mapping the enemies' power base in each city and nation is

strategically vital. As Wagner noted, spiritual mapping "is one of the most important things the spirit is saying to the churches in the 1990s."[201] How exactly do Professor Wagner and his spiritual warriors go about identifying the level of satanic power in your neighborhood? It's not terribly dissimilar to how Bill Murray and Dan Ackroyd did in *Ghostbusters*. First one has to understand that spiritual mappers believe, in the words of John Dawson, author of *Taking Our Cities for God*, that "One of the abilities or gifts of Jesus' Holy Spirit within us is the ability to discern or see the activity of spirits in the unseen realm (1 Cor. 12:10)."[202] In his thesis on spiritual mapping for the University of Utrecht, R. Holvast quotes Wagner from his Global Harvest Ministries website:

> Something new happened in the "waning months of the last decade" the Spirit introduced new dynamic spiritual warfare practices. Among them was the gift of prophecy. One of the greatest challenges the "mapper" faced was the analysis of data. Mapping was a research tool for the church of Christ. But now it became more than just that. Because of the prophetic gift Spiritual Mapping enables us to move into domains with valuable insights. God tells us through prophecy how to collect and interpret data.[203]

To enhance erstwhile spiritual detectives' discernment, hundreds of sleuthing techniques are offered in military-style manuals like Wagner's *Breaking Strongholds in Your City: How to Use Spiritual Mapping*, wherein prayer warriors are exhorted to:

do spiritual mapping that enables us to know so
far as possible the enemy's plans, strategies and
plots in order to go into battle with intelligence
and, as a result, be victorious within a minimum
of time, and with a minimum of risk and loss.[204]

Demon hunters are carefully coached to undertake exten-
sive research including making:
- A list or inventory of the names used for our territory
  and then ask ourselves the following questions:
- Does the name have a meaning?
- If the etymological name has no meaning, does it have
  any implication at all?
- Is it a blessing or a curse?
- Is it a native, Indian, or foreign name?
- Does it say anything at all about the first inhabitants of
  the land?
- Does it describe any characteristics of the people who
  live there?
- Is there any relation between the name and the attitude
  of its inhabitants?
- Do any of these names have a direct relation to the
  names of demons or the occult?
- Is the name linked to any religion, belief or local cult of
  the place?
- Does this territory have any special characteristics that
  distinguishes [sic] it from others?
- Is it closed or open to evangelism?
- Are there many or few churches?
- Is evangelization easy or hard?
- Is the socioeconomic condition of the territory uni-

form? Are there drastic changes?

- List the most common social problems of the neighborhood, such as drug addiction, alcoholism, abandoned families, corruption of the environment, greed, unemployment, exploitation of the poor, etc.
- Is there any specific area that draws out attention? For example, could we define this territory or its inhabitants with one word? What would it be?
- Are there events that have happened frequently such as deaths, violence, tragedies or accidents?
- Is there any factor that suggests the presence of a curse or of a territorial spirit?
- Are there frightening stories? Are they valid? What caused them?
- How far back does the history of the Christian church go in this place?
- How many churches do we have in the territory?
- Make an inventory of the places where God is worshiped and the places where the devil is worshiped.
- An extremely important question is: Are there "high places" in our territory?
- Are there excessive numbers of bars or witchcraft centers or abortion clinics, or porno shops?
- Study the socioeconomic conditions of the neighborhood, crimes, violence, injustice, pride, blessings and curses.
- Are there cult centers in the community? Does their location have any specific distribution?
- Can we discern a cover of darkness? Can we define its territorial dimension?
- Are there express differences in the spiritual atmo-

sphere over the regions of our territory? In other words, are the heavenly places more open or closed over different subdivisions, neighborhoods or communities in the area? Can we determine with accuracy these separations?

- Has God revealed a name to us?
- Does the information we have reveal a power or principality we can recognize?
- Has God shown us the "strongman"?[205]

As if all this is not enough, a myriad of websites associated with Wagner's movement offer even more detailed instruction:

- How has the City treated the poor and oppressed? Has greed characterized the City leaders? Is there evidence of corruption among political, economic or religious leaders and institutions?
- What natural disasters have affected the City?
- Does the City have a motto or slogan? What is its meaning? (Here the concern is influence from pagan or demonic sources like the Masons).
- What kinds of music do the people listen to? What is the message they receive from that music?
- Have any non-Christian religions entered the City in significant proportions?
- What secret orders (such as Freemasonry) have been present in the City?
- What witches' covens, Satanist groups or other such cults have operated in the City?
- Have any of the early or later Christian leaders been Freemasons?
- Is Christianity in the City growing, plateaued, or declining?

- Who were the City planners who designed the City? Were any Freemasons?
- Are there any significant discernible designs or symbols embedded in the original plan or layout of the City? (Once again, the search is for Masonic symbology).
- Is there any significance in the architecture, location or positional relationship of the central buildings, especially those representing the political, economic, educational and religious powers in the City? Did Freemasons lay any of the cornerstones?
- What is the background of the City's parks and plazas? Who commissioned and funded them? What significance might their names have? (Masons once again!)
- What other artwork is featured in the City, especially on or in public buildings, museums or theatres? Look especially for sensual or demonic art.
- Where are the areas that concentrate greed, exploitation, poverty, discrimination, violence, disease or frequent accidents?
- Does the position of trees, hills, stones or rivers form any apparently significant pattern?
- Do certain landmarks of the City have names that would not glorify God?
- How have God's messengers been received by the City?
- Has evangelism been easy or hard?
- What is the view of City leaders toward Christian morality?
- What is the identity of the ranking principalities seemingly in control of the City as a whole, or certain areas of the City's life or territory? [206]

Once a massive amount of information (this is only a small

sampling) has been painstakingly compiled, prayer warriors are advised to:

Work with intercessors especially gifted and called to strategic-level spiritual warfare, seeing God's revelation of:

- the redemptive gift or gifts of the City;
- Satan's strongholds in the City;
- territorial spirits assigned to the City;
- corporate sin past and present that needs to be dealt with;
- God's plan of attack and timing.[207]

Of course, before the Christian offensive can commence, the Strongman (Demonic Prince) must be revealed or, at the very least, the borders of the demonic territory must be defined. Wagner teaches that "Satan delegates high-ranking members of the hierarchy of evil spirits to control nations, regions, cities, tribes, peoples, groups, neighborhoods, and other significant networks of human beings throughout the world."[208] To date, Wagner's hypervigilant spiritual-mapping team has discovered these territories controlled by Strongmen: "Amsterdam, Kathmandu (Nepal), Tokyo, Cairo (Egypt), Tripoli (Algeria), Qom and Mecca (Islamic holy cities), Allahabad and Varanasi (India), Paris, New York, Pittsburgh, and of course, Hollywood, California."[209]

Specific demonic princes that the spiritual mappers have outed include those controlling Japan's Shinto religion, the Sun Goddess Amaterasu Omikami (who, if you remember, Wagner claims is destroying Japan's economy because the Japanese Emperor had intercourse with the demonic goddess), San La Muerte (Saint Death) in Argentina and the Princes of Greece and Persia (demons who rule Europe and Persia). Wagner associate Johnny Enlow claims the Prince of Persia rules a billion souls. Then there are princes Pombero, Curupi, and Piton (all in Argentina).[210] Then there's Satan's right-hand prince, Apolloyon in New York City.[211] And of course, the super demon known to prayer warriors as Mary—the Queen of Heaven— the demon to whom Catholics pray when they're hoodwinked into praying to Mary, mother of Jesus. This queen demon holds over a billion Catholics "in spiritual bondage."

Spiritual mappers, like many new agers, believe there are spiritual vortexes where heaven and earth meet, ideal for conducting warfare in the heavenlies. One such point is the Israeli Supreme Court building. It is believed to be a portal directly to Satan himself. Wagner cohort Martha Lucia explains:

> On September 15, 2005 we went to the new [Israeli] Supreme Court building which was built by the Rothchilds and contains every Masonic symbol and the Illuminati. *This place was built as a connection to the mind of Satan* as this connects to the Knesset and all the government buildings and is to house the Prime Ministers [sic] office next door. We knew we sat in a major axis of evil and made many declarations against the mind of Satan ruling this land and the earth.[212]

Another vortex is Mt. Everest. Taking the concept to its logical extreme, Wagner associate Ana Mendez, a former voodoo priestess, actually led a mapping expedition, dubbed by Ted

Haggard "Operation Ice Castle," up Everest to do war with
the Queen of Heaven. While their base camp at 18,000 feet
was "totally destroyed by demonic forces," Mendez claims her
team's prayer wreaked havoc on demonic agents and power
bases within Catholicism. The evidence? The next week an
earthquake destroyed the basilica at Assisi, Italy, and Mother
Teresa died.[213]

In case you're wondering about the attraction spiritual warfare offers to its practitioners, the benefits are a sense of power
and purpose for those otherwise powerless. For the most part,
the majority of spiritual mappers and warriors are not successful business people, professionals, or even ministers. The
movement's prime adherents are those with too much time
on their hands, mostly students, retirees, and those either un-
deremployed or unemployed. For these Americans, many of
whom feel powerless in the real world, the opportunity to be
victorious against God's enemies provides a very real sense of
purpose and empowerment. As Kevin Reeves, a former spiritual warrior explains, it can also provide quite a rush:

> It was all so exciting. Who wouldn't want to be
> on the biggest military operation geared toward
> setting the people of our valley free from Satan's
> influence? And military it was. Jason himself had
> said that the church office would be the base of op-
> erations from which sorties against our demonic
> enemies would be conducted. Like commandos in
> a hit-and-run guerrilla war, we would strike with-
> out warning and scatter the forces of darkness
> against the kingdom of God.[214]

While it's tempting to write this movement off as a small aberration, a fringe element within the Evangelical movement, it would be a mistake to do so. Reeves notes:

> Few other doctrines have gained as much respectability in the last decade as this new type of spiritual warfare: *spiritual mapping.* Crossing denominational lines, this teaching has gathered together a veritable army of adherents, all with the express purpose of freeing individual towns, cities, and even nations from bondage of Satan and his demonic *rulers, powers and world forces of this darkness.*[215]

Of course Sarah Palin's beloved Mat-Su valley did not escape contagion. In 1999, the valley's pastors prayer network, after watching a DVD called *Transformations*, invited the video's main star, a self-styled exorcist from Kenya by the name of Thomas Muthee, to teach them spiritual-warfare techniques, including mapping. Muthee would soon become a fixture at Sarah Palin's Wasilla Assembly of God Church (as we will see in the following chapter), culminating in the now infamous August 16, 2005 public ceremony where he sought to protect her against demonic forces just prior to her running for governor of Alaska. So, it shouldn't surprise us that Sarah Palin's mayoral records show she borrowed *Transformations* from her former Wasilla pastor in 2000.

Strange Bedfellows

To kick off the new millennium and take global his demon-blasting, spiritual mapping, warfare and prayer network, Wag-

ner partnered with no less of a personage than the president of
the National Association of Evangelicals, the official spokesman for 30 million Evangelicals, the Rev. Ted Haggard. In a
2005 cover story, *Harpers Magazine* noted that "no pastor in
America holds more sway over the political direction of Evangelicals than does Pastor Ted."[216] Harpers went on to note that
Haggard's New Life megachurch is equally influential as a
"crucible for the ideas that inspire the movement, ideas that
are forged in the middle of the country and make their way
to Washington DC."[217] In fact, Pastor Ted enjoyed access to the
President of the United States that many senior advisors would
envy, talking with fellow Evangelical George Bush on regularly scheduled phone conferences. Pastor Ted gained additional
heft from another 300 churches, members of his very own Association of Life-Giving Churches.

Pastor Ted began to "pastor" Wagner, and together they
constructed a multimillion-dollar prayer center on New Life's
11,000-member campus. The center features state of the art
communications technology connected to over 40,000,000
prayer warriors 24/7.[218] Prayer requests and suggested prayer
targets zip across giant TV screens while prayer warriors man
computers and phone banks. In the heart of the center, Pastor
Ted fielded urgent calls from the White House ("The President wants you in the Oval Office tomorrow!"). With Wagner's backing, Haggard wielded the prayer center nicknamed
"spiritual NORAD" (NORAD is the nation's most secretive
military command center buried deep in a mountain only a
few miles from Haggard's New Life Church) as a sword in his
war against the demonic forces.[219] Haggard claims that "it was
in the midst of these global prayer efforts that Peter Wagner
made the transition from seeing himself as a seminary profes-

sor to a person with an apostolic call."[220] Thus it was that Ted and Peter launched what would become a worldwide movement. As Wagner explains, "The New Apostolic Reformation is an extraordinary work of God that began at the close of the twentieth century and continues on. It is to a significant extent changing the shape of Protestant Christianity around the world."[221]

One's initial motivation for embarking on a pastoral career path often portends certain themes that the ministry will emphasize. For Ted Haggard, the defining moment came as a teenager when:

> One afternoon as I was walking through the church and praying, I saw a delivery room in a hospital. In the center of the room were the usual lights and equipment necessary to deliver babies, but around the walls were spirits. I could see them clearly. Some were tall and strong; others were like nervous animals. Some were confident; others were hyperactive. As the hospital attendants brought pregnant women into the delivery room and the doctors and nurses would deliver a baby, the strongest, most dominant demon would assign a demon to the baby. Sometimes the assigned demon would go into the baby's body; other times the demon would just hover around the baby and follow as the baby was carried out of the delivery room. Time after time, a demon was assigned to each baby who was newly delivered. As each demon was assigned, I intuitively knew its assignment: to instill or addict the person to hate,

drugs, immorality, self-centeredness, high-mind-
edness, greed, manipulation, lying, rebellion, mas-
turbation, pornography, witchcraft, idolatry, etc.
The spirits were assigned to keep these kids from
knowing Christ and to ruin their lives.[222]

Just a few years later Ted felt called by God to the ministry. He arrived in Colorado Springs at the tender age of twen-
ty-eight to wage spiritual war, posting a banner "SIEGE THIS
CITY FOR ME, signed JESUS" on his first church, located in a
lowly strip mall.[223] After being "anointed" for ministry by having a quart of oil poured over his head,[224] he began using spiritual-mapping techniques to target bars (especially gay bars!),
New Age centers, churches he didn't approve of, and government buildings for special treatment, employing increasingly
aggressive tactics including "violent confrontive prayer." Haggard soon became the keystone in Wagner's spiritual empire.
In fact, Haggard states his "New Life Church formed its mission for the 1990s—to support Luis Bush generally and Peter
and Doris Wagner specifically to build a network of prayer for
the lost—a calling that led to the creation of the World Prayer
Center and much more."[225]

Not only was he the pastor of the nation's fastest growing
megachurch and leader of the nation's Evangelicals, but he was
winning the war against Satan as well. In February of 2005,
Time magazine named him one of the twenty most influential
Evangelicals in America. But spiritual warfare, as many TV
ministers can attest to, is a risky business, since demons don't
take these assaults lying down. After flailing away at sexual
sins, especially homosexuality, and admonishing readers of
his pastoral "how-to" manual—enthusiastically endorsed by

fellow NAR apostles Chuck Pierce, Cindy Jacobs, John Kelly, Dutch Sheets, Luis Bush, and Francis Frangipane, and featuring a foreword by Peter Wagner, of course—to "keep no secrets,"[226] it turned out that Pastor Ted had been keeping quite a secret himself. Apparently, as an innocent baby in a hospital delivery room, he had been assigned a demon of homosexuality. In November 2006, Haggard was publicly outed by his male prostitute lover of some three years. His congregation, rather than forgiving him for getting tripped up by the very demons he waged war against, chose to hold him to the standard he set for himself and others:

> Certain lifestyles portray Christian maturity and give our witness credibility; other lifestyles do not. That's why the Bible lists qualifications for eldership and standards for Christian leaders. Personal sanctification validates His message. If we attempt to minister without internalizing His life to some degree, we can horribly embarrass the Body of Christ.

> First Thessalonians addresses this issue directly. It is God's will that you should be sanctified: that you should avoid sexual immorality; that each of you should learn to control his own body in a way that is holy and honorable, not in passionate lust like the heathen, who do not know God; and that in this matter no one should wrong his brother or take advantage of him. The Lord will punish men for all such sins, as we have already told you and warned you. For God did not call us to be impure,

but to live a holy life (4:3-7).[227]

So it was that after "horribly embarrassing the Body of Christ," he was unceremoniously banished from God's kingdom. Meanwhile his mentor Peter Wagner and his global prayer center continue on unfazed in their quest to restore America to its rightful moral heritage.

Second Stage: Strategic-Level Spiritual Warfare

This is an especially aggressive form of warfare to clear out the "territorial demons" that are represented by the "New Age, Freemasons and Eastern Religions," and that keep entire nations in bondage to Satan.[228] Wagner explains:

> This enters the invisible realm of the principalities and powers of darkness that often take the form of territorial spirits assigned to keep whole geographical areas, social spheres or cultural groups in bondage to evil. This is clearly the most demanding area of spiritual warfare. It can result in casualties if not done wisely, according to the spiritual protocol and under the specific direction and assignment of the Holy Spirit. Having said this, much of the warfare directly related to taking dominion and social transformation obviously will take place at the strategic level.[229]

Strategic-level spiritual warfare usually involves five steps:
- Establishing a "Godly perimeter" using prayer warriors.
- Expanding the perimeter—increasing the number of prayer warriors and culture warriors.

- Using spiritual mapping to identify Satan's exact power base within each city.
- Attacking that base through prayer and political organizing.
- Taking dominion of the city for King Jesus through political action, since all political structures either represent Satan or God.

While mapping and clearing out demonic strongholds is ideally done through strategic prayer and political action, the constant temptation is to carry the battle into a more violent realm. Max Blumenthal reports:

> Behind the Third Wave's histrionics lies an aggressive brand of Dominionism focused on purging "demon influence" from entire geographic areas through prayer or more forceful means if necessary. Becky Fischer, a Third Wave youth pastor who gained fame as the anti-hero of the 2006 award-winning documentary *Jesus Camp*, urged pastors to indoctrinate an army of spiritual suicide bombers to seize control of the country. "I wanna see young people who are as committed to the cause of Jesus Christ as the young people are to the cause of Islam," Fischer said in the documentary during an unguarded moment. "I wanna see them as radically laying down their lives for the Gospel as they are over in Pakistan and Israel and Palestine and all those different places, you know, because we have...excuse me, but we have the truth![230]

After all, demonic activity manifests itself through real people—Hindus, Muslims, Masons, Buddhists, liberal Democrats,
and basically anyone deemed ungodly. That's why several of
my colleagues condoned killing abortionists with one of them
actually pulling the trigger.

And that's how I almost got assassinated by one of my own
staff members in the early 1980s. A Pentecostal minister of
the NAR brand was convinced that during the heyday of my
political career—as I had been interviewed daily on network
news, *60 Minutes, Donahue,* and hundreds of talk shows—that
I was the Antichrist himself. As bizarre as it sounds, he was
convinced that my drinking and womanizing while leading
the infamous Christian Voice, combined with what he perceived as my rapidly growing political power, marked me at
least potentially as the Antichrist. Even weirder was that my
administrative assistant had to spend all night talking him out
of his deranged scheme. She certainly earned her pay that day!
While my career path as a potential antichrist was short-lived,
Dr. John Britton, an abortion provider, was not so lucky when
one of the Reconstructionist activists, Rev. Paul Hill, cut him
down in cold blood.

Taking Dominion over the Seven Mountains

Once a territory is cleared of demonic activity, in order to hold
the ground for Jesus, it must be garrisoned by Christian warriors. In this stage, the victory is to be consolidated by taking
dominion for God over each country. According to Wagner:

> Our theological bedrock is what has been known
> as Dominion Theology. This means that our di-
> vine mandate is to do *whatever is necessary,* by the

power of the Holy Spirit, to retake the dominion of God's creation which Adam forfeited to Satan in the Garden of Eden. It is nothing less than seeing God's kingdom coming and His will being done here on earth as it is in heaven.[231]

Neo-Pentecostals are, by and large, not any more interested in technical jargon, be it theological, philosophical, or scientific, than the average American. Like most of us, they are usually more moved to action by powerful metaphors than nuanced definitions. They also favor the practical over the esoteric— they want to know what can realistically be achieved in the here and now. So it didn't take long for these new millennial prophets and apostles to boil down COR's ambitious seventeen spheres of dominion to a more practical seven (God's perfect number according to some).[232] Likewise, the sterile academic term "spheres" was transformed into the more evocative imagery of "mountains"—a metaphor rich with biblical symbolism. The popular saga of how the term originated typifies the decision-making process in the neo-Pentecostal world. According to the official "Reclaiming the 7 Mountains" website, it happened this way:

In 1975 Bill Bright, founder of Campus Crusade, and Loren Cunningham, founder of Youth with a Mission, had lunch together in Colorado. God simultaneously gave each of them a message to give to the other. That message was that if we are to impact any nation for Jesus Christ, then we would have to affect the seven spheres of society that are the pillars of any society. These seven pillars are

business, government, media, arts and entertainment, education, the family and religion. About a
month later the Lord showed Francis Schaeffer the
same thing.[233]

Ironically, my former colleague Bill Bright was also the
founder of one of the worlds' largest *non*-charismatic Evangelical ministries and not normally given to receiving messages
directly from God.

God's people, led by his new apostles would indeed, as
Christ promised, "move mountains"—in this case, according
to Wagner, seven very specific mountains: "Human society is
regulated by seven supreme molders of culture—namely religion, family, government, arts and entertainment, media, business and education."[234]

Interestingly, Wagner reverts back to "COR-speak" as he
advises followers on strategies for taking dominion: "There
are many commonalities across the mountains for those of us
who live in America, but the differences are the crucial nuances for anyone attempting to go to the top and take dominion of
one particular *sphere*."[235]

One of those crucial differences, according to *The Seven
Mountain Prophecy* by Johnny Enlow and endorsed by Wagner,
is the various demons who now inhabit those lofty mountain
tops. Using a handy reference chart created by Enlow, one can
determine which demon controls which mountain: media—
Apollyon, government—Lucifer, education—Beelzebub, and
economics—of course, Mammon.

Enlow concisely outlines the next step: "This demonic en-
tity ... must be displaced from the mountains or seats of power. This is our mission that we were commissioned by Jesus to

do."[236] To control a mountaintop, one must first ascend to the summit. Consequently spiritual warriors emphasize various strategies to get there. Addressing the flock at City Harvest Church on August 16, 2008, Wagner urged listeners to become successful in one of the seven spheres (mountains) because "people at the top of their mountain have influence and dominion over their mountain."[237] He further advised them that "God wants us to take control of our mountain and let the values of the Kingdom of God be established in society."[238]

Third Stage: God's Apostles

By the turn of the millennium, Wagner realized that spiritual warfare alone was not a sufficient tool to establish total dominion. Once the demons were cleared, who would establish a garrison of Christian troops in the new "Christian colonies"? Wagner found his answer in the biblical role of apostle—men and women empowered and directed by God to rule in His name.

According to apostle Johnny Enlow, apostles enjoy "influence in heavenly places"[239] and are "called and anointed to take the tops of the mountains."[240] A secondary benefit is that apostles bring much needed order to rapidly devolving charismatic chaos. They could determine whether a prophet was false, a teaching in error, or a pastor out of line.

Thus was born, according to Wagner, the Second Apostolic Age (the first being Peter, Paul, John, and others from the New Testament), which would launch a new Protestant reformation represented by Wagner's New Apostolic Reformation,[241] with Wagner apparently playing a dual role of Calvin and Luther. To realize this new age of "Apostles on the level of Peter or Paul or John," Wagner formed the International Coalition of Apostles (ICA).[242]

According to Wagner, once prayer warriors have "cleared the pathway in the invisible world between heaven and earth," part of the apostles' job description is to utilize the spiritual authority "God has given them to bind and neutralize the demonic powers."[243] For additional impact, according to Wagner, they will, as the original apostles did, perform miracles—signs and wonders—including routinely raising the dead to life![244]

While we don't have the time or space to see how each of the 500 apostles presently walking the face of God's earth are implementing the Almighty's desires so that "His will may be done on earth as it is in heaven," several examples may suffice.

Dutch Sheets, one of the top five apostles and formerly a Colorado Springs megachurch pastor, was an outspoken advocate of both George Bush and Sarah Palin as "God's choice" for America, calling Palin "a true Esther in our generation" (more about Esther later). Like Jay Grimstead, Sheets believes America is already under judgment for "killing 50 million babies... exporting pornography, passing laws that reject His [laws]."[245] After Obama's impressive victory, Sheets declared that "God's judgment will increase...particularly for those in the church who aligned themselves with pro-abortion forces."[246] Sheets went on to call abortion a "blood sacrifice that empowers demons." In his post-election analysis, the apostle listed just a few of the judgments America can expect for electing Barack Obama, a self-described Christian, as you'll remember:

- Natural disasters (weather—tornadoes, hurricanes, floods, drought; fires, earthquakes)
- Terrorism (they will fear us much less now)
- War, perhaps on our own soil
- More economic woes

- More violence in an already violent nation
- Disease and death (Satan, who is responsible for these things will have greater inroads).[247]

In February 2009, Sheets warned that "America stands at the precipice. The future of our country and the destiny of our children's lives are before us." In his webcast, Sheets announced that after spending several days alone with the Lord, "God gave him a strategy to turn America back to its spiritual roots." Sheets believes God has shown him twenty-three states that contain "a root of God's righteousness that God can build upon." To help God, Sheets plans to recruit 10 million neo-fundamentalist youth—I doubt there are more than a few hundred thousand—to "transform the Seven Mountains." Sheets closes by reminding listeners that to "transform the mountains is to change the culture."[248]

Another influential apostle is apostle Mary Glazier of Alaska, who believes God Almighty taught her how "to ride the wind with Him," which was the impetus behind her founding the organization Windwalkers International. As one of Sarah Palin's spiritual counselors we might assume she also taught Sarah how to ride the wind, which would at least explain her extraordinarily fast rise to prominence. But that's a topic of its own which I will save for the next chapter.

A third apostle of note is apostle Martha Lucia, whose credentials include "traveling the world as an Eagle of God" and being "anointed as a general of intercession." Her major activity, other than identifying Israeli government buildings directly connected to Satan's mind, appears to be dispatching scores of prayer warriors to infiltrate various Masonic lodges and government buildings. Once behind enemy lines they combat demonic troops while receiving instructions from the Holy Spirit

to pray and sing while "whirling and twirling counter clock-
wise."[249]

A fourth important apostle is apostle Diane Buker, founder of The Battle Axe Brigade. Her website features a muscular
arm swinging a medieval spiked mace that smashes the words
"kingdoms of darkness" to bits. The site quotes Jeremiah 51:20,
"Thou art my battle axe and weapons of war: for with thee I
will break in pieces the nations" (KJV). Primary targets to get
axed are "corrupt religious systems" like Catholicism, Mor-
monism, Masons, Hinduism, as well as Evangelical "emergent
churches." Goals listed on her home page include:

- To bring change where the spiritual climate that pervades a people is held by darkness.
- Being informed through watchdog methods and spiritual mapping.
- To monitor the United Nations agenda because the UN
  is becoming the platform for a one world government
  [which] will work in conjunction with a one world religion and global economic system.[250]

The Battle Axe website also features dire warnings from
various NAR style "prophets." In a prophecy dated December
12, 2007, Rick Joyner, who we'll talk more about in the next
chapter, reveals, "Hurricane Katrina was discipline from the
Lord, intended to help wake up America and get us to turn to
Him." He worried that God may cause a massive drought if
America doesn't repent.

Finally, as we have seen apostle Dutch Sheets is one to
watch. He prohesized on March 17, 2000, that the warning
from the biblical prophet Joel, "What a day! Doomsday! God's
judgment has come" applies to America "because we have
turned from God and his ways." He cites as examples "homo-

sexuality, abortion, and socialism."[251]

It's not surprising that the scale of Wagner's new Apostolic Age requires a stage much larger than just the 500 apostles in his International Coalition of Apostles (ICA). Indeed the ICA comprises just one division in Wagner's Apostolic army, which includes at least eight other battalions, collectively forming the Global Apostolic Network that was publicly unveiled in April of 2007.[252]

Other components of this global army include my personal favorite, the International Society of Deliverance Ministries, consisting of over 150 "recognized deliverance ministries" specializing in naming, mapping and expelling demons. If you think 150 squads of exorcists might create a glut in the exorcism market, you would be wrong. Sensing that spiritual warfare represents *the* growth market amongst neo-Pentecostals, Wagner has plans to grow the group to 500 members as the next step.[253]

Wagner's empire doesn't stop there. He also created a training school for apostles and prophets, an apostolic prayer network with "high level prophetic intercessors" in all fifty states, and the Apostolic Council of Prophetic Elders—a group of "respected prophets" who meet with Wagner annually to discern, à la the Old Testament prophets, what God's will is for the following year. The counsel is led by high-profile apostle-prophet Cindy Jacobs.

Jacobs, who claims to be one of "God's generals," is Wagner's female counterpart and easily the most visible female prophet due to her prodigious "prophetic word" web postings. She coauthors with Wagner, teaches at his leadership institute, and leads his Apostolic Council of Prophetic Leaders, a post that positions her as Wagner's possible heir apparent. Jacobs is also the author of the NAR bestseller *Deliver Us from Evil,* which includes dire warnings about psychics, astrology, fortune tellers, Masons, Pokemon, and of course, Harry Potter. Whatever happened to poverty, injustice, starving children, and terrorism?

To give you a taste for the mindless magical "thinking" that characterizes NAR's paradigm—and, don't forget, people like Sarah Palin and Rick Perry—let's review a few of Cindy's "prophetic words." Or was that pathetic words?

In a December 7, 2009, post, she claims to be "a general of intercession" working directly under "The Holy Spirit—The greatest strategist in the universe ... [who] works in mysterious ways ... to undermine Satan's most intricately woven designs." She proceeds to blog about a trip to Spain which she notes is only 10 percent Christian—since she doesn't consider Catholics to be Christians. While driving through the hill country she saw

> a large black bull positioned on a high place...then I noticed another one. At this point my spiritual antennae went up as I sensed that I was looking at the strongman over Spain. At the same moment I realized that I had identified the strongman. I also heard the Holy Spirit say to me, Phoenicians and the word Baal.[254]

Cindy truly makes the science of determining who is the demonic strongman over a nation look easy. Just look around for any critter perched on a high place. I still haven't figured out the Holy Spirits' clues—the Phoenicians were neighbors of ancient of Israel and Baal was a pagan God worshiped in ancient Israel. But then, I'm not an apostle.

Another posting on her "Generals International" website cited a trip to South Korea where she realized their national emblem was the Rose of Sharon, which apparently grows in both Korea and Israel. This amazing clue led to "sharing the prophetic insights that I saw Korea as the Israel of Asia" and that as long as they stayed aligned with Israel as a nation, God would give them supernatural protection from an attack from North Korea."[255] That's certainly good news for our State Department and the White House. We can all relax now!

On July 26, 2010, Cindy posted a video with an urgent appeal for intercession, based on the Holy Spirit's urging. God was not happy "that the digression from a Biblical World is gaining momentum." The Lord revealed to her that the American Economy was "teetering" and if America didn't repent, there would be a depression. The solution: "working to elect pro-life, pro-family candidates who are fiscally responsible."[256] If Ms. Jacobs had been paying attention she could have saved herself a lot of anguish by realizing this prophetic word about an economic meltdown was almost two years after the fact.

Deliver Us from Evil is filled with similar gems. Within its pages she dispenses wisdom nuggets like, "We need to ask ourselves why don't kings and presidents regularly consult with people who have the gifts of prophecy, discernment and wisdom?"—like Cindy herself I suppose. She warns her female admirers against "Dreams that become extremely sexual," because they may experience a sexual encounter with "someone in astral form."[257] She also explains that if you're poor you "have a curse of poverty." Curses are caused by displeasing God in a number of areas, like not tithing to the church ("robbing God"), "praying to idols" (like Roman Catholics), or being named after a saint. [258] She also notes that it's "extremely dangerous" for children to read about turning into animals since "shape shifting" is an ever present danger. [259]

Going where angels fear to tread—Cindy seems willing to weigh in with God's opinion on any issue no matter how obscure. The residents of Beebe, Arkansas, woke up on New Year's Day 2011 to find that thousands of black birds had mysteriously dropped dead in mid-flight, plastering houses, lawns, and automobiles with their carcasses. Cindy thought this could be a "sign." She posted a video where she ponderously explored what prophetic word God might be bringing to America through the decimated black birds. She pointed out that Beebe also was the name of the Governor of Arkansas. Finally she realized that Bill Clinton was from Arkansas and he had initiated "Don't Ask, Don't Tell" to protect gays in the military. Cindy wondered if the dead birds could be warning us about the error of our ways.

According to an interview with researcher Rachel Tabachnick, a number of Wagner apostles, prophets, and allies have formed an alliance with the GOP's Palin wing. Prophet Lou Engle joined neo-fundamentalist senators Jim Demint and Sam Brownbeck and Tea Party darling Michelle Bachmann on a "prayer cast" to defeat Obama's health care legislation. As I write this in 2011, NAR activists are busy organizing grassroots support for both Michelle Bachmann and Rick Perry. Meanwhile, the queen of the NAR waits in the wings—mobilizing, encouraging, and inspiring millions of her followers to ensure that God's will be done in Washington, D.C. as it is in heaven.

8

Sarah Palin: Spiritual Warrior

"God has equipped Sarah for this hour." —Apostle
Mary Glazier

O F THE ESTIMATED 100 million worldwide adherents to
NAR's dominion theology, none is more powerful than
Sarah Palin, who as we previously noted has been voted the
second most popular woman in America. Who fed her soul
during her twenty-year Christian pilgrimage? Who or what informed her worldview? Who provides her with spiritual guidance? Who are the people and what are the ideas that have
molded one of America's most prominent political voices? The
answer unsurprisingly is the NAR and specifically one of its
apostles, Mary Glazier, who is not only Wagner's apostle for
Alaska but also a member of his Apostolic Prayer Network.

According to her website, Glazier "has been a powerful tool
in the hands of God."[260] Her ministry Windwalkers International, Glazier explains, was "birthed by the Holy Spirit...Many
years ago, the Lord drew me into His Presence and called me
'Wind Walker.' He revealed to me that He was teaching me

to ride the wind with Him." Glazier believes this is the same "wind of God" that Adam and Eve knew. It is the same "wind of His Spirit" that God is now sharing with Glazier and her Windwalkers as they "develop intimacy with the Holy Spirit" and learn "how to hear and respond to the Spirit."[261] Her official biography informs us that Glazier is also known as a powerful leader "on the subject of spiritual warfare." Indeed, Glazier is so adept at manipulating unseen spiritual powers that *Spirit Led Woman* magazine reported on what the apostle did when a self-styled witch applied to work as a chaplain in the Alaska State Prison system:

> Mary mobilized a prayer network for Alaska's prisons and began experiencing spiritual warfare as never before. She had received word that a witch had applied for a job as chaplain of the state's prison system. . . . Mary recalls, "As we continued to pray against the spirit of witchcraft, her incense altar caught on fire, her car engine blew up, she went blind in her left eye, and she was diagnosed with cancer." Ultimately, the witch fled to another state for medical treatment.[262]

Her unusual style of spiritual leadership is heartily endorsed by fellow apostles Dutch Sheets and Peter Wagner, who tout her "enviable track record of equipping others to move out to the front lines of the Kingdom of God." But Glazier's real significance lies in just *who* it is that she has trained to hear and respond to the Holy Spirit's orders to move out to the front lines of the war against Satan. In her sermon "Opening the Gates of Heaven on Earth," given at a conference entitled

"Receiving the New Prophetic Wind," she told her audience:
I believe in warfare. . . . our group hit our faces
and began to pray, give us a man of God. We began to shake that Gate of government. Father, you
said this is what you are going to do. We have to
have a Christian Government or to have this happen and by a miracle he won by a write-in campaign by a landslide. . . .

But while we were praying for him there was a
twenty-four year old woman that God began to
speak to about entering into politics. She became a
part of our prayer group out in Wasilla. *Years later,*
became the mayor of Wasilla. And last year she was
elected Governor of the state of Alaska. Yes! Hallelujah! At her inauguration she dedicated the state
to Jesus Christ. Hallelujah! Hallelujah![263]

So it turns out that one of Mary Glazier's Windwalkers
is none other than Sarah Palin. While that was over twenty
years ago, Wagner's apostle for Norway, Jan-Aage Torp, confirmed in a September 6, 2008, blog that Palin was still active
in the prayer network and remarked that:

Among the interesting things that have not received so much media attention is that Sarah Palin
is a member of one of the prayer networks under
Peter Wagner and his Alaska prayer-leader, Mary
Glazier.[264]

In broken English, Torp adds:

Todd and Sarah Palin has been his spiritual upbringing in the Pentecostal Church Wasilla Assembly of God, which is known as a congregation
with loudly and proklamativ [sic] worship and belief in spiritual warfare. Not one of the many silent
and politically correct white churches...[265]

Just two weeks later, on Sept 22, 2008, during Palin's vice-
presidential campaign, Glazier issued a "prophetic warning"
to her prayer warriors about "an imminent act of terrorism"
that would leave Palin alone to step into "an office that she
was mantled for,"[266] apparently insinuating that an act of God
would move Sarah Palin into the White House, presumably
over John McCain's dead body. As recently as December 15,
2008, Glazier issued a statement to *Charisma* magazine that
she and Palin's prayer warriors were convinced that the ar-
sonist who burned Palin's Wasilla Bible Church was politically
motivated.[267] *Charisma*, the authoritative voice for neo-fundamentalists and Charismatics, suggests that Palin often leans on
Glazier for spiritual support:

For several years, Glazier and other members of
Windwalkers have prayed for Palin regularly—
first when she was the mayor, then when she was
the governor of Alaska, and when she was a vice
presidential candidate. Last spring [2008], Palin
called Glazier and asked her to pray with her over
the phone, and they met at the governor's prayer
breakfast.[268]

"She asked me to pray with her for wisdom and direction,"

Glazier recalls. "I sensed a real heart of surrender to the will
of God in her. God often chooses the least likely people to be
at the forefront, and I do believe that God has equipped [Palin]
for this hour."[269] If Palin would call Glazier to pray with her for
"wisdom and direction" as governor, one can only speculate
as to what kind of wisdom and direction God's Windwalker
would offer to President Palin!

While Palin has not disclosed the exact process of spiritual
discipline she underwent during her two and a half decades in
the Pentecostal movement, we can venture an educated guess.
Unlike Barack Obama, she did not join her church as a discerning adult but as an eight-year-old child in 1972. Baptized at the
age of twelve in 1976, she spent her most intellectually forma-
tive years embracing a worldview taught by the leaders of the
New Apostolic Reformation. And unlike Barack Obama's former Chicago church, one cannot just warm the pews in an
Assembly of God church, tuning out a somewhat unhinged
pastor. For those assembled before God, religion is not a spec-
tator activity, but a whole-hearted immersion. Like many of
her fellow worshippers she felt that the messages from the pulpit were intended for her. When she prayed, she felt connected
and fed by a power beyond herself.[270] According to those who
knew her while she was mayor, Palin seemed "very conscien-
tious about applying the worldview she was taught at Wasilla
Assembly of God Church."[271] Indeed, anything less than a comprehensive approach was unthinkable, according to her former
pastor, Tim McGraw:

> I believe Sarah would not live in a fragmented
> world. ... The idea that Sarah would take this huge
> influence of the worldview that really only the Bi-

ble and the relationship with Jesus opens up...and
suddenly marginalize it and put it over on the shelf
somewhere and live apart from it—that would be
entirely inconsistent.[272]

So from what we've learned in the last few chapters, let's
see the neo-fundamentalist pillars and worldview in action in
Palin's life. For her, the Bible is God's direct verbatim revelation to her personally. It serves as her moral compass, direct-
ing her every decision. It provides a blueprint for a Christian
America—even a Christian world.

After committing her life to Jesus and getting baptized in
the frigid Alaskan waters of Beaver Lake, her first pastor and
NAR fellow traveler Paul Riley recounts, "I know that she did
receive an experience of the Holy Spirit . . . and that she received a calling on her life."[273] According to Charisma, "That
spiritual turning point came when Sarah's youth pastor told
her 'You are called by God for a purpose.' Years later, Palin
confided that the pastor's words were etched on her mind."[274]
As a "spirit filled" believer she would be filled with the Holy
Spirit who would teach her how to pray in God's special prayer
language. In fact, a few hours before Sarah's blowout speech
at the 2008 GOP Convention when she became John McCain's
vice-presidential candidate, her mother placed a call to her old
youth pastor to thank him for "launching Sarah toward this
moment."

Next, she would have learned defensive spiritual-warfare
techniques—how to keep her mind, soul, and family safe from
the devil. She also would have been taught how to detect and
eliminate demonic forces through spiritual mapping, a skill
particularly useful in clearing a path to the governorship and

the presidency. Her public mayoral records reveal that in 2000 she jotted a thank-you note to a friend for their donation of a manual on spiritual mapping and demonic warfare. Palin's constant reference to her "prayer warriors," "doing God's will," and waiting for God to "open a door" (to the presidency) are code words indicative of such training. A prime example was her answer on James Dobson's hard core Christian neo-fundamentalist radio program. When he told her he was asking his followers to pray for her, she responded in typical NAR code: "It is that intercession that is so needed. I can feel that strength that is provided through our prayer warriors across this nation."[275] Palin again acknowledges her debt to her prayer warriors, like Mary Glazier, in her book *America by Heart*. And finally, she would be reminded weekly of her God-mandated purpose—playing a pivotal role in the battle against Satan while preparing for the terminal battle between God and the antichrist. As *Newsweek* noted, "Palin's spiritual colleagues describe themselves as part of the final generation engaged in spiritual warfare to purge the earth of demonic strongholds. Palin has spent her entire adult life immersed in this apocalyptic hysteria."[276]

She had been taught that God speaks to her, even revealing the future. Just as He had told her fellow windwalker that she would "impact America," she prophesied to her fellow congregants, "God's going to tell you what's going on and what's going to go on."[277] This ability to foresee the future would certainly be indispensable for any candidate for higher office. And Palin, who turned Alaska's political establishment upside-down according to a definitive pre-presidential campaign biography by Kayleen Johnson, has good reason to trust in the Lord's divine guidance. After all, as the mayor of a small town with no political background, training, or significant financing, she defeated the incumbent Republican governor, who had also been a long-serving U.S. Senator, *in his own Republican primary*—a feat that has seldom occurred in the annals of American political history. She then went on to defeat a former Democratic governor to become Alaska's first female governor. Truly, she has reason to view herself as a giant killer *à la* David and Goliath.

And of course, Palin would be well-versed in the NAR's dominion theology with the specific mandate to capture the "top of the government mountain." Former spiritual mentor, Tim McGraw, states that "he has no doubt her religious beliefs will influence her decision-making when it comes to government policy."[278] If her swooning over Dobson is any indication, the beliefs of other Christian Right gurus would also hold sway over her. In an October 22, 2008, interview she told Dobson: "If it were not for you, so many of us would be missing the boat in terms of life and of ethics."[279]

As previously mentioned, when one considers that she, like many Evangelicals, not only believes Jesus Christ will return to judge (or destroy) the earth *in her lifetime*, but that she admitted that such a belief "guides me every day,"[280] the implications are as manifold as they are frightening. If Jesus is bringing his wrathful judgment against planet earth in a few years, why worry about the environment or global warming? Why waste public funds on futuristic scientific or medical studies when it could be spent on promoting abstinence or teaching creationism, which would please Jesus? Perhaps the most onerous aspect of Palin's eschatology is the belief that if Jesus is to return, someone needs to trigger Armageddon by inciting a war in the Middle East (perhaps by encouraging a hard-line neo-conservative foreign policy?).

The Smoking Gun

When I watched Sarah Palin's public anointing—meaning, as you'll remember, the impartation of spiritual authority, power, and God's "favor" by the Holy Spirit—any doubts I harbored about Sarah Palin's level of involvement in the New Apostolic Reformation's Dominion movement were quickly put to rest. The now infamous You Tube video features one of Wagner's lead apostles, a frequent guest speaker at Sarah Palin's home church, "Bishop" Thomas Muthee, who made his reputation in Kenya casting out demons and running witches out of town—which in fact turned out to be a giant hoax perpetrated by Muthee.[281] He delivers a Dominionist message, prophesying to Sarah and the rest of the faithful gathered together that "God is invading seven key areas." He then proceeds with the usual seven mountains litany. Explaining that God is particularly intent on seizing control of the "political dimension," he notes that's why he's "glad to see Sarah here." Immediately after acknowledging Sarah's presence he admonishes:

> We need God taking over our education system! . . . if we have God in our schools, we will not have kids being taught, you know, how to worship Buddha, how to worship Mohammed, we will not have in the curriculum witchcraft and sorcery. Is anybody hearing me?[282]

His remedy? Brigades of tongue-speaking, demon-casting young Christian warriors. He then directs the congregation to "talk to God about this woman, Sarah Palin," as she receives

God's anointing. Sarah is obviously familiar and comfortable with this mystical Pentecostal rite. Without hesitation she steps forward, mounts the platform, and confidently turns to face the congregation. She stands perfectly erect, wedged between her two spiritual authorities (Muthee and Pastor Kalnins), her head humbly bowed, arms outstretched, palms turned up to be filled with the power of the Holy Spirit.

The room is eerily quiet as the apostle speaks to God. In the easy manner of someone familiar with talking to the Almighty, he marshals God on Sarah Palin's behalf. "We say favor, favor" (meaning God opening doors on her behalf) "make a way for Sarah—make a way," he commands. Then, as he beseeches God to "use her to turn the nation...and protect her from witchcraft,"[283] Muthee dramatically places his hand on her forehead to impart God's anointing of spiritual power and privilege.

Palin has been well prepared for this moment. For almost her entire life, she has been trained to conquer in the name of the Lord. As a teen she was a leader in "The Fellowship of Christian Athletes" whose militantly triumphal creed states in part:

> I am a Christian first and last.
> I am created in the likeness of
> God Almighty to bring Him glory.
> I am a member to Team Jesus Christ.
> I wear the colors of the cross.
> I am a Competitor now and forever.
> I rely solely on the power of God
> I compete for the pleasure of
> my Heavenly Father, the honor of Christ

and the reputation of the Holy Spirit.
...I do not give up. I do not give in.
I do not give out. I am the Lord's warrior –
a competitor by conviction
and a disciple of determination.
I am confident beyond reason
because my confidence lies in Christ.
The results of my efforts
must result in His glory.
Let the competition begin.
Let the Glory be God's.[284]

As an adult she not only sat under the Third Wave NAR teachings of Pastor Kalnins, but numerous guest speakers as well—including Rick Joyner. In Joyner's signature book *The Call,* he purports to have had face to face conversations "with many New and Old Testament characters as well as prominent people in church history who are now dead."[285] These people include Adam (as in Adam and Eve), the apostle Paul and, of course, Jesus. He is guided throughout these numerous adventures by "my old friend, the White Eagle."[286] This is no ordinary talking eagle, but one who channels the Holy Spirit, as well as discerns Reverend Joyner's thoughts.

So basically, Sarah Palin has been taught by witch hunters (Muthee), windwalking spell casters (Glazier), and people who get their spiritual guidance from talking animals, all taken very seriously since "God works in mysterious ways."

Pastor Ed Kalnins himself is no slouch when it comes to indoctrinating his flock in hard-core dogma of Dominionism with his Ted Haggard-style insistence that Jesus "operates in a war mode!" Indeed Kalnins insists his flock, including Palin, also adopt a "war mode" because like Jesus, we are engaged in a giant cosmic war for souls, as well as for planet earth. After all, you don't defeat the devil and take Dominion as a Christian pacifist! Kalnins frequently warned the "end times" were just around the corner, and he also seemed eager to assign as many people to hell as possible, including anyone who voted for John Kerry in 2004 or who dared to criticize their pastor. Kalnins was so intent on taking Dominion, that his church offered a "Master's Commission" certification for young spiritual warriors who possessed the grit to complete a nine-month long spiritual boot camp where they are indoctrinated in the dogma of the New Apostolic Reformation. On both September 7, 2007, and June 8, 2008, Governor Palin traveled to her old church to bestow her blessing on the newest graduating class of spiritual warriors.

In 2008, while addressing the newest platoon of recruits, Palin spoke about how "powerful" the prayers of their church were, reminding her fellow warriors that just before her stunning upset in winning the governorship, apostle Muthee had publicly prayed, "Lord, make a way, Lord make a way." And, as she proudly told the graduates, that's exactly what happened. Pastor Kalnins topped the ceremony off by disclosing that God had chosen their very own state of Alaska to be a place of "refuge in the last days," presumably for those Christians fleeing the Antichrist in the lower 48. A video posted on the *Huffington Post* also shows that:

Masters Commission students were presented with Samurai swords, in a ceremony which mentioned the Samurai code of honor. Special note was made of the specific uses of the Samurai swords

gifted to the students, such as cutting down opponents from horseback, ground-level combat, and
in very close combat—as an auxiliary blade to be
plucked out for a sudden, killing blow.[287]

In the post Bruce Wilson reported that:
At the end of one of those events, young adults in
a church Palin had attended for over two decades
were presented with Samurai swords. "Warriors of
old were considered undressed if they were without their sword...Swords were worn in service to
the lord of the realm. Some of the most renowned
swordsmen were the Samurai," intoned a church
member officiating the sword ceremony, who then
quoted Psalms 149 verses 6–9:

May the praise of God be in their mouths and a
double-edged sword in their hands to inflict vengeance on the nations, and punishment on the
people, and to bind their kinds with fetters, their
nobles with shackles of iron, and to carry out the
sentence written against them.[288]

Queen Esther Reincarnated

Another indication of Sarah Palin's stellar standing in neo-Pen-
tecostal Dominion circles is her near cult-like status as a mod-
ern-day Queen Esther. According to one of her biographers,
Joe Hilley:
Shortly after taking office as governor in 2006,
Sarah Palin sent an e-mail message to Paul Riley,

her former pastor in the Assembly of God Church, which her family began attending when she was young.

"She needed spiritual advice in how to do her new job," said Riley, who is 78 and retired from the church. "She asked for a Biblical example of people who were great leaders and what was the secret of their leadership," Riley said.

He wrote back that she should read again from the Old Testament the story of Esther, a beauty queen who became a real one, gaining the king's ear to avert the slaughter of the Jews and vanquish their enemies.[289]

Subsequently, within neo-Pentecostal and Christian Right circles it is common to refer to Sarah Palin as a new Queen Esther—a favorite expression of Bishop Muthee. The metaphor is telling. Esther's saga is so important that she has her very own "book" in the Old Testament, the book of Esther.

The story begins by introducing Esther as a poor Hebrew girl, part of the Jewish tribe that had been carted off in captivity from Jerusalem by King Nebuchadnezzar of Babylon (present-day Iraq). At the time of the story, she was living in Persia under King Xerxes. It seems Xerxes' queen incurred the King's wrath, inspiring him to conduct a nationwide contest to select a suitable replacement. Scripture tells us that Esther "was lovely in both form and feature," like Sarah Palin, the second runner-up in the Miss Alaska beauty pageant. And like Palin, Esther was blessed by the Lord and immediately found favor

with Hagai, chief of the King's harem. With Hagai as her sponsor, she was awarded the finest suite in the harem, complete
with seven servants and twelve months of beauty treatments!
With the help of her new array of beauty consultants, Esther
proceeded to win favor with everyone who saw her. Finally,
her beauty won the favor of King Xerxes, who made her queen
of his empire.

Meanwhile, the king's number one advisor, the evil Haman,
was concocting a plot to pillage and murder every Jew in all of
Persia. Haman prevailed upon the pliable King who agreeably
dispatched orders to all his subordinates to kill and annihilate
all the Jews—young and old, women and little children—and
plunder their goods.

Enter Mordecai, Esther's adopted Hebrew father, who dis-
covers this diabolical plot and beseeches the queen to intercede
on behalf of her people. When Esther points out that such un-
invited intervention in the King's business might cost her life,
Mordecai none too subtly suggests that God has placed her in
such a pivotal position "for a time such as this." Esther then re-
solves to do the right thing for God, exclaiming, "If I die, I die."

As with Sarah Palin, God hadn't bestowed His favor upon
Esther or shown her the way to live (both familiar themes in
Palin's life) just so she could be queen (or governor). Rather,
God in His sovereignty had placed Esther/Palin in a position of
political influence for "a time such as this"—a time to save her
people from extinction (or to save neo-fundamentalists from
losing the culture wars). There's little doubt Sarah identifies
with Esther. A chapter in Sarah Palin's official biography is ap-
propriately entitled *For a Time Such as This,* and she reveals in
her autobiography *Going Rogue* that when she challenged the
incumbent Republican Governor of Alaska, risking an end to

her career, she thought to herself, "Well, If I die, I die." [290]

Now for the pivotal turn in Esther's story. What does she do when she is made aware of her enemy's plot? She uses her influence, beauty, and charm with the king to induce him to reverse his edict. Rather than putting Haman in charge of slaying the Jews, the king executes Haman, replacing him with none other than Esther's adopted father Mordecai. And here's where the story gets scary, especially in light of what we know of the ideologues that Palin and the like are associated with—the king awards Esther's people the right to seek vengeance against their would-be persecutors ("On this day the enemies of the Jews had hoped to overpower them, but now the tables were turned and the Jews got the upper hand over those who hated them." Esther 9:1, NIV). Scripture tells us that not only did Esther's new allies kill Haman, but her own people also killed all ten of his sons and quickly slaughtered 75,000 of their enemies!

What is the lesson that neo-fundamentalists draw from the Esther/Sarah analogy? That God in His wisdom has sovereignly, through showing "favor," raised Sarah Palin "for a time such as this" to save Christian America and to smite her enemies—whether demons or flesh and blood liberals. More to the point, what has Palin concluded about herself? Whatever it is, it's strong enough to move her to vacate the governorship during midsummer of 2009 to pursue a higher calling—a calling that is guaranteed to alter both politics and religion in the immediate future.

Rick Joyner himself reveals how Sarah's NAR troops hope to establish God's dominion over America:

Church leadership is about to be transferred from

the hands of professionals to the true warriors
which soldiers of the cross will all soon become.
. . . . Those who think the emerging generation is
soft will be shocked at the warrior nation that will
soon be revealed. God is a Warrior. He uses the
title "Lord of hosts" or "Lord of armies" ten times
more than all of His other titles. He is a martial
God. ... As this warrior generation emerges, it will
impact and bring transformation...so profound
that churches will start being thought of more as
military bases than congregations. . . . .There is "a
time for war, and a time of peace. . . . This is a
time for war. . . . True worship and warfare goes
together. How can one be a true worshiper of God
and not be provoked by the evil of our time and
stand for the truth by standing against the evil to
set its captives free? The warriors who are about
to arise will be provoked to action by every evil
stronghold that holds men in bondage, and they
will begin to bring them down with their divinely powerful weapons. . . . The world is about to
witness what true disciples are like—the true salt
and light of the world. When we are already dead
to this world, then there is nothing that the world
can do to us, and we will fear nothing on this
earth. Those who live without fear are the most
free and powerful people on earth. There is nothing that strikes more fear into the camp of the enemy than such a people walking the earth again.
They are already among us and will now begin
to emerge. It is a generation unlike any that has

walked the earth before. The Lord really has saved
His best for last. . . . Nations will soon bow their
knee to the irresistible power of the truth that is
about to be proclaimed by an irresistible army.
... The earth has never seen such an army as that
which will soon be released upon the earth. . . .
This army will strike fear into all who are not a
part of it. . . . The world has never seen anything
like this before.[291]

Or like Sarah Palin. She is a uniquely American phenomenon, which is why the media can't get enough of her and Christian conservatives adore her with the same intensity that others loathe her. She is part Ronald Reagan and part Joan of Arc,
part politician and preacher, part homemaker and part beauty
queen. She is a role model for millions of Evangelical women.
What almost no one (to my knowledge) has remarked on is
that Sarah Palin is the new standard bearer for the old Christian Right I helped to form and lead. As the old leaders died
off (Jerry Falwell, James Kennedy, R. J. Rushdoony) or were
discredited (Ted Haggard, Pat Robertson) or simply moved to
the sidelines (James Dobson), Sarah danced into the void. But
unlike the old Christian Right that led with moral issues like
abortion and gay rights, Sarah leads from a Tea Party influenced economic platform while dropping enough clues and
employing sufficient buzzwords (like "prayer warriors" and
"for a time such as this") to communicate to neo-fundamentalists that she is indeed one of them. Not just a run of the mill activist, Sarah Palin is the modern incarnation of Queen Esther—
waiting to claim the throne.

Part IV

Reconciliation

9

How to Replace Hubris with Humility

T O SAY THAT Americans are more divided, cynical, angry,
and poised for a fight than at any time since the Civil War
may be an understatement. For thirty years we have been em-
broiled in a culture war—two "nations" within a nation, both
committed to securing hegemony over the other, eerily reminiscent of tensions preceding Old Europe's "Thirty Years War,"
as well as our own Civil War. Our unrelenting toxic rhetoric,
incivility, lack of forgiveness, and refusal to recognize our opponents' decency or good intentions—or even their right to
exist—is threatening to irreparably divide America into a partisan wasteland.

Both sides' insistence on exploiting the fears and suscep-
tibilities of the unaligned middle has alienated the average
American from our political system, as anyone can see in our
normally low voter turnout. The result has been to increase an
already dangerous level of apathy toward vital issues affecting
our future. Voters trying to hear reasoned debate on issues of
national importance are instead subjected to fusillades of invective, character assassination, and pandemic levels of dissim-

ulation—artfully called "spinning." Many of us have turned
off and tuned out as a byproduct of the dogmatic rigidity and
ruthless tactics of both sides. Even appeals to "bipartisanship"
are now seen as nothing more than a ruse used by self-serving partisans to gain a momentary advantage over their opponents.

Unfortunately, this is a war I enrolled in as a child soldier.
As a neo-fundamentalist political strategist and propagandist
over four decades, it is a war I helped design, fund, and execute. *This is the America I helped create.*

And, like you, this is not the America I want to live in.

But I am an optimist. I see the stirrings of another possibility for all of us—a vision of a people once again living up to
the pluralism promised in our former national motto *e pluribus
unum*, out of many, one. This is an America where:

- Different worldviews are accepted and respected—
  where pluralism is a source of strength, not conflict.
- Culture warriors "agree to disagree" rather than seek
  to demonize and destroy each other.
- Politicians have been persuaded by an informed and active electorate to moderate their rhetoric and work together with true integrity on bipartisan solutions for
  the challenges of the twenty-first century.
- Americans serve as an example for the rest of the world
  in healing deep divisions through wisdom, dialogue,
  and goodwill.

The challenge that faces each one of us is *which America
will we choose?* Will it be a nation that provides hope for the
world? A hope that springs from realizing that the strength of
our commitment to pluralism is greater than the many issues
that divide us? A hope based on a nation united in its celebra-

tion of diversity?

Or, will we choose a nation ruled by apathy? Will we let our Thirty Years Culture War continue to escalate until it fully emulates the Thirty Years War fought on religious grounds that devastated Northern Europe so long ago?

If we choose the first America, the pressing question is what must we do differently? Clearly, we cannot continue thinking and acting the same way and expect to get different results. Change of course is difficult. Everybody says they are for change, but no one wants to work for it. The truth is, if we are to reconcile our broken nation we must be willing to make major changes.

Getting to the Root of the Problem

After analyzing so much of the social, political, and religious history behind the beliefs, worldviews, and mindsets of religious and secular neo-fundamentalists, hopefully you'll come to the conclusion I have, which is that the root problem beneath many of our conflicts is *not* the actual fundamentals of a particular belief.

In fact, not only are fundamentals not the problem, they may be part of the solution! If progressives and secularists would consistently practice their much-heralded celebration of pluralism, diversity, and tolerance when dealing with concerns of the millions of conservative Evangelicals as well as members of other faith traditions, they would all surely feel less threatened, and in turn be less reactive. Conversely, if neo-fundamentalists could *live* their faith (as opposed to merely *believing* it), if they actually *practiced* Jesus' prime directives of unconditional love and acceptance of everyone including one's opponents, dealing with their own sins and shortcomings before confronting everyone else about theirs, treating others as they'd like to be treated, and extending the benefit of the doubt ("Love believes the best." 1 Corinthians 13)—we just might be able to dial back the heated rhetoric of the culture wars enough to hear each other. *Then we could have a dialogue instead of a war.*

In my experience the biggest culprit is our *attachment* to the fundamentals we believe in—that is, we are more concerned about being "right" about our beliefs than about loving others. Too often our mindset tells us, "I know I'm right and I don't have the slightest doubt that I'm on the side of good—or God." In the case of many Christian neo-fundamentalists, their self-righteousness seems to flow from having the inerrant Word of God to stand on. More to the point is their often unacknowledged debt to René Descartes as well as ancient Greco-Roman philosophers we mentioned earlier, who taught that we are competent to objectively interpret universal truth. This is a critical point, so let's take a deeper look at the Cartesian paradox that, while invisible to us, runs our internal operating software.

Descartes—Father of Modern Certainty

As I mentioned in chapter 3, the seventeenth-century Catholic philosopher, lawyer, scientist, and mathematician René Descartes became frustrated by the inability of philosophers to employ a methodology that would allow them to discover objective truth. His quest was to find a way to establish not just confidence but *absolute certainty* about one's position on any given question. Descartes is widely recognized for being the first modern European philosopher to claim that by correctly utilizing our God-given gift of rational thinking, we could clearly perceive the truth. Thus, "error can be avoided and absolute certain knowledge can be achieved."[292]

What is not widely acknowledged, especially by the secular or scientific constituencies that base their epistemological models on Descartes, is that his entire premise—the objectivity of human perception—is based on the idea that God, the author of perception, guarantees it. He said, "It is impossible that God should ever deceive me... Its author [i.e. the author of clear perception] I say, is God...who cannot be a deceiver...hence the perception is undoubtedly true."[293]

Eventually, with the secularization of the modern mind, philosophers and people in general eliminated God from the equation but held on to the reassuring belief that their ability to objectively perceive reality or truth was untainted and stronger than ever. And it gets better. According to Descartes, not only do we recognize truth when we see it, but God has "molded" us so that we "are quite unable to doubt its truth."[294] In other words, "people cannot help but affirm their truth without doubting."[295] This, of course, is the recipe for absolute certainty: the prime culprit in our destructive commitment to being right and making everyone else wrong.

Ironically, secular fundamentalists are equally indebted to Descartes for their conviction that they too are perfectly able to objectively apprehend the right, true, or reasonable position on any issue. Since both sides are informed by Cartesian epistemology, each assumes the other has the ability to divine the universally "correct" answer to any problem. When one side fails to reach what the other "knows" is the correct answer— the opposing side all too often comes to one of three conclusions about their opponents who don't share the truth they see so clearly: They are willfully irrational, stupid, or downright evil for purposely refusing to acknowledge the truth.

This is one reason why I found it so easy to demonize those "damned secularists." After all, they could see the same truth we did, but they chose not to because they were "blinded by Satan." *That made them God's enemies—and mine.* And so it was open season on the forces of ungodliness, which of course meant anyone opposing the Christian Right agenda.

There is simply no way out of this circular labyrinth if all sides stay trapped in their "I'm right, therefore you must be wrong" paradigm. So, how do we extricate ourselves from it?

The first step involves investigating that "deep something" in our being that demands absolute certainty about how life works in order to insure our survival. Not too long ago, our ancestors' certainty about their world was essential to their survival. Mistaking a tar pit or quicksand for solid ground meant certain death. Miscalculating the speed or position of your prey meant going hungry, or starving to death, or maybe even being eaten yourself! Today our sense of certainty still provides us with the survival skills necessary to navigate our modern world. The certainty of cause and effect tells us not to play with fire, walk across a busy street without a crosswalk, or run a red light. Many of us also plan our lives on what appear to be certainties: If we study or work hard, we will get ahead; if we obey the law, we won't get in trouble; if we respect others, they will respect us. So we have learned that certainty, or at least a very high level of probability, is necessary to function well.

Why We Think We'll Die Without Our Worldview

Our world view is not simply the way we look at the world. It reaches inward to constitute our innermost be-

ing, and outward to constitute the world. It mirrors but also reinforces and even forges the structures, moorings, and possibilities of our interior life. It deeply configures our psychic and somatic experience, the patterns of our sensing, knowing and interacting with the world. No less potently, our worldview—our beliefs and theories, our maps, our metaphors, our myths, our interpretive assumptions—constellates our outer reality, shaping and working the world's malleable potentials in a thousand ways of subtly reciprocal interaction. Worldviews create worlds. —Richard Tarnas[296]

What we believe to be certain about our universe (purposeful or meaningless), about God (existent or not, sovereign or limited, nurturing or wrathful, forgiving or judgmental), about what constitutes good or evil, about humanity (fallen and sinful or evolving toward perfection), as well as a myriad other issues crucial to our understanding of the world and our place in it (who we are and why we exist), form our worldview. As we discovered in chapter 4, a worldview is essentially how we see or understand *our* world. Now let's explore more deeply the dynamic and the consequences of a worldview.

I find it's helpful to think of a worldview as a virtual "moral mapping system" similar to a global positioning unit that guides us as we navigate each day's challenges. Routes to various destinations are clearly indicated. The road marked Diligence, Hard Work, and Honesty guides us to Success Place, while Sloth, Arrogance, and Dishonesty take us to Dead End Circle

Along each highway are posted many warning signs like Be Honest, No Lying, No Cheating, and Treat Others with

Respect. If we carefully follow our map, we will safely reach our destination, which is whatever we believe our destiny, purpose, or legacy to be. If we deviate from the map, our life veers off course, ending up as a train wreck or a wasted life. Of course the key to our map's accuracy, which is necessary so we can rely on it with certainty, is the religious/philosophical presuppositions that we programmed into our mental GPS unit, which guides us according to the coordinates, or values, of our particular belief system. This map, or paradigm, in turn produces an individualized strategy for success, or at least for survival.

For myself, as well as for each one of us, this "winning strategy" is informed by the "pillars" of a worldview that is either religious or philosophical, as we explored in chapter 3. In other words, our worldview is an integration of the fundamental beliefs, truths, or axioms we take as a "given," or a presupposition, in order to provide us with a strategy for living the good life. Fulfilling our purpose or duty, how we raise a family, what kind of legacy we leave, being a force for good (or not)— all are dictated by our worldview.

But what happens when that worldview is challenged, our navigational system invalidated, our map torn up? Most of us are insecure with even a small amount of ambiguity in our lives. As my friend and fellow author Frank Schaeffer wryly comments:

> Embracing paradox—in other words, admitting the truth of our limits—is not good enough for many people, though, especially for pastors, religious leaders, and/or the New Atheists earning a living by selling certainty.[297]

Opposing beliefs, or even new ideas, can easily be interpreted as so threatening that our very survival is doubtful. After all, if the worldview we use *to filter* and evaluate the people, events, information, ideas, and decisions confronting us isn't 100 percent accurate, where does *that* leave us? What will become of us if we are deprived of the comfortable certainty afforded by our "life map"? That means we could also be wrong about other critical issues in our life, our values, even our most cherished religious beliefs! Indeed, if we're mistaken often enough, we may fear that our survival (at least spiritually or psychologically) may be threatened, or we may have to face up to choosing the wrong "fundamentals" to validate our life. Even the purpose of our existence, as we've defined it, may be called into question and our self-identity blurred or lost.

In my early twenties, when I was struggling with issues of faith, I turned to my mentor Billy James Hargis, who at that time was one of the nation's most prominent fundamentalist leaders. His sage advice to me was, "Don't ask too many questions—it might destroy your faith." I have heard this advice repeated by literally dozens of people who asked their pastors questions about faith, doctrine, and even church history. Several were admonished to "quit reading so much!" The bottom line of fear, even terror, is nicely summed up by popular megachurch pastor and author Adam Hamilton, "Some fear doubt. They fear that doubt might just be the tip of the iceberg and that if they allow themselves to doubt, they might very well fall away from God."[298] So there it is, the sum of all fears, the terror of terrors: losing one's connection to God, risking eternal damnation—all because you entertained a doubt about the truth you know to be true. Surely, this is why even Sarah Palin, when a friend handed her a book on philosophy, reportedly replied, "I never read anything that might conflict with my beliefs."[299]

So it should not surprise us that when our survival is linked to our worldview, or when our ego has completely identified itself with our beliefs, we are compelled to defend our self-preservation by either dismissing or prevailing over differing, even opposing, views that might introduce a sliver of doubt about our beliefs. Philosopher Robert Solomon observes that "we restructure our world in accordance with our needs and demands; sometimes our needs are such that they require a falsification of the world, a denial of certain intolerable facts."[300] In other words, as W. H. Auden said, *"We would rather die than let our illusions die."* Our very essence as human beings is focused on "being right"—a commitment we carry with a vengeance.

The consequences are clear. If we must be right, the "other" must be wrong. But that's not the end of the story. Because we often fear what we don't understand and despise what (or who) we fear, the possibility of an opposing view's validity threatens our own. According to neuroscientists like Drew Weston of Emory University, our brain circuitry is wired to insure our survival and it allows fear to bypass our logical processes.[301] It worked for the caveman confronted by a saber-toothed tiger, and it still works for a modern urban dweller faced with a rapist or mugger. We do not have the luxury of coolly and logically thinking all the options through in such circumstances. We need to get out of harm's way now! Consequently, as neurobiologist Michael Fanselow of UCLA observes, fear is "far, far more powerful than reason."[302] No wonder philosopher Edmond Burke claimed, "no passion so effectively robs the mind of all its power of acting and reasoning as fear."[303] In today's world, where fear runs roughshod over our rational checks and balances, the body's fight-or-flight response favors fighting over flight. After all, where would we flee to?

For the Love of Demonizing

Many Islamic radicals and inhabitants of "third world" countries use violence to express their fight response. In the West we are "too sophisticated" for such "uncivilized" actions. We prefer character assassination—the politics of personal destruction—over crude physical violence. Our weapons of choice are demeaning or demonizing—easy ways to dismiss any potentially upsetting challenges to one's certitudes. What do they know anyway? They're a bunch of "overeducated eggheads" or "undereducated crazies," "bleeding heart liberals" or "heartless conservatives." Or we write them off as hopeless: "they're all going to hell anyway" or "they're too stupid to ever get it." Condemning uncomfortable views and those who hold them to intellectual or spiritual oblivion is much more convenient than actually having to examine and test new concepts that could call into question our long-held presuppositions (secular or religious) and possibly have to (heaven forbid) deconstruct our worldview—something quite unthinkable for too many of us.

Demonization goes a step further than simple demeaning, with the implicit attribution of evil (or at least bad intentions) to our opponents. Those who challenge the security of our cozy worldview cocoon and threaten to upset our peace and comfort by advocating a different understanding of God, man, religion, politics, morality or who offer opposing solutions to vexing human problems are worse than ignorant or stupid. They are evil. Thus, the Pope can't just represent a different view of orthodoxy; he has to be the Antichrist, or at least a religious bigot! Eastern religious aren't simply exotic, they are demonic! George W. Bush isn't just incurious, mistaken, ignorant, or ill informed; he's a money-grubbing murderer! Barack Obama isn't just a liberal; he's a non-American Muslim Socialist!

Tragically, demonization seems second nature to all too many of us. How natural it feels for us "in the name of love" or "in the name of 'justice, freedom, and truth'" to demonize others. For the sake of the planet, we hate polluters or big corporations. For the sake of babies, we hate, or even kill, doctors who perform abortions. For the sake of women, we despise pro-lifers. For the sake of humanity, we put down fellow humans. For the sake of peace, we hate the "war mongers." Without a second thought we deny the "benefit of the doubt" and ascribe unquestioned evil (or at least bad intentions) to culture war symbols like Bill and Hillary Clinton, the George Bushs, Dick Cheney, Rush Limbaugh, Al Gore, Ann Coulter, Barack Obama, and even Sarah Palin. In a drastic reversal of American justice, they stand guilty until found innocent.

In my neo-fundamentalist case, liberals and secularists who denied the literal truth of God's Word (the Bible) and the lordship of Jesus Christ marked themselves as "the lost." They rejected God for the satanic "wisdom of this world." They were predestined for destruction and everlasting torment in the bowels of hell. In their rebellion against God, these "vessels of God's wrath" served their master Satan in murdering innocent babies, promoting (or tolerating) evil and degenerate lifestyles of porn addiction and homosexuality, and undermining families through their progressive agenda (pluralism, evolution, sex education). In my view and of many of my colleagues, demonizing the opposition was simply calling a spade a spade and honestly reporting who they were—agents of evil. God hated them because He hates evil. We could do no less.

The Necessity of Self-Awareness

As we have just seen, our reactions are all too often more visceral than logical. Recent psychological studies have shown that when logic and emotion collide, we go with our gut three times out of four! When our gut reaction is triggered to defend *our cherished values*, it seems all too easy for us mortals to abandon our *fundamental* values—like unconditional love and forgiveness and tolerance—to do it. What each one of us must ask ourselves is whether we are willing to exercise the discipline necessary to keep our commitment to the fundamentals of our beliefs in the face of our ego's survival instinct to do just the opposite. To accomplish this almost superhuman (Christlike?) feat we will need help and lots of it. In fact, we will need a whole new way of relating to new ideas and people.

We need a paradigm shift—from hubris to humility, absolute certainty to confident faith. Only then will love, compassion, and mutual tolerance have a chance to blossom.

Perhaps it would be more helpful to call the culture wars the "hubris wars." When we think of the unmitigated arrogance of secular fundamentalists claiming that they *know* there is no God and *all* faith is poisonous, or of the pontificating self-righteousness of your standard issue TV preacher, it isn't hard to see why the seeds of tolerance haven't taken root in such barren ground. Surely we can do better than this. In fact, we have no choice if we are to bridge our current chasm of fear, suspicion and demonization. *The antidote to hubris is humility,* and lots of it, as secular thinker Andrew Sullivan concisely summarizes,

The alternative to the secular-fundamentalist
death spiral is something called spiritual humility. . . . From a humble faith comes toleration of
other faiths. And from that toleration comes the
oxygen that liberal democracy desperately needs
to survive.[304]

Rabbi Michael Lerner warns his fellow liberal activists to
replace their "angry rhetoric" with "more humility and compassion for those with whom we disagree."[305]

Happily a new generation of postmodern Christian thinkers like Randall Balmer, Rob Bell, Ron Martoia, Theo Geyser, Adam Hamilton, Joel Hunter, Tony Jones, Tim Keel, Brian
McLaren, Claude Nikondeha, Doug Pagitt, and Leonard Sweet
are relentless in their calling Christians back to the love, compassion, and humility that Jesus modeled.

One way for us to experience a shift in our "humility paradigm" is to tune up our self-awareness. Have you ever noticed how some people seem to lack self-awareness, specifically, awareness as to how they impact others when they act
judgmental, arrogant, or self-righteous? One reason for low
self-awareness is a severely limited perspective. A healthy perspective reaches beyond our self-absorption and pays close attention to the feedback received from others. A mature perspective enables us to see in ourselves, if for only a moment,
the incongruence between our words and actions that others
may experience. As Aristotle first observed, a mark of intelligence is the ability to see things from another's perspective.
For instance, neo-fundamentalists like me saw themselves as
godly, compassionate, righteous, moral, even loving. But by
our actions we were often perceived as unloving, uncompas-

sionate, judgmental haters. Likewise, secular fundamentalists who see themselves as caring, thoughtful, enlightened, and tolerant need to get in touch with the reality that they too are often experienced as intolerant, close-minded, elitist ideologues.

Because we are experts at fooling ourselves, most of us at best have only moderate levels of self-awareness. We are largely unaware of how others perceive us: obnoxious or entreating, closed or open, arrogant or humble, giving or taking, wise or foolish, selfless or selfish, phony or authentic, congruent or incongruent, and so on. If we are to truly know ourselves, and if we want to successfully influence others—including friends and family—we must risk deflating our ego and begin to effectively calibrate how others (who we are not fooling) actually experience us. If you're still not sure, just ask your ex!

Perspective allows us to see the disparity involved in a 400-pound TV evangelist (the sin of gluttony) condemning homosexuals, or Christian groups supposedly representing the love of Christ proclaiming with placards that all "faggots" are hell-bound. Perspective enables us to perceive the disjuncture between advocating pluralism and Christian bashing, between celebrating tolerance while acting intolerant.

I have come to the conclusion that this age-old incongruent aspect of our humanity is no doubt why Jesus taught us to *remove the log from our own eye* before removing the splinter from someone else's. I think it is also why he taught us not to throw the first stone unless we ourselves are blameless. Armed with self-awareness and perspective, we can at last ask ourselves the question Jesus confronted us with: Who are we, with all our shortcomings, mixed motives, and deceitful hearts (hearts that lack perspective) to judge others? As one of the world's most profound observers of human nature, Alexander Solzhenitsyn, wrote in his famous *Gulag Archipelago*:

> The line separating good and evil passes not
> through states, not between classes, nor between
> political parties either—but right through every
> human heart—and then all human hearts. This
> line shifts. Inside us, it oscillates with the years
> and even within hearts overwhelmed by evil, one
> small bridgehead of good is retained. And even in
> the best of all hearts, there remains . . . an un-up-
> rooted small corner of evil.[306]

Working on our own incongruence, or the distance between our stated values and our measurable actions, before we
"set others straight" is a prerequisite if we are to dialogue with
each other in humility rather than hubris.

The Uncertainty of Certainty

Another important step in developing a more robust humility is coming to terms with our stark inability to achieve 100
percent, guaranteed, fool-proof, unquestionable certainty. Of
course we can have great confidence in the high probability of
things—that our spouse won't leave us, that our children will
love us, that friends won't betray us, that our job will be there
tomorrow, that our car will start in the morning. But we can't
be 100 percent certain. Neither can we be certain, in the sense
of empirical proof, of God's existence. Especially in the particular modes of being we project onto God—such as loving father, wrathful king, uninvolved creator, sovereign or limited.
That's of course where faith comes in. And of course I must
add that neither can we be scientifically certain of Darwinism

or other forms of faith that many secularists hold dear.

Christians had for 1500 years after Christ dutifully exercised something they called faith—and their faith enabled them to believe. Then along came the Enlightenment which birthed what we call the modern mind. Moderns didn't need faith to believe. They required cold, hard, scientifically-derived "proof," which they were confident they could objectively interpret to apprehend "truth" with a final certainty. Facts replaced faith. Then came postmodernism in the late twentieth century, which most fundamentalists—secular or religious—haven't quite caught up to, with its critical dictum that the old modern view of certainty was simplistic and naïve at best. Rather than being objective, infallible, and Spock-like, we are limited by our cultural mindset, unacknowledged bias, upbringing, presuppositions, and even our point in time. In other words, we can't escape the perception distortion that is part of our humanness. Social science is rife with recent studies that tell us that our political, even our religious disposition is influenced by a myriad of cultural and ontological factors beyond our control or even our awareness. For example, those of us more oriented toward individualism and respect for hierarchy tend to be solid Republicans, those preferring egalitarian and communitarian values are more likely to be "yellow dog" Democrats.

Richard Tarnas, in his highly acclaimed history of philosophy, *Passion of the Western Mind,* which tracks the evolution of epistemology (how we know what we know) from the beginning of modernism to our present postmodern era, asserts that our culture has already made the metaphysical turn from certainty to uncertainty:

From Hume and Kant through Darwin, Marx,

Freud and beyond, an unsettling conclusion was becoming inescapable: human thought was determined, structured, and very probably distorted by a multitude of overlapping factors—innate but not absolute mental categories, habit, history, culture, social class, biology, language, imagination, emotion, the personal unconscious, the collective unconscious. In the end, the human mind could not be relied upon as an accurate judge of reality. The original Cartesian certainty, that which served as foundation for the modern confidence in human reason, was no longer defensible. ... Despite the incongruence of aims and predispositions among the various schools the 20th-century philosophy, there was general agreement on one point: the impossibility of apprehending an objective cosmic order with the human intelligence.[307]

Specifically addressing Christians' tenuous ability to consistently and reliably discern ultimate truth, what the apostle Paul referred to it as trying to see through "a glass darkly," theologian Merold Westphal writes:

Because we cannot transcend the limited perspective of our location in time and in cultural history, knowledge can never be Truth. But cultural practices are not just finite and contingent; they are also fallen and corrupt, a point the postmodernists are not slow to point out (even if they don't speak the language of sin and the fall). . . . The truth is that there is Truth, but in our finitude and fallenness we do not have access to it.[308]

Conservative Bible scholar N. T. Wright adds, "We have had our noses rubbed in the fact that reality is not all it was cracked up to be; what we thought was hard fact turns out to be somebody's propaganda."[309]

Simply put, we need to recognize that literally everything we see or hear, including any possible revelation of truth, is filtered through our very own, one of a kind, personally created worldview lens. Whether we call it a worldview, paradigm, hermeneutic, or just plain old mindset, we all filter reality, and we each do it in our own unique way.

Not only do we filter what we look *at*, we filter what we look *for*. We are all familiar with this phenomenon. I was the happy driver of a jet black Mazda RX-8 sports car. While I never noticed them before purchasing one, now I could pick them out a mile away *without trying*. It seemed my brain filtered for RX-8's. When I was younger, it filtered for other things—like attractive women within my age range. Filtering is also at work when we assess those involved in public policy debates. For instance, if my lens for viewing Democratic candidates or spokesmen for progressive causes is that they avoid the question, "spin" like crazy, dissimulate, and are generally disingenuous, what do you think I will be listening for? Bingo. And I assure you that most of the time my expectations will be met, my suspicions confirmed once again, my intense dislike heartily reinforced. Conversely, if my filter for conservatives is more positive, I will for the most part not notice when they indulge in much the same dance as their liberal counterparts. If I do notice, I will give them a "pass" because they represent the good guys, and after all, they deserve to win. The fate of the nation depends on us!

To drive the point home, my friend Monte Wilson, who lectures around the world on human behavior, relates this story:

> I recently read a study about how, during the 2004 elections (Kerry v Bush), some researchers at Emory University used functional magnetic resonance imaging brain scans (fMRI) on 30 voters: 15 committed Democrats, 15 committed Republicans. While viewing multiple instances where their candidate of choice had clearly contradicted himself, the researchers monitored the 30 brains.

> And what did the men and women at Emory discover?

> While the viewers watched and listened to the self-contradictory statements of their candidate, that part of the brain where we reason was inactive! And what part of the brain was active? The emotional circuits were all firing away.

> People pretty much hear what they want to hear. If I like you, I will place what you do and say in a particular frame. You weren't contradicting yourself; you were adding a nuance to a previous statement. You weren't staking out an entirely different position than previously taken; you were merely reframing the same position you had always held to for a different segment of the voters.

Psychologists call this confirmation bias.

The powerful polarizing effect of confirmation bias was recently documented by Farhad Manjoo in his book *True Enough: Learning to Live in a Post-Fact Society*. According to columnist Nicholas Kristof, Manjoo cites a more recent study by Stanford University psychologists of students who either favored or opposed capital punishment. The students were shown the same two studies: one suggested that executions have a deterrent effect that reduces subsequent murders, and the other doubted that.

Whatever their stance, the students found the study that supported their position to be well-conducted and persuasive and the other one to be profoundly flawed. "That led to a funny result," Mr. Manjoo writes. "People in the study became polarized."

A fair reading of the two studies might have led the students to question whether any strong conclusions could be drawn about deterrence, and thus to tone down their views on the death penalty. But the opposite happened. Students on each side accepted the evidence that conformed to their original views while rejecting the contrary evidence—and so afterward students on both sides were more passionate and confident than ever of their views.[310]

Manjoo poses the question, "What happens when people are presented with information that contradicts their core beliefs?"[311] His answer, based on a host of studies: People "tuned out information that conflicted with their beliefs. . . . Both sides were choosing what comforted them."[312]

Confirmation bias, the tendency to unconsciously filter out information that doesn't fit into our preconceived notions, provides us with one more reason to question our objectivity.

Disillusioning Ourselves

To give up the comfortable illusion that our sense of certainty provides (in other words, to *dis-illusion* ourselves) is not a complex task, but it does take a certain amount of inner security and courage. For me, it happened over several years as I was deeply engrossed in writing *The Late Great Evangelical Church,* a "reformed" (i.e., Calvinist) critique of the evolution of certain aspects of Evangelical theology. About five years into my project I started asking myself how it was that my particular faith tradition could objectively interpret "God's Word" and everyone else was so obviously subjective (since they disagreed with my point of view). Slowly it dawned on me that perhaps "we" did not have a corner on the truth! My friend Brian McLaren explains this crucial postmodern epiphany:

> Most modern people love to relativize the viewpoints of the others against the unquestioned superiority of their own modern viewpoint. But in a way, you cross the threshold into postmodernity the moment you turn your critical scrutiny from others to yourself, when you relativize your own modern viewpoint. When you do this, everything changes. It is like a conversion. You can't go back. You begin to see that what seemed like pure, objective certainty really depends heavily on a subjective preference for your personal viewpoint.[313]

But the challenge is larger than just a preference for our personal viewpoint that holds us in a type of mental captivity. It's our whole cultural thought pattern that conditions us to see, hear, and interpret in its own peculiar way. Like a fish unaware that it spends its whole life in water, we don't realize that we spend our life in a sea of presuppositions we have never examined.

Spending my entire life in a culture that embraced Cartesian rationality leading to absolute certainty, I had never before thought to question my own objectivity. But as both McLaren and N. T. Wright suggest, once I scrutinized my own beliefs with the same rigor I applied to others, there was no return. As Wright says, "There is no way back to the easy certainties of modernism, whether Catholic or Protestant, fundamentalist or liberal."[314] And he adds, "The only way is forward."[315]

10

What Would Jesus (or Richard Nixon) Do?

MILLIONS OF NEO-FUNDAMENTALISTS were fond of sporting "WWJD" (What Would Jesus Do?) bracelets a few years ago. Why have they gone out of style? Isn't this the perfect time to bring them back?

For Christians, this is really the point at which we need to stop talking and start doing. We need to quit criticizing and condemning and renew our love for Jesus and God's creation. When asked what was the most important of all God's commandments, Jesus unhesitatingly offered, "Love the Lord your God . . . and love your neighbor as yourself" (Matthew 22:37-39, NIV). His short statement summarized the entire Jewish Scripture (the Old Testament) from which he taught. The question that has plagued his followers, beginning with the scholars who heard this answer down to us today, is, "How are we to follow Jesus' prime directive to love our neighbor?" According to Jesus, by not throwing the first stone (withholding judgment), by treating others as we would be treated (the Golden Rule), by forgiving our enemies, and of course, by extending mercy as Jesus did when he forgave the woman caught in an apparent act of adultery (punishable by stoning) and when he told his famous parable of the Good Samaritan. *Jesus was an inclusivist.* He didn't exclude "sinners" or "non-believers" from his inner circle. On the contrary, he was notorious for hanging out with corrupt and unpopular tax collectors, prostitutes, and thieves. In fact, the only people Jesus seemed to exclude were the religious leaders of his day!

One of the themes running through Jesus' teaching is to extend to others the benefit of the doubt, something I sometimes still have to force myself to do. But I am helped by realizing I cannot truly understand the motives (hearts) of others because I am not God. If we can learn to extend to our fellow humans the benefit of the doubt, if we can refrain from confusing disagreement with enmity and acrimoniousness with debate, we may find ourselves practicing patience, kindness, and tolerance by default. This is the only way we can truly claim to "love," which a commentary of the Bible defines as an "outgoing, selfless attitude that leads one to sacrifice for the good of others."[316]

Can We Trust Jesus?

Let me repeat the question—Can we trust Jesus? Which is stronger, our faith in Jesus or our faith in our own judgment? Will we choose to follow the all-encompassing, incomprehensible, counterintuitive, countercultural love of Christ, or give free reign to our fears, revulsions, and insecurities? Or as Brian McLaren observes, will we continue to develop "systems that [teach] us how to avoid many of Jesus' teachings and reinterpret those we couldn't avoid."[317] Ironically, it is through these "made in America" theological systems that many of us remade Jesus in our own image. Handsome, white, right-wing, and comfortable—and so very nonthreatening to the status quo.

As McLaren pointedly remarks, "the Jesus who is preached, pasted on bumper stickers, serenaded in gooey love songs on religious radio and TV, and prayed to is an imposter."[318]

Why not make Jesus' number-one command of love the test of who's truly a "Born-Again Christian?" To paraphrase the Book of James, "Let us be judged by our actions, not just our words," that is, by how we live and love, not by what beliefs we give mental assent or lip service to. As I wrote earlier, when I left my neo-fundamentalist Washington power trip long enough to devote an uninterrupted week to pray and recenter myself on Jesus' priorities, his message hit me hard. So hard, in fact, I was driven to write a plea to my Christian Right colleagues published in 1989 as *The Samaritan Strategy: A New Agenda for Christian Activism.* Within its 200 pages I argued:

> An active, expressive love for all people is one of the main commandments to us as Christians. "This is the message you heard from the beginning: 'we should love one another'" (1 John 3:11).

The Secular Challenge

The challenge for secular fundamentalists is no less daunting. What can liberals and secularists do to build bridges in order to avert an escalation of hostility? We could start by following the sage counsel of world religions expert Karen Armstrong.

> If fundamentalists must evolve a more compassionate assessment of their enemies in order to be true to their religious traditions, secularists must also be more faithful to the benevolence, toler-

ance, and respect for humanity which characterizes modern culture at its best, and address themselves more empathetically to the fears, anxieties,
and needs which so many of their fundamentalist neighbors experience but which no society can
safely ignore.[319]

Following Armstrong's counsel will entail a change of both
heart and strategy on the part of many, if not most, secular or
liberal culture warriors. Liberal pundit E. J. Dionne Jr. speculated that if the great twentieth-century liberal thinker Rein-
hold Niebuhr were alive today, he might counsel his fellow liberals to "abandon their prejudices about people of faith, even
those who vote the wrong way."[320] Fortunately, progressive
thinkers like Rabbi Michael Lerner have already taken the first
step in extending the benefit of the doubt: "What I will not do
. . . is attribute evil motives to those on the Religious Right."[321]
He also urges fellow progressives to "reject the tendency to regard people who are not part of the liberal culture as stupid,
demented, or evil. Instead [we] must affirm the fundamental
decency of people."[322]

The big question, of course, is whether the myriad ideological and theological militias in the culture war are willing to establish a détente, providing a time-out to deescalate hostilities
long enough to find common ground.

Détente

Those of us old enough to have lived through the 1970s remember the Cold War. Communist China, now our major
trading partner, was then our implacable enemy. Killing tens
of thousands of GIs and consigning others to a life of horror in

secret slave labor camps in North Korea, supporting their fellow communist revolutionaries in the war against capitalism
and imperialism in Viet Nam, Laos, and Cambodia, threatening to invade "Free China" (Taiwan), the Chinese were widely perceived as a major threat to American interests as well as
to world peace. Chairman Mao, the Chinese Supreme Leader
was not a nice person. After murdering an estimated 50 million of his own citizens, he turned his fanatical (fundamentalist!) "Red Guard Youth Brigades" loose on his own leaders. To
eliminate any potential opposition, mayors, governors, generals, even communist party leaders were humiliated, sent to
concentration camps, or simply "liquidated."

We were next on Mao's hit list—at least conservative Republicans and anticommunist Democrats thought so. Enter Richard Milhouse Nixon. Surely Nixon is an unlikely role
model, which is precisely why I've selected him. Nixon is one
of those uncommon politicians roundly demonized by *both*
sides, a point worth pondering for Boomers who still suffer
from Nixon-phobia. Nixon was certainly a flawed character
(and who isn't?), but like so many people we demonize, he still
made some positive contributions. In 1969, enveloped by the
heat and paranoia of the Cold War, Nixon decided to journey
to the stronghold of our sworn enemy to find common ground
and a chance for peace. How was it that in a highly charged political environment, a lifelong "communist fighter" could get
away with pursuing a nonadversarial strategy with the communist enemy—a strategy that fortuitously led to the strong
symbiotic relationship that unites the common interests of
China and the U.S. today? Nixon built his political reputation
(congressman, senator, vice president, and finally president)
as a vehement anticommunist, earning the undying hatred of

the left. With that record, the average American trusted that Nixon would not "roll over" for the communist Chinese leadership and "give away the store," as some accused Roosevelt of doing at Yalta, where the Soviets were awarded hegemony over Eastern Europe after World War II.

So after a quarter century of an American diplomatic and economic quarantine on the Chinese, Nixon went to China. He was immediately assaulted by the hard Right for even talking to the enemy. In fact, I still remember the reaction of my friend Congressman John Schmitz of Orange County, California, a member of the John Birch Society and the sponsor of my college Young Republican Club. At a dinner with several dozen local GOP leaders, including myself, he quipped that he wasn't concerned that Nixon went to China. He was only worried that he might return!

But despite the hysteria of the political extremes, Nixon was determined to pursue a new paradigm to change the rules of the game between these two world powers. Think for a moment of the obstacles faced by both sides. To start with, they literally spoke different languages. Despite skilled interpreters, many of the nuances of diplomacy can get "lost in translation." An even more formidable challenge was their use of different metaphors and symbols. Mao, as a dedicated, even fanatical, Marxist Leninist, and Nixon, a dedicated lifelong capitalist, held worldviews that were totally opposed at every point—spiritually, politically, sociologically, and economically. Consequently, they literally demonized each other as the epitome of evil. Mao even pondered if any good could come from a parlance between "the capitalist Devil and the Marxist Devil."

And yet somehow, both sides learned to listen and understand the other. Both sides were committed to move forward

until they could find common ground. What do you think the
two sides had to do to come to this historic agreement? Since
I wasn't invited to this particular party, I'll just have to speculate:

First of all, they had to *suspend their judgments about each other.* They would not have gotten far if Nixon saw only a blood-
thirsty dictatorship and Mao—who Henry Kissinger, Nixon's
foreign affairs guru, described as "being in some anguish over
dealing with the enemy"[323]—saw only a heartless representative of the exploitative bourgeois class.

Second, they had to *listen to each other very carefully.* The
usual name calling, sloganeering, and inflammatory rhetoric
would have been counterproductive. They had to learn to actually empathize with each other's concerns, fears, and aspirations. In this case both nations shared a deep fear of the expan-
sionist designs of the Russians—a fear on which Nixon adroitly
capitalized.

Third, to get beyond their history of mutual demonization and polarization, they had to *reframe their conflict.* After re-
spectfully listening and empathizing, they needed to set aside
their built-in bias and see each other with "new eyes." Nixon
did exactly this by forthrightly recognizing the two nations'
past enmity and their current significant differences. He then
pointed out that events and interests had dramatically changed
for both parties in the last quarter of a century and it was now
time "to break out of the old pattern."[324]

Fourth, they had to *extend to each other the benefit of the doubt*
rather than questioning or vilifying the other's intentions.

After they worked their way through these first four stages,
they were able to build enough trust and find enough common
interest to move to the fifth and final stage: *they had to compro-*

mise. Neither side got 100 percent of what they wanted. Here is perhaps the biggest obstacle. For many culture warriors, the very term "compromise" denotes everything wrong with the political system, with America, and the world. Compromising on "principles" is seen as "selling out" at best, or a betrayal bordering on treason at worst. While compromising on issues that do not affect one's principles is acceptable, negotiation on matters involving foundational principle is *verboten.* Why? Because fundamentalists, whether religious or secular, regard their fundamental principles as inviolable. They have absolute certainty that their fundamental principles are either self-evident to any rational person or, conversely, are clearly stated in God's revelation to man (the Bible, Pentateuch, Koran). How then do we dare compromise "the truth" or "God's Word?"

As an example, the Christian Right's aversion to compromise on abortion was so severe; they refused to do so even to avoid a greater evil. As Dr. Everett Koop, Ronald Reagan's conservative Evangelical pro-life Surgeon General commented:

> If the pro-life people in the late 1960's and the early 1970's had been willing to compromise with the pro-choice people, we could have had an abortion law that provided for abortion only for life of the mother, incest, rape, and defective child; that would have cut the abortions down to *three percent* of what they are today. But they had an all-or-nothing mentality. They wanted it all, and they got nothing."[325]

The pro-lifers' principles remained intact—and millions of babies continued to be aborted.

The most powerful motivator for compromise in fact may be to avoid "mutually assured destruction" if the conflict is allowed to escalate or somehow get out of control. Perhaps the newly discovered common ground between Nixon and his arch enemies was a fear of mutually assured destruction. The "MAD" theory in vogue at the time postulated that nuclear war could be best avoided by the specter of the absolute and complete destruction of each side in a nuclear exchange. Perhaps they both saw a chance to keep a more immediate enemy—the Soviet Union—off balance. Or maybe the Chinese were simply charmed by Nixon's warmth, integrity, and charisma! While this last possibility is highly dubious, what isn't questionable is that these implacable foes found a way to call a time-out in the cold war—a "détente" of sorts.

What our world would look like today if these long time antagonists had not found common ground? Would the backyard concrete bomb shelter building frenzy of the 1950s and '60s have continued until the fateful day we actually had to use them?

Don't breathe a sigh of relief too soon. *Peace is not yet at hand.* The Cold War has morphed into the culture war and the new millennium finds many of us taking shelter down in our mental bunkers—isolated, paranoid, and tossing verbal grenades at any "enemy" who strays within range.

11

Finding Common Ground

I F WE ARE to do what President Richard Nixon did and, in spite of ourselves, climb to higher moral ground to initiate a dialogue of hope, healing, and reconciliation, we must first find some common ground from which to begin that journey. It *is* possible, against all odds. After all, if Bob Beckel, a top Democratic political strategist, and Cal Thomas, a former leader of Jerry Falwell's Moral Majority, can find common ground in their frequent *USA Today* column, *where they dialogue together in a civil manner,* there is hope for the rest of us! But we do need to be realistic about the challenges confronting us by acknowledging them and then contemplating how best to get beyond them.

Here is my short list of obstacles we will need to overcome:

Addiction to wedge-issue politics. To regain their cherished position as arbiters of culture, the religious and secular neo-fundamentalists know that they must pull enough of the middle to their side to prevail. Yet, many on the extremes of the culture wars have given up hope of winning over enough of the great "unthinking mass" of people to their side. They

are satisfied with peeling off enough votes on various "wedge"
issues to give their side a temporary advantage, which hopefully can be parlayed into something more long-term, such
as the appointment of Supreme Court Justices. Both sides are
committed to manipulating people or manufacturing "facts"
in order to do an end run around the opposition.

Demonizing the opposition. Both sides distrust, resent,
anathemize, and demonize the other. Many are sincerely convinced that those on the other side are basically Nazis, as liberal author Gore Vidal once publicly labeled William F. Buckley,
the nation's leading conservative intellectual. During a nationally televised debate on abortion in my heyday as a political hit
man, I couldn't resist inferring that Rev. Charles Bergstrom,
the political spokesman for the Lutheran Church, was taking a
neo-Nazi stance. Neo-fundamentalists and conservatives easily
let "politically correct Nazis, eco-Nazis, and femi-Nazis," roll
off their tongues while their progressive opponents were not
hesitant to return the favor, calling the conservatives Ayatollahs, theocrats, and even terrorists.

Proselytization paranoia. Both sides rightly accuse the
other of attempting to foist their personal philosophical or religious beliefs on the other. They each also seem to be committed to straight-jacketing the rest of us with their ideas of
"the moral life." The politically correct thought police want to
outlaw smoking, drinking, fatty foods, free speech (at least for
military recruiters, religious fundamentalists, and right-wing
talk show hosts), homophobia, ethnic jokes, polluters, atom-
ic energy, tree cutters, anti-abortion protesters, and fun. The
theologically correct ayatollahs want to outlaw drugs, pornography, homosexuality, tree huggers, off-color jokes, eco-Nazis,
flag burners, abortions, and fun. No wonder each side appears

edgy and defensive. No wonder the rest of us in the middle are worn and weary.

Intimidation via threats of government intervention. Both secularist and religious communities react with moral indignation, if not outrage, when the other side attempts to use the coercive power of government to enforce a position they perceive as an assault on their values. For example, regarding their children's education, neo-fundamentalists demand prayer in school, the Ten Commandments posted on the wall, intelligent design taught as an alternative view to evolution, and abstinence taught in place of sex education. Secularists or progressives want all religions taught as equally valid (or nonvalid), evolution to monopolize the field, and sex education to include approval of "alternative" sexual preferences. The most intense point of the conflict, where overheated partisans rush to battle, is reached when *both* sides insist that the government should be employed to force everyone's children to accept their values, whether "politically correct" or "theologically correct."

Clinging to the emotional security blanket of certainty. As we discussed in chapter 9, both sides cling to unquestioned certainty that they have cornered the market on truth and are 100 percent on the "right side" of any question. It's like a security blanket. Trying to snatch away (or shred) that blanket is likely to send them into paroxysms of hysteria and retribution that would embarrass even Linus from the *Peanuts* comic strip.

Perpetuation of conflict by special-interest groups and media. At a (hopefully) subconscious level, the powerful special interests represented by the various militias of the culture wars—pro life, pro choice, gay rights, anti gay rights, the secular left, the religious right—simply *don't want peace. They can't afford it.* Their entire existence is dependent on fundraising from their "base," which is usually highly radicalized. The base does not want its donations, often given with some degree of sacrifice, used to find common ground or promote détente. They see themselves as combatants in a war and they expect total victory, sooner rather than later! The financial support of "public interest" lobbies that don't deliver withers away. If an advocacy group is not on the attack or being attacked, its donors may perceive it as ineffective, and its leaders may be accused of going soft—or worse, compromising with the enemy.

To illustrate, when several of the Christian Right organizations I led experienced a downturn in fundraising, I would simultaneously ratchet up our attacks while baiting the enemy to attack back—a tactic that was usually successful. Sometimes it was too successful, as when the Metropolitan Community of Churches threatened to sue me for demonizing them as "The Church of Sodomy."

Just as conflict translates into a bigger war chest to fund the embattled armies, it also means better ratings for the ubiquitous talking heads of TV land. Whether entering the "no spin zone" of Fox's "fair and balanced" network, debating with the pundits of CNN: "the network you can trust," or playing "Hardball" with Chris Matthews on MSNBC, conflict stimulates while thoughtful discussion bores. The fact that the very format of these programs is designed to be fast-moving and exciting makes rational, comprehensive dialogue all but impossible. Those are relegated to C-Span and the snooze zone. Visceral conflict and name calling is the currency of the media realm, not reasoned discourse.

Examples of Burying the Hatchet

Reviewing these six obstacles to finding common ground admittedly is sobering. They can seem, both on the surface and especially when viewed collectively, to be insurmountable. But surmount them we must. We must do it for ourselves, our families, and our nation.

The secret to finding our common ground is deceptively simple. We have to start looking for what we share in common *before* we focus on what separates us.

If our starting point is what divides us, we will be blind to what unites us.

Let's take a very sensitive issue—how we raise our children—and see how this might work. Surely one of the most divisive and inflammatory issues in the culture wars is the right of parents to raise their children the best way they see fit, including choice of discipline techniques, religious training, and educational content and techniques. Specific points of contention include teaching intelligent design vs. evolution, religious pluralism, sex education, and the appropriateness and/or acceptance of various sexual life styles.

Quite naturally some of these perspectives may seem bizarre, even harmful, to parents on the opposing side, which is why we must empathize with the fears, anxieties, and beliefs that lead to specific positions if we are serious about finding common ground. And if we are willing do the work necessary to understand our opponents' presuppositions, their positions may even appear logical, *given their particular paradigm*. Liberal scholar Stephen Carter provides us with an excellent example of discerning the motivations and legitimate fears of many religious parents:

It is not that they want the public schools to pros-
elytize in their favor; it is rather that they do not
want the schools to do what Dewey implied, that
they must press their own children to reject what
the parents believe by calling into question a central article of their faith. The parents are fighting
to preserve their sense of community, a sense en-
gendered in part through a shared religious faith.
The response of the creationist to the teaching of
evolutionary theory, like the resistance to AIDS
education or condom distribution, might be best
viewed as a reaction to a fear of indoctrination: religion demands one intellectual position, and the
state seeks to command another. Liberalism, in
this case, is curiously intolerant of what certainly
may be viewed as a classic case of conscience inter-
posed before the authority of the state.[326]

He adds:

On this vision, a public school curriculum perceived as secular and modernist is a grave and
obvious threat to the efforts of parents to raise
their children in their religious belief with its hermeneutical implications. Thus, the question that
moves the debate—who shall control the education of children?[327]

It seems to me that in this example if just one side possessed
the wisdom and courage to admit their opponents may have
legitimate concerns, it could cause the opposition to recipro-

cate, a natural reaction I've witnessed on numerous occasions.

So where might we find common ground in conflicting methods of child-rearing? If we break free from our normal left-right, religious-secular bias, a "pro-family" agenda offers the perfect opportunity. Just as fundamentalist families diligently guard the status of their traditional nuclear family, other types of families, such as blended marriages, single parents, or gay couples, do not want to see their families' status demeaned. Can we have a conversation where representatives of different family structures agree that they all care about their children's well-being? Where they agree to respect the diversity of the other? Where they agree not to seek punitive legislation or sanctions against the other? In other words, can we agree to avoid the "mutually assured destruction" of family integrity that both sides of the conflict are capable of inflicting?

No family, however constituted, wants the government to deprive them of their right to raise their children as they deem best. Religiously conservative as well as progressive and/or secular parents have fundamental beliefs that they don't want violated, such as the right to control or at least approve how their tax dollars are spent in regard to their children's education. Just as conservative parents may not want their young children taught sex education, evolution, or the equality of all religions, secularists may not want their children receiving religious instruction, reciting school-crafted prayers, or being taught creationism. And no parent wants government bureaucrats to dictate how they discipline their children in the privacy of their own home.

Can every parent in twenty-first-century America "grow up" and agree to follow the same rules they teach their children about relating to other children—to respect the fundamental beliefs and choices of

*others, and not throw a tantrum when others want to play by differ-
ent rules?*

It's more likely to happen if we can remember that we share
the universal experience called parenting, and that it is our
love for our children that binds us together as members of the
human family.

Another area where we can find agreement between religious fundamentalists and progressives and/or secularist fundamentalists has to do with human rights. Most Christians
are strong believers in the dignity and rights of individuals because they believe each person was "created in the image of
God." That Christians often ignore or even violate this belief—
through apathy toward the civil rights movement or the demonization of gays, for instance—should not negate the manifold positive consequences that have flowed from this same
conviction.

For two millennia the Christian concept of humanity has
inspired hundreds of thousands of saints, prophets, radicals,
reformers, and average people to help their fellow humans
secure increasingly greater degrees of equality and liberty. A
very short list of examples include:

- Contravening the Roman Empire's view of women as
  their husbands' personal property by demanding that
  Christian husbands treat their wives as "equal before
  God," with love, kindness, and respect. In fact, the
  apostle Paul was the first major voice of the ancient
  world to boldly proclaim the equality of all races and
  economic classes.

- Salvaging thousands of unwanted babies from being devoured by wild animals when they were discarded like
  so much trash by their Roman parents.

- Leading the fight for abolition of slavery and child labor in Great Britain (portrayed so powerfully in the 2007 film *Amazing Grace*).
- Initiating and leading the movement to abolish slavery in America (abolitionism).
- Leading the women's suffrage movement that gave American women the right to vote—a right still not recognized in many Islamic nations.
- Inspiring and leading the Civil Rights movement.

Of course, this is by necessity a very brief list. The interesting thing to note is that in many of these great moral crusades, non-Christians, mainly Deists (those who believe in a universe produced by a removed but Intelligent Designer—sometimes referred to as God) and their modern more secularist cousins, marched shoulder to shoulder with the Jewish and Christian community. Perhaps their commitment flowed from our founding fathers, many of whom were Deists, who believed that everyone's right to "life, liberty and the pursuit of happiness" was "self-evident." Of course, these virtues can't be proven to be self-evident, and in fact are denied by many. Nevertheless, they can and do provide us with common ground.

And there is more encouraging news in that today, perhaps more than ever, Christians of all persuasions are joining secularists as well as members of other faith communities to address a number of important human rights crises. Whether it is to end genocide and slavery in the Sudan or child sexual slavery in Asia and elsewhere, people are transcending differences in background, belief, and borders to work together.

Something good is *happening*. As *Washington Post* columnist and author E. J. Dionne Jr. notes:

American politics is at a turning point. Evangelical Christians are an increasingly diverse group.
Many in their ranks are broadening their tradition's agenda to include a commitment to the poor,
an engagement with international human and religious rights, opposition to genocide in Darfur, a
passionate commitment to relieving the burden
of AIDS on the African poor, and a deepening belief in the obligation of stewardship toward the
environment. Mainline Protestants are battling
through the moral approaches of their churches
toward homosexuality even as they maintain powerful and long-standing commitments to peace, social justice, and a strong version of the common
good.[328]

On social justice issues like poverty, both liberal and conservative Christians are beginning to work together. Two recent efforts, Christian Churches Together (CCT) and The Poverty Forum, headed by progressive spokesman Jim Wallis and
former Bush speech writer and policy advisor Michael Gerson,
are dedicated to finding common ground in relieving the specter of poverty for millions of Americans who have lost their
jobs or homes or both in the most recent economic tsunami.
*What's the common ground of these initiatives? A deep respect for hu-
man life, for nature, and for this planet we all call home.*

Even finding common ground on abortion may not be as
daunting as it once was, now that 60 percent of Evangelicals
support some type of compromise.[329] If pro-lifers can respect
pro-choicers' concern with the rights of women to exercise
sovereignty over their own bodies, and conversely, if pro-

choicers can respect how pro-lifers similarly value the rights of an unborn child, *both sides can start from a mutually respected concern for human rights.* Perhaps then they can begin to appreciate how their opponents' understanding of when life begins logically dictates their position.

As 2004 Democratic presidential nominee Senator John Kerry observed,

> If you really believe that life begins at conception and that that's a living person with full ensoulment, and that is the image of God, then for that person, whatever number of abortions are a Holocaust, and I have to be prepared to say, "I respect that." Now, if you do respect that, then the language of "It's my body, I can do whatever I want with it" is frankly not correct. It doesn't mean you don't have the right to make a choice.... But it still means there is a morality that we have to acknowledge in that choice.[330]

Hillary Clinton also has taken a public stand for opening dialogue and seeking common ground, saying "I, for one, respect those who believe with all their heart and conscience that there are no circumstances under which abortion should ever be available."[331] Have Kerry and Clinton converted to the pro-life cause? Hardly. Have they learned to empathize with and respect pro-life concern? Definitely! What a splendid example these bona-fide progressives have set in showing us how to engage with great civility those with whom we disagree.

Of course pro-lifers also will need to reach out from a place of respect and try to appreciate the belief in a woman's right to

control her body and her life without demonizing those who
hold that belief as "baby killers." Respecting an opponent's
convictions is a huge step in the right direction, and if Hillary Clinton and John Kerry can make the leap, the rest of us
should be able to follow. Indeed it seems that some other liberal Democratic leaders, normally hostile to pro-lifers even
within their own ranks, are actually beginning to practice the
pluralism they have so long advocated. After famously deny-
ing Bob Casey, the popular *Democratic* governor of Pennsylvania, a chance to address Bill Clinton's 1992 Democratic National Convention because of his pro-life stance,[332] and after
consistently refusing any contact with "Democrats for Life,"[333]
in 2006, Democratic leaders later cleared the way for Casey's
pro-life son, Bob Jr., to gain the Democratic nomination for
U.S. Senate as opposed to a popular pro-choice candidate. Consequently Casey won the general election against the incumbent senator, Christian Right hero Rick Santorum. Casey was
propelled into his new Senate office thanks to winning 30 percent of the white Evangelical vote.[334] Today, Democrats for Life,
with the help of pro-life Democrats in Congress, is sponsoring
a "95-10 Initiative" to reduce abortions by 95 percent within
ten years.

The Third Way Project, representing a wide spectrum of
progressives and Evangelicals, including Rev. Joel Hunter, a
former leader of Pat Robertson's Christian Coalition, hopes
that progressives and Evangelicals can both agree that given
the high number of abortions, we should join together to reduce the need for abortion. Third Way leaders are working
with both pro-life and pro-choice members of Congress to find
common ground around the idea of "reducing the number
of abortions in America through reducing the need for abor-

tions...by both preventing unintended pregnancies and supporting pregnant women who wish to carry their pregnancies to term."[335]

Another hopeful sign comes from Evangelical leaders like Adam Hamilton, the bridge-building pastor of a 14,000-member church, who has proposed seven points that he believes offer common ground for moderates on both sides of the abortion divide:

1. Pro-choice advocates and pro-life advocates each have legitimate concerns.
2. Abortion is both "not ideal" and yet, occasionally "necessary" (at the very least, most pro-life advocates would allow abortion to save the life of the mother).
3. Decreasing the number of abortions in America would be desirable.
4. Adequate information about and access to birth control can reduce abortions.
5. The longer a pregnancy progresses, the more morally problematic an abortion becomes.
6. No one should be pressured into having an abortion.
7. If an abortion occurs, it should be safe.[336]

From even these few examples, *it's clear that we can find common ground if we truly choose to.* But like all history-changing quests, our task will not be easy. In addition to the obstacles listed earlier and in spite of our newfound optimism in finding common ground based on respect for individual and human rights, serious questions persist.

What happens when respecting your tradition means disrespecting another's? When guaranteeing the rights of one group is perceived as violating the sacred principles of a competing group—the very principles that provide the foundation of their life and purpose? What do we do when, in exercising freedom of religion, one group teaches that homosexuality is a sin? What if, in exercising their freedom of speech, they use the word "gay" in a negative sense, and such use is considered hate speech by progressives? What do we do when secularists or liberals, in the interest of eliminating discrimination, teach that "gay is OK" to kindergarteners or elementary students, which fundamentalist Jewish, Islamic, or Christian parents may perceive as holding their child hostage and "brainwashing" them to oppose their parents' religion, perhaps even their parents themselves? Secularists may have similar feelings if their children are asked to pray in school and look at the Ten Commandments on the wall. What do we do about abortion when protecting the rights of an unborn child is equated with oppressing the rights of a woman and vice versa? Unfortunately, the solution is not as simple as just asking our public schools to remain neutral, to stay away from prayer in school, and to not teach "gay is OK" in an effort not to offend fundamentalists in either camp.

But, as complicated as peace is, it takes two (or more) willing combatants to throw a war. In the culture wars no side can credibly claim the moral high ground of being above the fray. As Karen Armstrong summarizes:

> But the fundamentalists did not have a monopoly on anger. Their movements had often evolved in a dialectical relationship with an aggressive secularism which showed scant respect for religion and its adherents. Secularists and fundamentalists sometimes seemed trapped in an escalating spiral of hostility and recrimination.[337]

The question that should now be in the forefront of our minds is how can we call a halt to this self-perpetuating cycle of distrust, acrimony, and mutual recrimination?

How do we strike a compromise so we can move ahead—together—toward a national dialogue of hope, healing, and reconciliation?

12

Moving Forward

In John Gray's words, the way forward is to search for
means of coexistence rather than for a consensus. . . . At
the level of faiths, our differences will always be deep, ir-
reducible, and incompatible. —Os Guinness[338]

IT'S TIME FOR us to move forward, with confidence in our
positions, but not with absolute, unquestionable certainty.
Hopefully we desire to keep searching and learning, expanding, updating, and modifying our worldview, remembering
that knowledge is a journey, not a destination. We have seen in
this book that we will need to identify and modify, or at least
actively "manage," our presuppositions that so readily lend
themselves to polarizing rhetoric and positions.

For Christian neo-fundamentalists, that means *not* fram-
ing every argument within the parameters of "God's Word,"
such as citing biblical passages that define human life as beginning at conception, or sodomy as a sin. That form of argument is simply not admissible as evidence in the postmodern
court of public opinion where any ideology that lays claim to

fundamental truth is suspect. According to his son Frank, even Francis Schaeffer, the theologian who arguably did the most to augment neo-fundamentalism, "hated circular arguments that depended on the Bible when used against secular people who didn't acknowledge biblical authority. He believed that you should argue on a level playing field, where both people stay on common ground."[339] For secularists, relying on arguments claiming objective rationality or science as "the last word" is equally inappropriate and demonstrably counterproductive, as we have seen over the last century or so. As Frank Schaeffer observes, "The New Atheists pit religion's literalistic truth claims against their own literalistic truth claims. In that sense the New Atheists turn out to be secular fundamentalists arguing with religious fundamentalists."[340]

We will need to remember that perceived threats to the status quo, or to our dead certain belief about how things are or ought to be, catapult our fear-driven, fight-or-flight response right past our more reflective reasoning and better judgment. We need to reconnect with and practice our fundamentals of love, tolerance, and respect.

But respectful tolerance should not be limited to lofty, self-serving gracious feelings about different but benign worldviews—the proof is in the pudding of direct opposition. For instance, some secular fundamentalists who identify themselves with tolerance and pluralism often seem to have great difficulty consistently practicing either. Many seem tolerant only of those ideas and practices that differ from, but do not directly oppose, their own ideals. The rest they label as intolerant, ironically failing to be tolerant themselves. In the tradition of true pluralism, tolerance must involve an eyes-wide-open acceptance of the legitimacy of paradigms diametrically opposed to our own. This of course must be coupled with a respect for the rights of ALL humans to celebrate their respective beliefs.

Similarly, neo-fundamentalists often seem fundamentally incapable of following Christ's example of love, compassion, and withholding condemnation. While some Christian neo-fundamentalists practice benign neglect toward philosophies or religions which do not seem to pose a direct threat—such as, Buddhists and Jews—they are less generous to those they deem "ungodly" or even "demonic" for undermining or opposing "Scriptural truth"—such as, Mormons, secular humanists, Muslims, and homosexuals.

How can both sides and all the rest of us as well, practice these noble concepts when it is all too natural for us (especially myself!) to violate the thin line between "hating the sin" and "hating the sinner?"

It is always difficult for the two sides in any conflict to truly empathize with the other's motivations, especially when this involves a complex and somewhat incongruent mix of fears and hopes, commendable aspirations and dubious tactics, good intentions and deplorable rhetoric. Empathizing is also challenging when we essentially inhabit not just different worlds, but worlds where moral compasses seem reversed—where light in one world is darkness to the other, where morality to one is perceived as immorality to the other. With these obstacles, even communicating clearly and civilly can seem like a daunting feat. But we must make the effort.

To do so will require all of us to learn new ways of hearing and responding, of seeing and doing—in essence, a new way of being. And isn't one of the prime purposes of *all* religions, as well as secular wisdom traditions, to change not just our beliefs, or even our *behavior*, but to elevate us to a better state of *being human?* As the Bible declares: "Faith without action is

dead" (James 2:26). The way we conduct ourselves should reflect our deepest beliefs with the goal of being better humans.
Hopefully then, the challenge of acting or reacting differently
will be made easier by renewing our commitment to the "fundamentals" of our belief systems.

We Need a New Attitude

What many of us know but may fail to fully appreciate is how
much our attitude directly affects our behavior, and how our
behavior translates into actions that can cause unintended or
even unwanted reactions. For instance, the obnoxious hubris-
tic behavior of *both* sides of the culture wars has often driven
people to the *other* side rather than to a tolerant and hopeful
middle.

*To create the possibility of a national dialogue of hope, healing,
and reconciliation will require a radically new attitude of openness,
humility, and mutual respect.* Stopping the condemnation, hostility, and consequent demonization will also be necessary to create a safe space for *a civil* exchange of conflicting convictions
and concerns.[341] Something seemingly so simple as respectful
listening is one of the first things we must master if we are to
engage in meaningful dialogue. As Pastor Hamilton points
out:

> The culture wars we're experiencing now, and the
> polarization in our society and in the church, are,
> in large part, a result of our unwillingness to lis-
> ten to others and acknowledge that they may have
> something important to say. Consequently, we
> talk past one another, but seldom really attempt
> to learn from one another, or to see if there is any

place where, despite our differences, we might come to find common ground. . . .

The key is to listen to both sides and look for ways to integrate the legitimate concerns of each side, often forging a new way forward, or at least plowing forward while taking seriously the views of the other. This willingness to listen to those with whom we disagree, and to take seriously their legitimate concerns, is critical for people of all religions and nationalities. Until we can learn to do that, there will be no hope for resolving the culture wars here at home, nor the broader international conflicts that threaten our world.[342]

On the right, many former or even current activists like former Robertson operative James Muffet seem to be taking Hamilton's advice to heart:

Sometimes [members of the Religious Right] convey that "We're Christians, we read the Bible, we know the truth and you don't; therefore, we're right and you're not." There's a self-righteous air that we have to get away from. And I see people on the other side who are more moderate or liberal, and they have an air of "We know what's best." There's an elitism there. I think everybody has to get rid of that and just sit down and say, "OK, let's talk." I, for one, want to do that.[343]

On the left, Jim Wallis, provided us with an excellent example of how to avoid our all-too-common preference for *ad hominum* attacks in his civil critiquing of George W. Bush. Rather than polarizing a dialogue before it begins by assailing our nation's former president as evil, duplicitous, and conniving (all things the Christian Right accused Bill Clinton and currently Barack Obama of), Wallis balanced his criticism by extending the benefit of the doubt and not questioning the president's intent while firmly sharing his own heartfelt sentiment:

> From what I have seen and heard of George W. Bush (including in small meetings and personal conversations I've had with the president) I believe his faith to be both personal and real. And I also believe that he has a heart genuinely concerned for poor people. But I think the president is often guilty of bad theology. On the issue of poverty, George Bush believes in a God of charity, but not a God of justice.[344]

Whether one agrees with Wallis' assessment of the president's theological deficiencies is not the point. The lesson is that we can disagree—even strongly—without assassinating the other's character. Wallis has taken an important step in encouraging others to follow his example. His "Covenant for Civility" to launch a "civil national discourse" was signed by scores of Christian leaders representing a broad spectrum of perspectives. In part, the Covenant reads:

> We pledge that when we disagree, we will do so respectfully, without falsely impugning the other's motives, attacking the other's character, or ques-

tioning the other's faith, and recognizing in humility that in our limited, human opinions, "we see
but a poor reflection as in a mirror." . . . We recognize that we cannot function together as citizens
of the same community, whether local or national,
unless we are mindful of how we treat each other in pursuit of the common good in the common
life we share together.

Since attitude is so important, it's encouraging to see that
it's not just progressives or "bleeding heart liberals" like Wallis who have learned to pay respectful attention to those with
whom they differ. Frank Schaeffer reports that his father, the
towering intellect of the Christian Right, was "tough on issues"
he disagreed with, "but not on people,"[345] adding that "Dad's
sparring partner of the moment would be stunned by my father's kindness."[346]

Closer to home, my first mentor, David Noebel was, along
with Schaeffer, the fiercest as well as the most prolific intellectual critic of "secular humanism." For four decades he relentlessly identified humanists as "the enemy" in textbooks, articles, and in lectures to over 30,000 students. And yet today he
maintains a cordial personal relationship with many of these
same humanist leaders. In fact, when one of the nation's most
prominent humanists was hospitalized with a life-threaten-
ing illness, David wrote him an extremely kind letter sharing
the news that "even though I know you don't believe in God,
I want you to know we have a lot of friends praying for your
full recovery." Why the stark contradiction between David's
approach and that of the Christian Right jihadist "imprecatory
prayer warriors?" Could it be that one attitude is rooted in the

God of love and mercy, while the other in demonizing one's opponent?

What each of these men, representing different faith traditions, is demonstrating is the lost grace of civility and Christian charity. Os Guinness, a scholar and long-time observer of the culture wars, suggests in his *The Case for Civility* that the road to civility lies

> . . . through *covenant pluralism*: everyone in the world is free to believe what they choose to believe, on the basis of freedom of conscience; but, as with the civil public square, they have to accord the same freedom to others, and learn to live with a double eye—one to the integrity of their own faiths, and the other to the responsibility of seeing and dealing with other through the lens of their faith. In short, recognizing and respecting the difference of others, without relinquishing the integrity of one's own faith, is a prerequisite for global freedom and justice.[347]

In other words, as Guinness points out, the right to be wrong must be consistently defended. After all, our humanness guarantees all of us will be wrong at least some of the time. [348]

Replacing an attitude of religious self-righteousness or secular arrogance with civility is something we all need to work on. As Guinness concludes, "Civility is a key not only to civil society but to civilization itself."[349]

Questioning Our Own Authority

Hopefully most of us agree with Socrates—"the unexamined life is not worth living." And many of us, including myself, would also have to admit we have invested insufficient time and effort examing our own life and belief system and the inevitable disconnect between the two.

It seems to me that before we attempt to engage the many competing worldviews that make up our community, we need to judiciously examine what are the underlying assumptions of our own worldview and exactly how and why we arrived at them. Was it an essentially unconscious process of mental osmosis from family, friends, teachers, and religious figures, many who no doubt offered contradicting notions? Or did we consciously build a coherent paradigm that required study, analysis, and trial and error? As we have seen, our certainties can lead us to imagine we have "arrived" with full knowledge of "the truth," rather than seeing ourselves as humble pilgrims on a journey which will, in all likelihood, take a lifetime and probably more.

If we are serious about dispassionately testing our cherished beliefs against new or opposing concepts, we will have to stop taking the path of least resistance and get out of our comfort zone. But most of us don't have the time, energy, curiosity, security, emotional strength, or intellectual skill to constantly test our beliefs. New ideas, particularly if they challenge long-held beliefs, are perceived to be stressful because if valid, they might involve change. Since most of us quite understandably don't need any more stress in our lives, our tendency is to dismiss new ideas rather than do the necessary hard work to investigate, and then either integrate or disregard them. What "new" learning we do undertake is usually to confirm or reinforce our existing views, making them even more impenetrable to any challenge regardless of its merits! This, along with the "confirmation bias" discussed earlier, is one more reason why we tend to interpret any new information in a way that supports our presuppositions.

Consequently, we need to get better at questioning authority—our own! Most of us seem to have a built-in reticence to question authority, even when we have subconsciously christened *another's interpretation* with our own authority. Neo-fundamentalists are proud that they "don't question God's Word," but what they are really saying, unbeknownst to them, is that they are not questioning their *interpretation* of Scripture. Similarly, secularists are often unwilling to question the "rational" conclusions drawn from their "scientific" worldview. The possibility that they may be subjectively interpreting a paradigm which itself has been constructed on subjective presuppositions is never even entertained.

Embracing Reality

Another help in adjusting our attitude is what I call a *reality check*. Can we start by embracing the reality that pluralism is here to stay, please? None of the culture war combatants are going to disappear anytime soon—not Sarah Palin, not Richard Dawkins, not anyone of their ilk.

Second, achieving a *national consensus* is the only possibility for long-term stability. Secularists and progressives need to come to grips with the fact that they no longer have a clear playing field. After a 50-year "time out"—from the Scopes trial in 1925 to the rise of the Christian Right in 1978—the other team has taken to the field. And they are scoring points—most recently in the 2010 elections. Likewise, Christian neo-funda-

mentalists need to accept the obvious—that the Christian consensus that once dominated American culture has been sup-
planted by a diverse array of voices. As ministry leader and
author Tim Keel advises:

> We can no longer assume privilege, position, or
> control. We cannot assume a divine *imprimatur* be-
> cause we have the power to back up our convic-
> tions. Post-Christendom tells us we no longer live
> in a society that by default shares the same lan-
> guage, beliefs, values, or structures that we believe
> ought to shape American identity.[350]

And yes, the majority still may hold—somewhat loosely
to be sure—to Judeo-Christian principles, and Evangelicals
may be the largest voting bloc in the country, and yes, they
might be able to achieve "majority rule." But majority rule, if
it is perceived as oppressing the deepest desires of the minority, doesn't work well in the long term. Neo-fundamentalists
should also remind themselves that eighteen years of conservative presidents (Reagan, Bush, and Bush Jr.) failed to achieve
major goals of the Christian Right, especially outlawing abortion, pornography, and gay marriage, reducing sex and violence on TV, and mandating prayer in schools. Each side must
get out of denial, acknowledging the fact that they no longer
dominate the field as they once did during a particular phase
of our national journey. Here's a reality check—*nothing lasts
forever.* No team or party can hang on to unchallenged power
or preeminence over an extended period of time. Just ask my
home team, the San Francisco 49ers!

Part of embracing reality is to lower our expectations. It

should be clear after three decades that the culture war is unwinnable in the long run. The fact is that neither side can, or should, win, which should remove the desire to repress the other side. The last thing any of us really want is to fan the flames of desperation that has spawned the violence in East Africa, the Middle East, or in Eastern Europe. Readers my age who experienced the Vietnam War may recall months on end when it seemed like buildings were either blown up or burned down by antiwar protestors who felt their best or only recourse was violence.

Embracing reality will demand we learn to live with each other as we are—not as we would like others to be. Since the French Revolution, we have believed that we have the power to change everything—ourselves, others, institutions, and even culture—in a short period of time. We think we can "reconstruct" each other. This has proven to be one of history's biggest fallacies, and it has led to the greatest horrors of the twentieth century. Ask infamous Marxist tyrant Mao Tse-Tung who, after a half century of ruthlessly "revolutionizing" the world's largest nation, complained that he had essentially changed nothing. Confirming the Chairman's pessimism, today's China is essentially a capitalist nation.

A Trial Prescription

As we've seen, hubris is the diagnosis for our cultural malady, and humility (starting with myself) is the likely prescription. All cultural spheres—religious, secular, political—need to acknowledge their unfaithfulness to their guiding ideals and their counterproductive and unfair demonization of each other.

I propose that neo-fundamentalists need to, as I have done,

read 2 Chronicles 7:14 with new eyes: "If my people, who are called by my name, will humble *themselves* and pray and seek my face and turn from *their* wicked ways, then I will hear from heaven and will forgive *their* sin and will heal their land" (NIV, emphasis added). This Scripture clearly does not expect nonbelievers to turn from their "wicked ways." Rather it admonishes "believers" (my people) to humble themselves and admit *their* evil ways: arrogance, lack of compassion, selfishness, consumerism, bigotry, ignoring the poor, and so on.

Another step toward humility, in my experience, is to understand, as I think Jesus taught, that my first priority is to fix myself rather than trying to fix others. In my case, this task seems to be so formidable at times that one lifetime may be insufficient! It seems like it should be easier to force someone else to change. But after four decades of trying to change the world, I have come to appreciate how hard it is to just change myself, let alone anyone else!

For progressives and secularists, I can find no wiser advice than that offered by historian Karen Armstrong:

> We have to try to make the *huge* imaginative effort to put ourselves in the shoes of the fundamentalists because they threaten our values just as we threaten theirs. If we understand a bit more clearly what the fundamentalists really mean, if we learn to read the imagery of fundamentalism, we take the first step in learning about and understanding each other. You can make war in a minute, but peace takes a long time.[351]

And finally, let's all admit we make judgments about everyone and everything—nonstop—people's looks, weight, social attributes, intellect, politics, and ideas. And if we're not judging on these levels, we're judging them for being judgmental. We are judgment machines—our mindless brain chatter constantly spewing forth opinions on this or that. The point is, if we can "get off it," for even a few seconds, we will realize that our judgments are nothing more or less than our opinions. They are not ultimate truth. History—even very recent history—often proves that what we "know" to be true is simply not true. With that in mind, we can follow Frank Schaeffer's prescription: "Take the one overarching lesson from reality—humility—to heart, and move forward together."[352]

Is Peace Possible?

The overarching question I think we must ask ourselves is this: Is peace possible? Short of entering a rehab clinic for arrogance, what will it take to get the warring parties to repent of their lack of compassion and tolerance, and of their bogus claims to objectivity and infallibility? Just this book alone probably will not do it! Nor must we count on a miraculous change of heart. What is required is a paradigm shift. But as science philosopher Thomas Kuhn observed, such shifts usually are not the result of adherents of the old paradigm rigorously reexamining their own presuppositions and methodologies.

As we discussed earlier, old warriors will likely discount or reinterpret questions, challenges, or dogmatic inconsistencies in such a way that they support their previous conclusions. So, paradigm shifts are more apt to occur as the old guard gradually dies off and an upcoming generation with new ideas is elevated to power. I am at once hopeful and excited that I see this change of the "generational guard" happening even now. The

282   Christian Jihad

postmodern generation with its weariness of absolute truth claims—whether secular, scientific, or religious—and its wariness of all those who represent themselves as truly "objective," is rapidly replacing my generation of boomers who tended to rigidly adhere to and fiercely defend the absolute correctness of their assumptions.

This generation—filled with hopeful idealism and energized by love, compassion, and inclusion—is ready to place itself in the shoes of others, as Armstrong suggests. It is composed of visionaries like my twenty-one-year-old son, Brant, who asks, "If we do not speak the same language, how can we understand each other?" And then he adds, "My hope is that people will eventually be able to understand others that reside on opposite sides of the spectrum without telling them they're wrong." There's also twenty-five-year-old Melisse Harris, who helped research this work and who envisions an America where we

> . . . stop obsessing over ourselves and focus on taking steps toward peace—even if it means we must be as passionate about listening and making efforts toward understanding as we are passionate about speaking and fighting for what we believe in. If we are willing to take drastic measures to protect our identities, we need to be willing to question ourselves in order to be sure our identities are worth protecting—before we destroy each other trying to protect ourselves. Let the identity crisis begin.

Brant and Melisse, less than half my age, have learned in a

few years a perspective that took me decades to understand. Their insights, and those of many of their peers, are our true national treasure.

If we are not to end up as a merely more sophisticated version of the Palestinian-Israeli, Sunni-Shia, Muslim-Hindu debacles, we will need the next several generations to call a halt to America's thirty-year culture war. Let us pray they hasten to act.

Of course, the rest of us cannot—must not—abdicate our *own* responsibility to act. We cannot expect "our kids" to salvage the house we have set afire, or through our apathy and ambivalence have allowed to burn. But their idealism, their freshness and purity of heart, their readiness to embrace change can serve to inspire us. At this writing I am struck by how many leaders of the "old guard"—congressmen; senators; Maria Shriver, the former First Lady of California; and even a former President of the United States, Jimmy Carter—have credited their children, even their grandchildren, with getting them to consider new possibilities. If we can muster the humility to listen with an open mind to the wisdom our nation's future leaders are discovering, we may find hope and charity rekindled in our own hearts.

For my part, once I realized that my objectivity was nothing more than illusion, the consequences were clear—my new paradigm required me to grant others the benefit of the doubt, to strive for confidence rather than certainty, to embrace pluralism, and last—but definitely not least—to follow Jesus in loving people rather than condemning them.

I had been born again, this time as a post-conservative, post-fundamentalist, postmodern Christian.

I was also fortunate enough to be in a perfect position, as

CEO of Children's Hunger Relief Fund (chrf.org), one of America's leading charities, to practice my newfound sense of empathy, compassion, and pluralism. I refocused my strategic and organizational building skills on helping to launch a dozen charities on four continents—all committed to transforming lives around the world by breaking the self-perpetuating cycle of illiteracy, disease, and poverty. A decade and over $500 million of aid later, I'm happy to report that my colleagues and I are busily engaged in providing millions of meals a year for hungry children, helping thousands of families start self-sufficient businesses, creating clean water systems for African villages, providing medical and immunization services where there have been none, building schools, and teaching people to get along with their neighbors. As we bring them God's love, we expect them to "pass it forward," sharing God's love and compassion with friends, strangers, even enemies. And we do all of this with no concern for race, gender, religion, or political affiliation.

I've come home to God's love at last. *I am truly born again.*

In the end, the choice between allowing our certainties and hostilities to continue to separate us, and embracing a new paradigm of grace and humility is up to us. As Brant asked me this morning at breakfast, *"What sort of world would we live in if we took responsibility for the choices that lead to our actions?"* Indeed.

Endnotes

Chapter 1

1   James S. Cutsinger, ed., *Reclaiming the Great Tradition* (InterVarsity, 1997), 23.

2   Dan Wakefield, *The Hijacking of Jesus* (Nation, 2006), 5.

3   Mel White, *Religion Gone Bad* (New York: Tarcher/Penguin, 2006), 213.

4   Jim Wallis, *God's Politics* (New York: Harper, 2005), 7.

5   Earl Black and Merle Black, *Divided America* (New York: Simon and Schuster, 2008), 19.

6   Jim Wallis, *The Great Awakening* (New York: Harper, 2008), 247.

7   E. J. Dionne Jr., *Souled Out* (Princeton, NJ: Princeton University Press, 2008), 35.

8   Jim Wallis, *Who Speaks for God?* (New York: Delacorte Press, 1996), 165.

9   Dionne Jr., 34.

10   Dionne Jr., 48.

11   Jeff Sharlet, *The Family* (New York: Harper, 2008), 367.

12   Glenn H. Utter, *The Religious Right: A Reference Handbook* (Amenia, NY: Grey House, 2007), 88.

13   Joel Carpenter, *Revive Us Again: The Resurfacing of American Fundamentalism* (New York: Oxford, 1999), 242.

14   Bruce Barron, *Heaven on Earth?* (Grand Rapids, MI: Zondervan, 1992), 116.

15   James Davison Hunter, *Before the Shooting Begins* (New York: Free Press, 2007), 5.

16   Hunter, 8.

17   Randall Balmer, *Thy Kingdom Come* (New York: Basic Books, 2006), 64.

18   Charles Kimball, *When Religion Becomes Evil* (San Francisco: HarperSanFrancisco, 2003), 44.

19   Karen Armstrong, *The Battle for God* (New York: Ballantine, 2000), 367.

20   Jim Wallis, *God's Politics* (New York: HarperCollins 2005), 67.

21   Gary McCuen, *The Religious Right* (GEM, 1989), 42.

22   Dionne, 32-3.

23   Armstrong, 371.

24   John Avlon, *Wingnuts* (New York: Beast Books, 2010), 18.

25   Avaln, 129.

26   Avaln, 1.

27   Avaln, 1.

28   Avaln, 63.

29   Wallis, *God's Politics*, xxiii.

Chapter 2

30   Glenn Utter, *The Religious Right: A Reference Handbook* (Amenia, NY: Grey House Publishing, 2007), 88.

31   Utter, 88.

32   Frederick Clarkson, *Religious Right Update*, www.publiceye.org, May/June 1997.

33   Judy Bachrach, "What a Top Religious Rightist Believes." *San Francisco Chronicle*, November 17, 1980.

34   John Buchanan, "Alliance with Religious Extremists Threatens Integrity of GOP." *The Courant*, February 4, 1985.

35   "Nationalist Federal Fascism or Protecting the Flag?" *The Roundhead Watch* www.geocities.com/CapitolHill/Senate/9526/against.html?20069.

Chapter 3

36   Mark A. Noll, *America's God* (New York: Oxford University Press, 2005), 380.

37   1 Corinthians 7:12, *The Living Bible.*

38   Karen Armstrong, The History of God (New York: Ballantine, 1994), 289. Karen Armstrong, The Bible (Atlantic Monthly Press, 2007), 167.

39   Rob Bell, *Velvet Elvis* (Grand Rapids, MI: Zondervan, 2005), 62.

40   Alister McGrath, *The Intellectual Origins of the European Reformation* (Hoboken, NJ: Wiley-Blackwell, 2003), 162.

41   Noll, 414-16.

42   Bell, 63.

43   Gary Dorrien, *The Remaking of Evangelical Theology* (Louisville, KY:

Westminster John Knox Press, 1998), 130. Emphasis added.

44   Gary Dorrien, *The Word as True Myth* (Westminster John Knox Press, 1997), 237-38.

45   Dorrien, 233.

46   Dorrien, 141.

47   Stanley Grenz, Roger Olson, *20th Century Theology* (Downers Grove, IL: Intervarsity, 1997), 108.

48   Karen Armstrong, *The Battle for God* (New York: Ballantine, 2000), 144.

49   Karen Armstrong, *A Short History of Myth* (Canongate U.S., 2006), 135.

50   Karen Armstrong, *The Bible* (Boston: Atlantic Monthly Press, 2007), 199.

51   The problem lies not only with the different thought forms of Eastern and Western cultures, but the fact that words in Greek, Hebrew, or even German may have multiple possible translations in English.

52   Carl Raschke, *The Next Reformation* (Ada, MI: Baker, 2004), 121.

53   Fuller Seminary, *Theology News and Notes*, Winter 2008, 12.

54   Alister McGrath, *Reformation Thought* (Hoboken, NJ: Wiley-Blackwell, 2001), 52.

55   Richard Tarnas, *The Passion of the Western Mind* (New York: Harmony Books, 1991), 239.

56   Armstrong, 175.

57   John Armstrong, *Your Church Is Too Small* (Grand Rapids, MI: Zondervan, 2010), 127.

58   Mark A. Noll, *America's God* (Oxford University Press, 2005), 231.

59   Alister McGrath, *Reformation Thought* (Wiley-Blackwell, 2001), 144.

60   A. C. Grayling, *Descartes: The Life and Times of a Genius* (Walker & Co, 2006), 169.

61   Noll, 383.

62   The Bible was meant to be read by believers collectively, which is what the constant reference to "thee" in older translations like the King James infers. "Thee" addresses whole communities of believers, not lone readers. Following rabbinical tradition, the early church, as a community, would explore the possible meaning of each text. As Rob Bell, former pastor of one of the fastest-growing churches in America writes: "The Bible is a communal book. It came from people writing in communities, and it was often written to communities. Remember that the printing press wasn't invented until the 1400s. Prior to that, very few if any people had their own copies of the Bible. In Jesus' day, an entire village could probably afford only one copy of the Scriptures, if that. Reading the Bible alone was unheard of, if people could even read. For most of church history, people heard the Bible read aloud in a room full of people. You heard it, discussed it, studied it, argued about it, and made decisions about it as a group, a community" (Rob Bell, *Velvet Elvis*, Zondervan, 2005, 52). Pastor Bell, one of Evangelicalism's most prominent new voices draws a conclusion that stands the modern American approach to Bible reading on its head: "I don't think any of the writers of the Bible ever intended people to read their letters alone" (Bell, 53).

63   Tim Keel, *Intuitive Leadership* (Ada, MI: Baker Books, 2007), 124.

64   Tarnas, 279.

65   Raschke, 115.

66   Raschke, 116.

67   Raschke, 29.

68   Noll, 381.

69   Noll, 381.

70   *Newsweek,* August 19, 1986.

71   Colonel Doner in *Christian Life,* October 1984.

72   Derek Prince, *Rules of Engagement* (Grand Rapids, MI: Chosen, 2006), 156.

73   Mark Juergensmeyer, *Terror in the Mind of God* (Berkeley, CA: University of California, 2003), 164–165.

74   John P. Newport, *The New Age Movement and the Biblical Worldview* (Grand Rapids, MI: Eerdmans, 1997), 591.

75   George M. Marsden, *Fundamentalism and American Culture* (New York: Oxford, 2006), 210.

76   *The Scofield Reference Bible* (Oxford University Press, 1945), 1350.

77   Noll, 380.

78   Ray C. Stedman, *Spiritual Warfare* (Waco, TX: Word Books, 1978), 37.

79   Stedman, 49.

80   Colonel Doner in *Christian Life,* October 1984.

81   Stedman, 49.

82   Michael Lienesch, *Redeeming America* (Chapel Hill, NC: University of North Carolina, 1993), 91–2.

83   Colonel Doner in *Christian Life,* October 1984.

84   Gary North, *Backward, Christian Soldiers* (Tyler, TX: Institute for Christian Economics, 1984), 13.

85   North, 12.

86   Hosea 8:7 (NIV).

87   Deuteronomy 28:15-22, 27-29, (AMP).

88   Deuteronomy 28:25-26 (AMP).

89   Judges 2:10-14 (NIV).

90   Bart D. Ehrman, *Lost Christianities* (New York: Oxford University Press, 2005), 177.

91   Jay Grimstead, "An Urgent Message to a Few Christian Leaders," undated.

92   Colonel Doner in *Christian Life*, October 1984.

93   James B. Jordan, ed., *The Covenant Enforced* (Tyler, TX: Institute for Christian Economics, 1990), jacket copy.

94   Joshua 6:21 (niv).

95   Judges 8:4-19 (niv).

96   Judges 1:7.

97   Noll, 258.

98   Brian McLaren, *The Last Word and the Word After That* (San Francisco: Jossey-Bass, 2005), xii.

99   McLaren, xii.

100   Jonathan Kirsch, *A History of the End of the World* (New York: HarperOne, 2007), 219.

101   *USA Today*, front page, September 12, 2006.

102   *USA Today*, front page, September 12, 2006.

103   Karen Armstrong, *The Bible*, 209.

104   O.J. Grooms, *Russia Invades Israel When?* (Lynchburg: Thomas Road Baptist Church, 1983).

105   Jerry Falwell, *Nuclear War and the Second Coming of Jesus Christ* (Old Time Gospel Hour, 1983), 14.

106   John MacArthur, *The Truth War* (Nashville: Thomas Nelson 2007), 130.

107   MacArthur, 130.

108   North, 13.

109   *USA Today*, October 24, 2006.

110   *Newsweek*, May 12, 2008, 34.

111   Kirsch, 220.

112   *Newsweek*, May 12, 2008, 34.

113   Psalm 103:6-8; 99:4.

114   Isaiah 58:6-7, (tlb).

Chapter 4

115   Thomas More, *Care of the Soul* (New York: Harper Perennial, 1994), 236.

116   http://www.lbgstore.com/migagilebeet.html.

117   Eric Hoffer, *The True Believer* (New York: Harper Perennial, 1951), 82.

118   Frank Schaeffer, *Crazy for God* (New York: De Capo Press, 2007), 151.

119   Jeff Sharlet, *The Family* (New York: HarperCollins, 2008), 374.

120   William Martin, *With God on Our Side* (New York: Broadway, 1996), 215.

121   John MacArthur, *The Truth War* (Thomas Nelson, 2007), 183.

122   P. Andrew Sandlin, "Hyper-Realized Epistemology" AndrewSAndlin.net, 19 January 2006, http://www.andrewsandlin.net/?p=124.

123   Judges 2:17.

124   Frank Schaeffer, *Patience with God* (New York: De Capo Press, 2010).

125   MacArthur, 40.

126   Pastor Ock Soo Park, "Enter the Ark:" *New York Times*, October 23, 2006, A-15.

127   *Newsweek* May 12, 2008, 34.

Chapter 5

128   Nathan Hatch, *The Democratization of American Christianity* (New Haven, CT: Yale University Press, 1989), 35.

129   Leonard Sweet, *The Three Hardest Words* (Colorado Springs, CO: WaterBrook, 2006), 122.

130   Joel Carpenter, *Revive Us Again* (New York: Oxford University Press, 1999), 87.

131   Carl F. Henry, *The Uneasy Conscience of Modern Fundamentalism* (Grand Rapids, MI: Eerdmans, 2003).

132   Jon Meacham, "Pilgrim's Progress" *Newsweek*, Aug. 14, 2006.

133   Joseph Ratzinger, *Without Roots* (New York: Basic, 2007), 7.

134   Fawaz Gerges, *Journey of the Jihadist* (New York: Mariner, 2007), 16.

135   *Webster's New World Dictionary, Second College Edition* (New York: Simon and Schuster, 1980), 1288.

136   Curtis W. Reese, *Humanist Sermons* "The Faith of Humanism" (Chicago: Open Court, 1927), 39.

137   Sweet, 21–22.

138   *Newsweek* June 18, 2007, 14.

139   Julian Huxley, *Religion Without Revelation* (Mentor, 1957), 94.

140   Roy Wood Sellars, PhD, *Religion Coming of Age* (New York: Macmillan, 1928), 125.

141   John Dewey, *Education Today* (New York: Putnam, 1940), 84.

142   Dewey, 17.

143   Dewey, 86.

144   Dewey, 145, 147.

145   Roy Wood Sellars, PhD, *The Next Step in Religion* (New York: Macmillan, 1918), 215–16.

146   *Free Inquiry*, February/March 2007, 64–65.

147   Paul Kurtz, ed. *Humanist Manifestos I and II* (Amherst, NY: Prometheus 1973), 3.

148   Kurtz, 13.

149   Robert C. Solomon, *The Passions* (Cambridge, MA: Hackett, 1993), 65.

150   Michael Lerner, *The Left Hand of God* (New York: Harper, 2006), 130–31.

151   Lerner, 131.

152   Ken Wilber, *Integral Spirituality* (India: Integral Books, 2006), 188.

153   Lerner, 151.

154   Wilber, 189.

155   Huston Smith, *Forgotten Truth* (New York: HarperOne, 1992), 16.

156   Richard Tarnas, *The Passion of the Western Mind* (New York: Harmony, 1991), 361, 397.

157   James Davison Hunter, *Before the Shooting Begins* (New York: Free

Press, 2007), 5.

158   Smith, 16.

159   Joseph Ratzinger, *Without Roots* (New York: Basic, 2007), 88.

160   David Horowitz, *Hating Whitey and Other Progressive Causes* (Dallas, TX: Spence, 1999), 242.

161   Ratzinger, 128.

162   Jim Wallis, *God's Politics* (New York: Harper, 2005), 69.

163   Stephen L. Carter, *The Culture of Disbelief* (New York: Anchor, 1994), 229–30

164   P. Andrew Sandlin, *Totalism* (Vallecito, CA: Chalcedon, 2001), 104.

165   Lerner, 29.

166   Wilber, 188–90.

167   Wilber, 198.

168   Wallis, 67.

169   Hunter, 5.

Chapter 6

170   George Marsden, *Fundamentalism and American Culture* (New York: Oxford University Press, 2006), 86.

171   Stephen L. Carter, *The Culture of Disbelief* (New York: Anchor, 1994), 86.

172   Joel A. Carpenter, *Revive Us Again* (New York: Oxford University Press, 1999), 37. (Emphasis added.)

173   Steve Bruce, *The Rise and Fall of the New Christian Right* (Clarendon, 1988), 192.

174   Bruce, 170.

175   Karen Armstrong, *The Battle for God* (New York: Ballantine, 2000), 269.

176   Armstrong, 268–69.

177   Armstrong, 278.

178   Bruce, 171.

179   Bruce Barron, *Heaven on Earth?* (Grand Rapids, MI: Zondervan, 1992), 136.

180   Michael Duffy, "Jerry Falwell: Political Innovator" *Time*, May 15, 2007, http://www.time.com/time/printout/0,8816,1621300,00.html.

181   Armstrong, 277.

182   Jay Grimstead, "A Brief History of C.O.R." *Crosswinds*, Summer 1995, vol. III, no. 1, 4.

183   Dr. Jay Grimstead, ed. *The Christian World View Documents* (Coalition on Revival, Inc, 1986), 1–7.

184   Warren Hinckle, Associate Editor *San Francisco Examiner.*

185   COR Update, December 2008.

186   Frederick Clarkson, "Christian Reconstructionism" *The Public Eye* Vol 8, No. 1, March/June, 1994, online www.publiceye.org/v08n1/chrisre3.html.

187   R. J. Rushdoony, *God's Plan for Victory* (Chalcedon Foundation, 1997), 24.

Chapter 7

188   http://www.huffingtonpost.com/bruce-wilson/media-gives-palins-strang_b_182295.html

189   C. Peter Wagner, *The Third Wave of the Holy Spirit* (Ann Arbor, MI: Servant, 1988), 16.

190   Wagner, 18.

191   Wagner, 18.

192   C. Peter Wagner, ed., Breaking Strongholds in Your City (Ventura, CA: Regal, 1993), 127.

193   R. Holvast, *Spiritual Mapping: The Turbulent Career of a Contested American Missionary Paradigm*, 1989-2005, http://igitur-archive.library.uu.nl/dissertations/2008-0710-200706/holvast.pdf, 134.

194   Wagner ed. *Breaking Strongholds in Your City*, 62.

195   Wagner, *The Third Wave of the Holy Spirit*, 68, 65, 67.

196   Wagner ed. *Breaking Strongholds in Your City*, 33.

197   Doris M. Wagner, *How to Cast Out Demons* (Berrien Springs, MI: Renew, 2000), 123-26, 130, 144.

198   Doris M. Wagner, 128-29, 134, 137-39, 145-48.

199   Wagner, ed. *Breaking Strongholds in Your City*, 40.

200   Wagner ed., *Breaking Strongholds in Your City*, 80, 39.

201   R. Holvast, *Spiritual Mapping: The Turbulent Career of a Contested American Missionary Paradigm*, 1989-2005, http://igitur-archive.library.uu.nl/dissertations/2008-0710-200706/holvast.pdf, 82.

202   John Dawson, *Taking Our Cities for God* (Lake Mary, FL: Charisma House, 2001), 9.

203   R. Holvast, *Spiritual Mapping: The Turbulent Career of a Contested American Missionary Paradigm*, 1989–2005, http://igitur-archive.library.uu.nl/dissertations/2008-0710-200706/holvast.pdf, 82 (quoting Wagner).

204   Wagner ed., *Breaking Strongholds in Your City*, 138.

205   Wagner ed. *Breaking Strongholds in Your City*, 139–43.

206   www.graceandmercyministries.co.uk/breaking_strongholds_home.htm.

207 www.graceandmercyministries.co.uk/breaking_strongholds_
home.htm.

208 John P. Newport, *The New Age Movement and the Biblical Worldview* (Grand Rapids, MI: Eerdmans , 1997), 591.

209 Wagner ed., *Breaking Strongholds in Your City*, 36, 45.

210 Wagner ed., *Breaking Strongholds in Your City*, 69, 87, 35, 175.

211 Johnny Enlow, *The Seven Mountain Prophecy* (Lake Mary, FL: Creation House, 2008), 58.

212 Watchman Network, http://www.watchmannetwork.org/ Israel_2005_trip_reportl.htm (emphasis added).

213 "The Ana Mendez Story" http://www.transformingmelbourne. org/au/index.php?option=com_content&%20 ;view=article&id=122:the-ana-mendez-story&catid=54:testim%20 onies&Itemid=74.

214 Kevin Reeves, *The Other Side of the River* (Eureka, MT: Lighthouse Trails, 2007), 61–2.

215 Reeves, 61.

216 Jeff Sharlet, "Soldiers of Christ," *Harpers Magazine*. May, 2005, 43.

217 Sharlet, 43.

218 Ted Haggard, *The Life-Giving Church* (Ventura, CA: Regal, 1998), 34.

219 Sharlet, 46.

220 Haggard, 35.

221 Haggard, 14.

222 Haggard, 31.

223 Sharlet, 44.

224   Haggard, 34.

225   Haggard, 35.

226   Haggard, 30.

227   Haggard, 74.

228   C. Peter Wagner, *Dominion!* (Chosen, 2008), 127.

229   C. Peter Wagner, *Dominion!* (Grand Rapids, MI: Chosen, 2008), 127.

230   Max Blumenthal, *Republican Gomorrah* (New York: Nation Books, 2009), 293.

231   C. Peter Wagner, letter to friends of Global Harvest May 31, 2007 (emphasis added).

232   In December 2007 COR proudly announced that one of Wagner's associates, Luis Bush, had been granted permission to distribute COR material. COR Year End Report, December 2007.

233   http://www.reclaim7mountains.com.

234   Wagner, *Dominion!*, 12.

235   Wagner, *Dominion!*, 147 (emphasis added).

236   Enlow, 9.

237   Wagner, "Applying the 7M Mandate" http://the-holy-express. blogspot.com/2008/08/applying-7m-mandate.html.

238   Wagner, "Applying the 7M Mandate" http://the-holy-express. blogspot.com/2008/08/applying-7m-mandate.html.

239   Enlow, 71.

240   Enlow, 65.

241   Wagner, *Dominion!*, 127.

242   Wagner, *Dominion!*, 26.

243   Wagner, *Dominion!*, 26.

244   Wagner, *Dominion!*, 112–13.

245   Letter from Dutch Sheets, Oct. 20, 2008.

246   Dutch Sheets open website letter Nov. 6, 2008 http://www.dutchsheets.org/index.cfm.

247   www.dutchsheets.org.

248   www.dutchsheets.org webcast, Feb. 19, 2009.

249   www.watchmannetwork.org.

250   www.battleaxe.org.

251   Battle Axe Brigade, "What are the Prophets Saying," www.battleaxe.org.

252   "A Message from Peter Wagner" e-mail, April 11, 2007.

253   "A Message from Peter Wagner" e-mail, April 11, 2007.

254   Cindy Jacobs, www.generals.org. *Fighting The Toro-Report On Spain*, 2009.

255   Cindy Jacobs, www.generals.org. *Discovering The Rose Of Sharron*, 2009.

256   Cindy Jacobs, www.generals.org. Video-*Urgent Appeal For Intercession*, 2010.

257   Cindy Jacobs, *Deliver Us from Evil* (Ventura, CA: Regal), 131.

258   Jacobs, 213.

259   Jacobs, 87.

Chapter 8

260   www.windwalkersinternational.org.

261   www.windwalkersinternational.org.

262   Max Blumenthal, *Republican Gomorrah* (New York: Nation Books, 2009), 293–94.

b   She's referring to Walter Hickle, elected to the governorship on the ultra-right Alaska Independent Party ticket

264   Pastor Torp's Blog http://translate.google.com/ translate?hl=en&sl=no&u=http://pastortorp.blogspot.com/&sa=X&o i=translate&resnum=2&ct=result&prev=/search%3Fq%3Dpastor%2 Btorp%2Bsarah%2Bpalin%26hl%3Den%26rls%3DGFRC,GFRC:2007- 18,GFRC:en.

265   Pastor Torp's Blog.

266   Bruce Wilson, "Palin Ties to Militant Religious Movement Confirmed," Talk to Action, July 16, 2009, www.talk2action.com.

267   Paul Steven Ghiringhelli, "Did Politics Fuel Arson at Palin's Church?" *Charisma Magazine*, December 15, 2008, www.charismamag. com.

268   Paul Steven Ghiringhelli, "Did Politics Fuel Arson at Palin's Church?" *Charisma Magazine*, December 15, 2008, www.charismamag. com.

269   Julian Lukins, "The Faith of Sarah Palin," *Charisma Magazine*, January 1, 2009, www.charismamag.com.

270   Manya A. Brachear, "How Religion Guides Palin" September 6, 2008, chicagotribune.com.

271   Brachear, "How Religion Guides Palin."

272   Brachear, "How Religion Guides Palin."

273   Lukins, "The Faith of Sarah Palin."

274   Lukins, "The Faith of Sarah Palin."

275   Blumenthal, 305.

276   *Newsweek* September 29, 2008, 34.

277   *Newsweek* September 29, 2008, 34.

278   http://www.cnn.com/2008/POLITICS/09/08/palin.pastor/index.html.

279   Blumenthal, 305.

280   Michael Patrick Leahy, *What Does Sarah Palin Believe?* (Thompson Stations, TN: Harpath River Press, 2008), 258.

281   http://www.youtube.com/watch?v=5ccmRuCpFjY

282   From a transcript of Muthee's appearance at Wasilla Assembly of God, May, 2005, www.talk2action.org.

283   From a transcript of Muthee's appearance at Wasilla Assembly of God, May, 2005, www.talk2action.org.

284   Leahy, 275.

285   Rick Joyner, *The Call* (Fort Mill, SC: Morningstar Publications, 1999), 14.

286   Joyner, 133.

287   Bruce Wilson, "Palin Attended Church Event with Samurai Sword Ceremony," www.huffingtonpost.com, July 17, 2009.

288   Wilson, "Palin Attendee Church Event With Samurai Sword Ceremony."

289   Joseph H. Hilley, *Sarah Palin: A New Kind of Leader* (Grand Rapids, MI: Zondervan, 2008), 70.

290   Sarah Palin, *Going Rogue* (New York: HarperCollins), 98.

291   Rick Joyner, "The Warrior Nation," June 26, 2006, www.etpv.org.

Chapter 9

292   Justin Skirry, *Descartes: A Guide for the Perplexed* (New York: Continuum, 2008), 99.

293   Skirry, 95, 99.

294   Skirry, 100.

295   Skirry, 100.

296   Richard Tarnas *Cosmos and Psyche: Intimations of a New World View* (New York: Plume, 2007), 16,

297   Frank Schaeffer, *Patience with God: Faith for People Who Don't Like Religion (or Atheists)* (Cambridge, MA: Da Capo Press, 2010), 152.

298   Adam Hamilton, *Seeing Gray in a World of Black and White* (Nashville: Abingdon, 2008), 134.

299   Joe McGinniss, *The Rogue: Searching for the Real Sarah Palin* (New York: Crown, 2011).

300   Robert Solomon, *The Passions: The Myth and Nature of Human Emotion* (New York: Doubleday, 1976).

301   Sharon Begley, "The Roots of Fear," *Newsweek*, December 24, 2007.

302   Sharon Begley, "The Roots of Fear," *Newsweek*, December 24, 2007.

303   Sharon Begley, "The Roots of Fear," *Newsweek*, December 24, 2007.

304   Andrew Sullivan, "When Not Seeing Is Believing," *Time*, October 9, 2006, 59–60.

305   Michael Lerner, *The Left Hand of God* (New York: Harper, 2006), 40.

306   Jim Wallis, *The Great Awakening* (New York: Harper, 2008), 261.

307   Richard Tarnas, *The Passion of the Western Mind* (New York: Harmony, 1991), 353.

308   Merold Westphal, *Overcoming Onto-Theology* (New York: Fordham University, 2001), 84, 87.

309   N. T. Wright, *The Challenge of Jesus* (Downers Grove, IL: InterVarsity, 1999), 167.

310   Nicholas Kristof, "Divided They Fall," *New York Times*, April 17, 2008.

311   Farhad Manjoo, *True Enough* (Hoboken, NJ: Wiley, 2008), 27.

312   Manjoo, 28.

313   Brian McLaren, *A New Kind of Christian* (San Francisco: Jossey-Bass, 2001), 35.

314   Wright, 170.

315   Wright, 170.

Chapter 10

316   Edward E. Hindson, Daniel R. Mitchell, *Zondervan King James Version Commentary---New Testament* (Grand Rapids, MI: Zondervan, 2010), 759.

317   Brian McLaren, *A Generous Orthodoxy* (Grand Rapids, MI: Zondervan, 2004), 86.

318   McLaren, 85–6.

319   Karen Armstrong, *The Battle for God* (New York: Ballantine, 2000), 371.

320   E. J. Dionne Jr., *Souled Out* (Princeton, NJ: Princeton University, 2008), 34.

321   Michael Lerner, *The Left Hand of God* (New York: Harper, 2006), 8–9.

322 Lerner, 16.

323 Richard Nixon, *The Memoirs of Richard Nixon* (Buccaneer, 1994), 354.

324 Nixon, 565.

325 William Martin, *With God on Our Side* (New York: Broadway, 1996), 240.

Chapter 11

326 Stephen L. Carter, *The Culture of Disbelief: How American Law and Politics Trivialize Religious Devotion* (Harpswell, ME: Anchor Books, 1993), 179.

327 Carter, 179.

328 E. J. Dionne Jr., *Souled Out* (Princeton, NJ: Princeton University, 2008), 196.

329 Jon Meacham, *Newsweek*, October 15, 2007.

330 Dan Gilgoff, *The Jesus Machine* (New York: St. Martin's Griffin, 2008), 251–52.

331 Gilgoff, 262.

332 Gilgoff, 262–63.

333 Gilgoff, 262–63.

334 Gilgoff, 262–63.

335 "Come Let Us Reason Together" a Third Way Report, October 2007, 21–2.

336 Adam Hamilton, *Seeing Gray in a World of Black and White* (Nashville: Abingdon, 2008), 158.

337 Karen Armstrong, *The Battle for God* (New York: Ballantine, 2000), 370–71.

Chapter 12

338 Os Guinness, *The Case for Civility* (New York: HarperCollins, 2008), 149.

339 Frank Schaeffer, *Crazy for God* (Cambridge, MA: De Capo Press, 2007), 78.

340 Frank Schaeffer, *Patience with God* (Cambridge, MA: De Capo Press, 2010), 8.

341 One such safe space civilly presenting multiple dimensions of various issues is www.civilpolitics.org.

342 Adam Hamilton, *Seeing Gray in a World of Black and White* (Nashville: Abingdon, 2008), 46, xvi.

343 William Martin, *With God On Our Side* (Broadway, 2005) 369

344 Jim Wallis, *God's Politics* (New York: Harper, 2005), 13.

345 Schaeffer, *Crazy for God*, 78.

346 Schaeffer, *Crazy for God*, 79.

347 Guinness, 160–61.

348 Guinness, 157.

349 Guinness, 163.

350 Tim Keel, *Intuitive Leadership* (Grand Rapids, MI: Baker, 2007), 143.

351 Karen Armstrong, *A Battle for God* (Ballantine, 2000), in the Reader's Guide.

352 Schaeffer, *Patience with God*, 154.

353 See www.chrf.org for how you can help.

Index

N